Severn

by

Richard Hayman

LOGASTON PRESS
Little Logaston, Woonton, Almeley
Herefordshire HR3 6QH
www.logastonpress.co.uk

First published by Logaston Press 2012

ISBN 978 1 906663 66 7

Typeset in Garamond by Logaston Press
Printed and bound in Poland
www.polskabook.pl

❧ Contents ❧

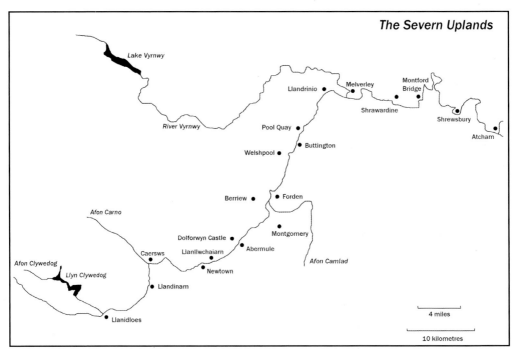

The Severn Uplands

Lake Vyrnwy
River Vyrnwy
Llandrinio
Melverley
Montford Bridge
Shrawardine
Shrewsbury
Atcham
Pool Quay
Buttington
Welshpool
Berriew
Forden
Afon Carno
Montgomery
Dolforwyn Castle
Abermule
Caersws
Llanllwchaiarn
Afon Camlad
Afon Clywedog
Llyn Clywedog
Newtown
Llandinam
Llanidloes

4 miles
10 kilometres

River Avon
Ripple
The Severn Vale
Tewkesbury
Deerhurst
Tirley
Ashleworth
River Wye
Maisemore
Gloucester
Minsterworth
Westbury-on-Severn
Longney
Newnham
Arlingham
Framilode
Saul
Awre
Frampton-on-Severn
Lydney
Slimbridge
Purton
Sharpness
Berkeley
Tidenham
Sedbury
Chepstow
Oldbury-on-Severn
Portskewett
Aust
Redwick

4 miles
10 kilometres

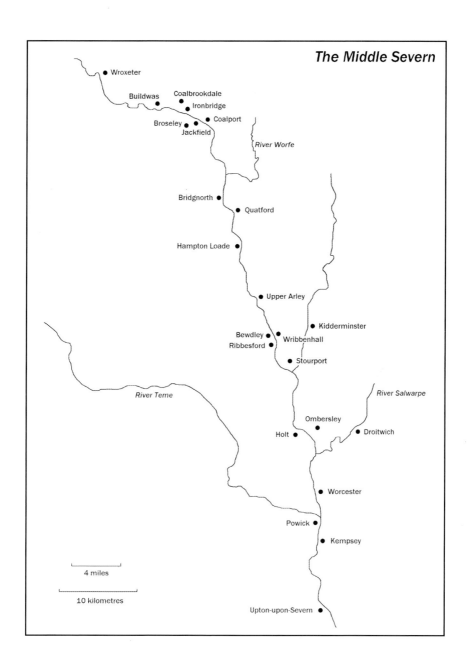

The Middle Severn

Wroxeter

Buildwas
Coalbrookdale
Ironbridge
Broseley
Coalport
Jackfield

River Worfe

Bridgnorth
Quatford

Hampton Loade

Upper Arley

Kidderminster
Bewdley
Wribbenhall
Ribbesford
Stourport

River Teme

River Salwarpe

Ombersley
Holt
Droitwich

Worcester

Powick
Kempsey

4 miles

10 kilometres

Upton-upon-Severn

❧ Acknowledgements ❧

I am indebted to the staff of several institutions who have helped me in research for this book, and I would like to thank especially the staff at the Cadbury Research Library at Birmingham University and Shropshire Archives. Permission to reproduce illustrations has been given by the University of Birmingham Special Collections, Ironbridge Gorge Museum Trust, Shropshire Archives, Gloucester Museums Service and Worcester City Museum.

❧ Introduction ❧
Queen of Rivers

The past is usually written in terms of people, events or monuments and it may therefore seem unusual to look for our history in the course of a river, but for those of us who through long years live or have lived in mid Wales or near the England-Wales border, the Severn has dominated where we live, how we move around, how we have made our livings and fought our internecine wars. It could be argued, however, that since we no longer need the Severn as a mode of transport, the river now literally passes us by. In riverside towns and cities like Worcester, Shrewsbury and Newtown, the riverbank is populated by grandparents pushing buggies, sweaty runners and people drinking beer out of cans. In Gloucester the dock has become the waterfront, while the river it supplanted flows quietly on unnoticed, except at the times of the bore. Despite the popularity of rowing and the occasional triathlon or coracle race, the Severn has largely been relegated to the status of scenery. It is possible to live in a Severnside town and hardly be conscious of the river at all. But every couple of years over the past two decades the river has risen up and devastated parts of its riverside communities, a reminder that it remains a powerful force of nature that two thousand years of civilisation and civil engineering has failed to domesticate. Millions of pounds have been spent on flood defences in Bewdley and Upton. In Shrewsbury in 2009 more people drowned in the Severn than died on the town's roads. And yet if it now seems that we live here in spite of the river, the reason people settled here in the first place was *because* of the river. This book, then, is about when and why the river mattered, and why it still matters even though we may take it for granted.

The Severn has not simply been the setting for events great and small, but often an active player in them. The river has been a giver and taker of life, the economic lifeblood of the region, a political and symbolic boundary. From the Iron Age to World War II, regimes have built fortresses and other defences to ensure their control over it, and throughout the Civil Wars, Royalists and Parliamentarians fought bitterly for possession of it. Three of Britain's finest bridges were built over the Severn – the medieval Welsh Bridge in Shrewsbury, the 18th-century Iron Bridge and the modern Severn Bridge, all of which have transcended their practical functions to become icons of their age. Along the riverbank are also the smaller details of history, the redundant slipways, stone quays, canal

Etched glass in the windows of the Anchor Inn at Upton-upon-Severn.
The inn, built in 1601 on the High Street leading to the old bridge, is a reminder that
Upton was once a port town.

Three 19th-century warehouses on the quayside at Worcester. All have been converted
to new uses but were built when the Severn was a working river and not the quiet and
picturesque site that it has now become.

interchanges, mills and warehouses revived as apartments and restaurants, all of which are remnants of once vibrant riverside industry. But there are also a Roman city, castles of Marcher lords and Welsh princes, numerous churches and one of Britain's finest cathedrals, all of which are where they are because of the river, and all evidence of how powerfully the river drew human life to its bank, even though it has largely been forgotten, is worth recovering and appreciating.

The Severn is one of the few British rivers big enough to have engendered its own culture. In Bewdley the Severn can boast Britain's finest river port, a familiar sight on the European continent, perhaps, but a rarity in these islands. Trows and barges were built on the Severn and adapted to the specific conditions of the river. Likewise, coracles were Severn boats that evolved for use on specific small stretches of the river. The stop nets and lave nets of estuarine fishing were especially adapted to suit the needs of the estuary bed and the behaviour of migrating salmon. Other rivers have tidal bores, but none as remarkable as that of the Severn, from which bore-surfing has grown into a global sport. Throughout this book the standard grammatical convention is followed, in which the river is described as 'the Severn'. But along the English river it was once referred to only as 'Severn' – hence 'twenty feet into Severn', 'drowned in Severn' and so on – a usage that is now fading but testifies that the Severn has been a fundamental fact of life to those who have lived by it.

The river retains two names that sum up a body of water that begins in Wales, flows through England and receives the waters of many tributaries before it reaches the sea near the English-Welsh border. *Hafren* is undoubtedly the oldest name but was rendered as *Sabrina* by the classical authors Tacitus and Ptolemy. Writers once liked to translate Hafren as 'queen of rivers', because it appeared to be an agglomeration of the Welsh words *afon* (river) and *frenhines* (queen). 'Sabrina' too has enjoyed its own interpretations. One is that it is an old British word for 'sandy', alluding to the muddiness of the Severn waters, a description that could be applied to most of Britain's rivers, but perhaps suggested by Shakespeare's reference to the 'sandy-bottomed Severn' in Henry IV Part I.[1] 'Severn' seems to have derived from Hafren and its tributary Efyrnwy (River Vyrnwy). It is the most recent name and, perhaps inevitably, the most prosaic.

Bewdley is Britain's finest river port.
It retains an 18th-century waterfront with Thomas Telford's bridge of 1796.

The strategic importance of the Severn has been recognised for at least as long as the land of Britain has been written about. According to the Roman historian Tacitus, the governor Ostorius singled out southern England, as bounded by the Trent and Severn, as his first priority in establishing the colony of Britannia after the Roman invasion of AD 43. In his description of Britain written in the 6th century, the historian and monk Gildas characterised it as being influenced by two noble rivers, 'two arms by which foreign luxuries were of old imported', a point echoed by Nennius in the 9th century and Geoffrey of Monmouth in the 12th century. Geoffrey added the Humber to the Severn and Thames and described the three rivers as the three great arms of Britain that opened up the interior of the nation by virtue of their navigability. The Severn has been a provincial river ever since the nation had a recognised capital on the Thames, but it was not always so. William I wore his crown once a year at three places in England – Winchester (the royal capital of Wessex), Westminster (on the Thames) and Gloucester (on the Severn).[2] Gloucester had been home to kings since Anglo-Saxon times. Athelstan, the first king of all England, died there in 939; and Ethelred II was crowned there in 978 and Henry III in 1216. Henry II consolidated his grip on power by being re-crowned in Worcester Cathedral at Easter 1158, when he and his queen Eleanor of Aquitaine laid their crowns on the shrine of St Wulfstan. Edward II was killed at Berkeley Castle in 1327 and is buried beneath a golden effigy in the abbey at Gloucester. King John is buried at Worcester Cathedral, as is Prince Arthur, Henry VII's eldest son and heir. Llywelyn ap Gruffudd, Prince of Wales, married Elinor de Montfort in Worcester Cathedral in 1278, with Edward I in attendance. Five years later his brother Dafydd ap Gruffudd was executed upriver at Shrewsbury.

Like all great rivers, the Severn has been seen not just as a conduit of trade but as a giver of life in a more mystical sense. Daniel Defoe acknowledged the Thames as the only rival to the Severn as 'the richest, most fertile and most agreeable part of England'. But in Montgomeryshire he went further and claimed that 'some are of opinion, that, the very water of the Severn, like that of Nile, impregnates the valley, and when it overflows, leaves a virtue behind it, particularly to itself; and this they say is confirm'd, because all the country is so fruitful, wherever this river does overflow, and its waters reach'.[3] The Honourable John Byng, the future fifth Viscount Torrington, agreed. On a tour to north Wales in 1784 he recommended that 'all travellers should go up the vale to Newtown, to see this luxuriant country'.[4] To its native people the Severn entered the bloodstream. Edward Elgar never relinquished his attachment to the Severn, which became stronger and more important to him as he advanced in years. When he moved into a smart London home he had it re-named 'Severn House' and later expressed his desire to be buried at the confluence of Severn and Teme. He wrote in 1921, aged 64, 'I am still at heart the dreamy child who used to be found in the reeds by the Severn side'.[5]

The facts of the river are no less impressive. The Severn is Britain's longest river, at 220 miles (354 kilometres) from source to sea. It has the largest catchment of any British river system (which includes that of its tributary rivers) at 3,820 square miles (9,895 square kilometres). Its average flow is 107 cubic metres per second, exceeded in Britain only by the river Tay.[6] Beginning in the mountains of central Wales it flows through nearly every type of landscape that is found in the British Isles – mountainous scenery, broad fertile valley and vale, a gorge and estuarine levels. On its course to the sea it flows through only four counties: Montgomeryshire (part of Powys since 1974), Shropshire, Worcestershire and Gloucestershire. The Environment Agency recognises only three stages of the river. The Severn Uplands is the Welsh river, extending from the source to just over the English border; the Middle Severn is roughly its course through Shropshire and Worcestershire; and the Severn Vale is approximately its course through Gloucestershire to the sea.

The river rises in the Cambrian Mountains on Plynlimon at 620 metres above sea level. Its headwaters flow over peaty moorland, part of which is now forested, and then in a valley of pasture before the river reaches its first town, Llanidloes, which is nine miles below the source. Llanidloes is approximately 165 metres above sea level, so by this point the river has already made over two thirds of its descent to the sea. Llanidloes stands at the confluence of the Severn's first important tributary, Afon Clywedog, from whose reservoir the level of the Severn is now controlled. From there the river flows

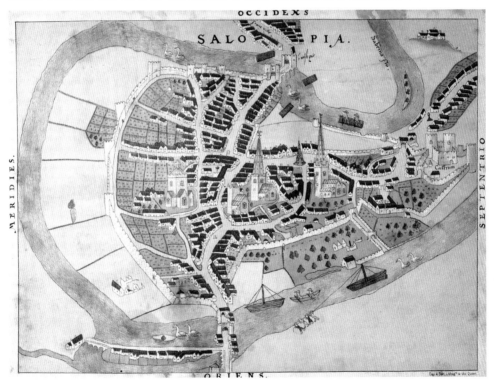

No town has a more intimate relationship with the river Severn than Shrewsbury, as is shown in this 19th-century copy of Lord Burleigh's map of Shrewsbury, c.1575. The Severn acts as a moat around the town, with the castle defending the open side. At the bottom of the picture is the Stone Bridge, near the confluence with the Rea brook, and Coleham Island, which subsequently ceased to be an island when the river bed silted up. At the top of the picture is the Welsh Bridge. On the left-hand side, beyond the town walls, are open fields on which the ruins of the former Greyfriars church can be seen. (© Shropshire Archives)

The river Severn in the Shropshire Plain at Cound, with the Wrekin in the distance, drawn by Samuel Ireland in the late 18th century.

Samuel Ireland's view of the Severn at Ashleworth in the Severn Vale

eastwards, passing Llandinam, joined by Afon Carno at the small town of Caersws, to Newtown. Beyond Newtown the river opens out into a broad floodplain, passing the town of Welshpool, before skirting around the north side of the Breidden Hills and its confluence with the river Vyrnwy on the border with Shropshire. The Vyrnwy is the last of the major Welsh mountain rivers to join the Severn. In Lake Vyrnwy it incorporates the largest artificial reservoir in Wales, and at its confluence with the Severn it is of almost equal size to the main river.

The Middle Severn flows through two distinct landscapes, divided by the Ironbridge Gorge. At the upstream end the Severn meanders across the Shropshire Plain in broad loops. Shrewsbury stands within one of these loops, created by an outcrop of rock rather than the mechanics of river flow, and has the most visually dynamic relationship with the Severn of all of its towns and cities. The gateway to the Ironbridge Gorge is today marked by the Ironbridge Power Station, and the subsequent three-mile stretch creates one of the river's most dramatic spectacles: a steep wooded gorge and a unique industrial landscape of factories and cottages. Beyond Coalport, which is at the downstream end of the gorge, the river flows again through an undulating landscape, its course diverted by large outcrops of red sandstone at Pendlestone above Bridgnorth and Blackstone near Bewdley. There are important river towns along this stretch at Bridgnorth, Bewdley and Stourport near the confluence with the Stour, before the Severn opens into a flood plain again at Worcester, near which is the confluence with the Teme, with Upton-upon-Severn the small town beyond it.

The Severn at Westbury on Severn, in a stretch of the Severn Vale below Gloucester that is far more built up than the Middle Severn and Severn Uplands.

The west, or Maisemore, channel of the Severn completely bypasses Gloucester
and is seen here at Maisemore Bridge, built in 1710.

The Severn Vale begins above Tewkesbury, where the river Avon joins the Severn. At 85 miles in length, the Avon is the longest Severn tributary. The Severn Vale is a far more open landscape than the Middle Severn and Severn Uplands, with meadows, or 'hams', on the flood plain that are liable to flooding and have required towns like Tewkesbury to be built further back from the river bank than the Middle Severn towns. It also supports a greater number of settlements than upriver. Downstream of Tewkesbury there is Gloucester, then Minsterworth, Longney, Westbury-on-Severn, Newnham, Arlingham, Purton, Sharpness and Lydney. Yet more Severnside villages have been cut off from the river by the Gloucester and Sharpness Canal, as at Frampton-on-Severn and Slimbridge. Since at least Roman times Gloucester has been the most important settlement on the river because, until the 19th century, it was the lowest point downriver at which the river could be bridged.

Just above Gloucester the river splits into two channels at Upper Parting, and then reunites at Lower Parting, creating a river-bound body of land known as Alney Island. The west or Maisemore channel completely bypasses Gloucester, and the east channel passes the west flank of the city, where there is a junction with Gloucester Docks, which was an interchange basin between the Severn and the Gloucester and Sharpness Canal. Below Gloucester the river is tidal and broadens considerably towards the estuary, which is characterised by two road bridges, the Severn Bridge and the Second Severn Crossing. The Severn Bridge in fact crosses two rivers: a smaller channel on the west side is the river Wye, which flows into the Severn estuary, having also sprung from Plynlimon. With the establishment of long-distance footpaths it is now possible to walk the entire course of the Severn from Plynlimon, then cross the Severn Bridge and walk the entire course of the Wye, ending back on the tract of peaty moorland from which both rivers spring.

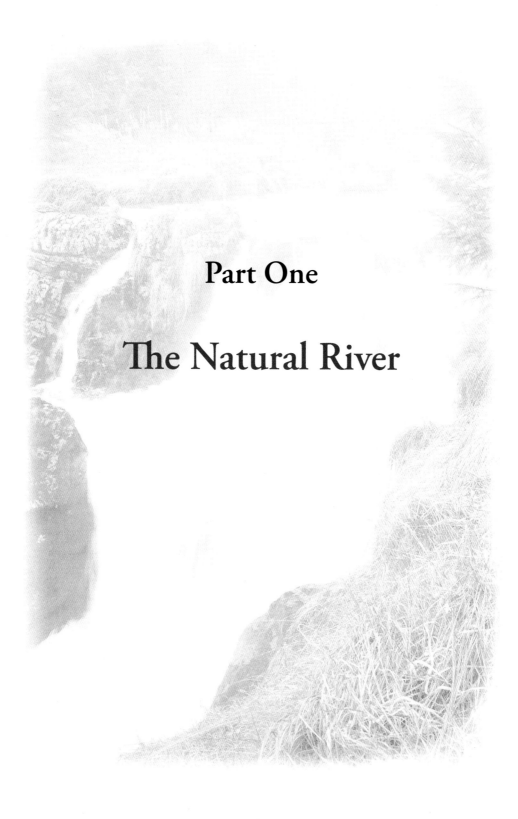

Part One

The Natural River

❧ 1 ❧
The Natural River

In the early morning of 27 May 1773, at about four o'clock in the morning, there was an earthquake at Buildwas, and so opened a dramatic final chapter in a period of flooding on the river. Samuel Wilcocks, who lived at The Birches, close to the river, heard the sound of the earthquake and got up to see an amazing sight. A copse of about twenty oak trees had been wrenched from the hillside and were sliding down the bank into the bed of the river. The river bed, meanwhile, was so convulsed that part of it was thrown up, revealing boulders and a large tree trunk that had been buried in mud for many years. Worse, a chasm had opened that took up the river water so that for a moment Samuel Wilcocks thought that the river was flowing backwards. Samuel Cookson, who lived slightly further downstream, woken by the same noise, looked out of the window to see if the level of the floodwater in his fields had abated, only to find that the river had disappeared altogether.

Crowds of people flocked to the scene the following morning, among them the Reverend John Fletcher, vicar of the neighbouring parish of Madeley (and widely acknowledged as the foremost Methodist preacher after John Wesley).[1] He walked through a field of oats and saw fissures in the ground, but they were nothing compared to a chasm higher up the bank which was, so he was informed, 396 yards long, 42 yards wide at its widest and 10 yards deep at its deepest point (362 by 37 by 9.1 metres). Into a similar cavern a field barn had fallen, more or less intact. But the river dominated the conversations of onlookers. The oak trees that had slid down the bank choked the river, causing floodwaters to rise fast on the upstream side. On the downstream side the flooded meadows and the riverbank drained so quickly that fish were left high and dry. So were moored vessels, which tipped over on to the dry bed. Worse was to follow. As the river level built up behind the temporary dam, a weak point emerged that began as a cataract but soon became a torrent that, in a matter of hours, carved a new channel for the river Severn about 300 yards long (274 metres). The stranded vessels, tipped on to their sides, duly flooded and sank.

That natural catastrophes cast light on the spiritual condition of human beings is a superstition even larger and more ancient than Christianity. By the end of the 18th century it had a long pedigree in Protestant rhetoric, and was certainly consistent with the Methodist view of the world. 'I concluded that the God of nature had shaken his providential iron rod over the subverted spot before me', was Fletcher's first reaction. The preacher quickly turned the event into a sermon, which he preached to the crowds gathered by the river. Having speculated on the cause of the event according to the laws of nature, which he quickly satisfied himself was an earthquake, he began to think more deeply. 'Whatever the second, or natural cause of our phenomenon was, it is certain that the first or moral cause of it was twofold; on our part aggravated sin; and on God's part, warning justice.' Had not Moses told the Israelites, when the men of Korah were swallowed up by the earth, that if 'the earth opens its mouth and swallows them, with everything that belongs to them, and they go down alive into the grave, then you will know that these men have treated the Lord with contempt'?[2]

Even so, in apocalyptic terms, the stoppage of the river Severn was only a gentle warning. 'You stand in the deepest part of her channel and yet you are in a wood: Large oaks spread their branches, where bargemen unfurled their sails: You walk today on solid ground where fishes yesterday swam in 20 feet of water.' The fish left high and dry reminded Fletcher of the coming Day of Judgment, when shoals of impenitent sinners would suffer a similar fate. The river had appeared to Samuel Wilcocks to flow backwards, which sounded decidedly Biblical, and Fletcher, as skilled as the best of preachers, was quite capable of making the events on the river Jordan and the river Severn appear one and the same. The Jordan may have turned back on itself in the presence of God guiding his people to Israel, but the Severn had different reasons for reversing its course: 'Did the impiety of the inhabitants of Madeley-wood, and Broseley, shock thee back to thy source?' If there was an overriding moral to be drawn it was the need to stand on solid ground. 'If the Severn, at a moment's warning, left the deep, favourite part of her bed, should you not be ready to leave your houses, your estates, and this world itself, for Christ's sake?'

The episode reminds us that 'natural' is a subjective term. This remains the case even though the formation of a river is now understood as a sequence of physical processes. A scientific explanation of how the river came to be the phenomenon it is today is comparatively recent, however, and the long road to this way of understanding it can seem like the triumph of science over superstition that was played out in Victorian society. Not until the late 19th century was the course of the Severn understood as a piece of history over which there was no divine or human influence.

As long ago as 1818 a Mr Aikin noticed that the Severn descends from the mountains of mid Wales into the Shropshire plain and then, instead of turning north and draining towards the Cheshire plain, cuts through the end of a ridge of hills known as Wenlock Edge. Geologists of the time still sought their interpretations from divine intervention rather than natural processes. Professor William Buckland (1784-1856), for example, claimed that rivers had no power to cut their own valleys but flowed through the spillways carved out by waters of the biblical Flood. Explanation of fluvial processes by reference to the Flood receded in the 19th century, but geologists, including George Maw, owner of the famous tile factory in Jackfield, were puzzled that small stones and boulders appeared to have been deposited in the Severn valley from north-west Wales. The glacial origin of this material was not accepted until the 1880s. Aikin was proved right in his speculation that once the river flowed northwards to the Dee Estuary. The Severn as we know it is a comparatively recent amalgamation of two rivers, one flowing from mid Wales north to the Dee estuary, and the other flowing south and then west from the English Midlands. In its present form, therefore, the Severn is less than 20,000 years old.[3]

About 28,000 years ago, ice sheets moved across north Wales from a north-westerly direction, blocking off the lower valley of the original Upper Severn. The break from its original course occurs in Buildwas. From here meltwater streams at the base of the glacier cut channels across Wenlock Edge as far south as Eardington, which was the limit of the ice sheets. When the climate warmed and the ice began to melt, water was prevented from following its natural course northwards because ice sheets still covered the ground. Instead it slowly cut deeper into the channel across Wenlock Edge to form what is now known as the Ironbridge Gorge. In doing so it also exposed minerals such as coal and iron ore that would be exploited from here many centuries later. The Gorge is nearly three miles long, and below it the glacial meltwater flowed into a pre-existing river at Apley, which now became the principal channel of the Severn as we know it. It was first suggested in 1907 that there was a glacial lake at Buildwas, but this is still the subject of debate, as is the question of how significant such a lake might have been.[4]

The river upstream of Shrewsbury is depicted in a watercolour of 1912 by F.W. Seville,
a rare view of the river that sees it as a purely natural phenomenon.
(Courtesy of Shrewsbury Museum and Art Gallery)

Our knowledge of geology does not mean that we can now know the river objectively; we are bound to see it from our own human point of view. One of the obvious ways of characterising a river is to imagine its course like that of a human life span, and this is how Francis Brett Young's portrait of the Severn is constructed. By the time the river reached Shrewsbury, for example, its youthful exuberance was far behind:

> … But Severn flows
> With the graveness of a deepening stream,
> Till her waters part – and high in air
> The steeple vanes of Shrewsbury dream
> Caught within her silver snare,
> And her voice is stilled; for now she hath
> Forgotten the madrigals that she sung
> In the dalliance of her downward path
> And the lilt of the valleys where she was young,
> But hath put away such childish things
> With their merriment of light-hearted youth;
> And the memory of her mountain springs
> Is all forgotten – for now in sooth
> She floweth mantled in her sober state.[5]

Just by naming features of the river we draw them into our culture. For example, there are the Severn's many natural islands and the words used to describe them – bylet, eyot, naight. By natural we usually mean things that exist independent of human agency, but when we apply the term 'disaster' to episodes of very high or very low river levels, nature is measured purely in human terms. Nevertheless, nature is what we expect to find when we visit the river, and it is one reason why so many picnic sites are provided at riverside spots. The riverside is the democratic version of the landscape park.

The Severn largely conforms to our idea of the classic British river, flowing through a pastoral landscape, much of which was once water meadow but has been well drained since the 18th or 19th century. It retains important examples of ancient woodland in places, notably in the steep-sided Ironbridge Gorge, and in Wyre Forest, which in the Middle Ages was the chase, or hunting ground, of the powerful Mortimer family. In Benjamin Williams Leader's painting *Smooth Severn Stream*, painted in 1886, the river is at the heart of a rural idyll, which is to live in perfect harmony with nature. It is the sort of place that engenders nostalgia, nature that we like to think is unchanging, giving some semblance of stability in an otherwise shifting world. Ivor Gurney retained this feeling in his nostalgia for the river:

> If England, her spirit lives anywhere
> It is by Severn, by hawthorns and grand willows …
> There in the brakes of May Spring has her chambers,
> Robing-rooms of hawthorn, cowslip, cuckoo-flower.[6]

Once, willows lined the banks of the river in the Severn Vale, but the river was not the permanent fixture that Gurney longed for. Daniel Defoe noted another characteristic feature that is no more. On the bank of the Severn between Tewkesbury and Worcester 'we had the pleasing sight of the hedgerows, being fill'd with apple trees and pear trees, and the fruit so common, that any passenger as they travel the road may gather and eat what they please; and here, as well as in Gloucestershire, you meet with cider in the publick-houses sold as beer and ale in other parts of England, and as cheap'.[7] Nature is indivisible from culture, and the river has never been as timeless as the poets would have us believe.

The rise of the Romantic appreciation of nature was paralleled by the rise of the naturalist. They can be found on the estuarine river looking for the birds that thrive in wetland environments, and especially congregate at Slimbridge, where Sir Peter Scott founded in 1946 what is now the Wildfowl and Wetlands Trust. There are other riverside nature reserves. Wetland habitats are being restored at Llandinam, where otters live. Otter, snipe and water rail inhabit the damp meadows downstream of Newtown. Conservation tries to reduce the rate of change as a response to the decline of habitats, but the way the word 'change' in nature is often associated with 'decline' needs to be challenged. It is not a very helpful way to imagine the river as a whole, given that a river's natural tendency is to change all the time, and it would change more if left to its own devices. The scouring effect of glaciation effectively lowered the level of the river bed to the extent that the Severn has a very low gradient for a long river, but this only slows the rate of change, it cannot stop it.

Benjamin Williams Leader's painting, 'The Smooth Severn Stream', unconsciously pays tribute to the work of his father, the engineer Edward Williams Leader, in managing the river between Worcester and Gloucester.
(Image from Worcester City museum collection)

Changes in the natural river tend to happen either very slowly or very quickly. The formation of the Ironbridge Gorge is an example of the former, while the Buildwas earthquake is a classic case of the latter, and another is the creation of the west, or Maisemore, channel of the Severn by Gloucester. This occurred in the late 15th or early 16th century – possibly as a direct result of the duke of Buckingham's flood in 1483 (which is described in chapter 13), when the river broke through the levee into a lower backwater. In the process the Severn took in the smaller river Leadon and broke through the causeways at Over and Maisemore, where bridges were subsequently built. In the 1540s it was described as 'a great arme of the Severne called Owesburne or Overse Burne'.[8]

The anatomy of the Severn is typical of British rivers in its general characteristics, which show the evolution of the river in progress. The upper section of the river is the steepest. As is typical of most upland rivers, this is the section where the river is noisiest and where it often flows over the natural bedrock. The phenomenon can be seen easily by following its course up through the modern plantation near the source known as Hafren Forest, where the blanket forest has obscured the effect of the deeply incised valley that the river has created. It also flows over gravel beds that release small stones which excavate the channel and congregate in beds where the current is not strong enough to wash them downstream, except when in spate. When the river passes over a band of rock particularly resistant to erosion, a waterfall is formed, although in geological time it is only a temporary obstacle that the river will eventually overcome. At Blaen Hafren water cascades down an inclined shelf of rock, but the only vertical fall is downstream from there, at a place known as Severn-break-its-neck, just over three miles

The cascade at Blaenhafren is the first of its waterfalls, less than a mile below the summit.

The waterfall at Severn-break-its-neck is the only true vertical waterfall on the Severn.

below the source. Over the falls the river has cut a deep ravine in the bedrock, although it is now difficult to appreciate since a wooden footbridge has been built across it to give a good view of the waterfall. This is a common characteristic of waterfalls: because they cut deep ravines it is often impossible to find a safe vantage point from which to appreciate them aesthetically.

Upstream of Llanidloes the river flow is in its natural state but the environment is still managed. Dams in the forestry around Plynlimon help to maintain the moorland peat bogs from which the river springs, and the heather in which the grouse and hen harrier live. Below Llanidloes the river enters a broad valley; past floodwaters have brought down the silt that has made the valley fertile. Here the river no longer flows on bedrock but on the sediment that the river has itself washed down its course.

Once a river reaches its middle section and the gradient is only very slight, it has a natural tendency to meander. It has been calculated that a river cannot flow in a straight line for much longer than ten times its width, the result of a dynamic relationship between the water and the sediment it carries.[9] The Severn is thus a river of meanders for most of its course between mid Wales and the sea, except where it is affected by other factors, like the Ironbridge Gorge or large rock formations like Blackstone Rock near Bewdley, which it flows around. The river winds with variable degrees of stability, and between Caersws and Welshpool there have been marked shifts in the past 200 years, the period in which the course of the river has been accurately mapped. A combination of alluvium in the river and a certain flow rate causes meanders to change and it is in these middle reaches below the mountainous country, sometimes called the 'piedmont zone', that optimum conditions for changing meanders prevail. For the Severn, that means the stretch between Llanidloes and Welshpool, where minor and major changes in the course of the river happened during the 19th and 20th centuries. Two river loops

The confluence of the rivers Severn and Vyrnwy

near Aberhafesp were cut off between 1900 and the early 1970s, and their residual small lakes – the oxbow lakes of geography text books – can still be seen. The most accessible landscape of old meanders is at Dolydd Hafren, now a nature reserve near Forden. The river at Welshpool cut a new straighter channel through its previously sinuous course as a result of the flood of 1795. Since then its meanders have been redeveloping. At Llandinam, although the meanders have been stable in the past two centuries, the beds of gravel within them have shifted considerably.[10]

A well-defined series of meanders is visible in sections upstream and downstream of Shrewsbury. Upstream is a large loop nearly closed at the south end which encloses a private enclave of farmland where there are neither roads nor public footpaths, appropriately named the Isle. Downstream, the fine sequence of meanders near Leighton is clearly visible from the road between Leighton and Buildwas. In both sections the meanders are interspersed with sequences of pools and riffles, where the stream has not been strong enough to erode the banks and form loops, a consequence of its shallow gradient. Rivermen understood this phenomenon empirically. Eustace Rogers, the Ironbridge coracle-maker, described the river above Ironbridge as a similar sequence, except that he used the terms pool or hole for the deeper pools, and ford for the shallows: hence names such as Painter's Hole, Gother's Hole, Edge Pool, Buildwas Low Ford, Buildwas Top Ford, Milking Fawd, Ash Fawd, Clapham Ford and Sludge Hole, all of which are on a two-mile section upstream of Ironbridge.[11] The shallows have a tendency to develop into islands, causing the river channel to braid, and these islands, or bylets, have often been exploited for the construction of fish weirs, since they left one of the channels free for the navigation. A number of them can be seen on the river, including those at Montford, Castlefields and Pimley in Shrewsbury, Wroxeter, Bridgnorth, Highley and Bevere. But they are not necessarily permanent fixtures. A bylet is shown on 19th-century plans of the Madeley Wood ironworks in the Ironbridge Gorge, but it has since been washed away and is now no more than a riffle.

There are many relict river channels on the Welsh section of the river, such as here at Dolydd Hafren.

Meanders are vulnerable to erosion, but wherever sediment is removed from one section of river it is deposited in another. There is plenty of evidence for this in the river below Gloucester. Longney – long island – received its name in Saxon times, when the ridge of land was bounded on the west by the river and on the east by marshy ground that was probably an older river bed. At Saul Warth the line of the former sea wall indicates how the river retreated in the 17th century. Salmon traps known as putchers were laid there in 1595 but the change in the course of the river by 1615 left them high and dry. At about the same time 30 acres of ground were abandoned by the river and became known as Bromwich's Warth.[12] On the estuary at Lydney level the shoreline is unstable, and although there has been settlement on the floodplain, there have been at least six episodes of sea-bank construction over the past two millennia. The reclaimed coastal marshes have typically been meadows but from about the 12th to the 14th centuries they were dry enough to be ploughed for crops.[13] Just as the river has cut new channels in historic times, so it has created new pieces of solid ground. Two examples are well recorded from 17th-century Gloucestershire. New Grounds near Lydney was formed by the deposition of silt when the river channel narrowed. As it was seemingly a product of the river – the king's great highway – Charles I began a ridiculous and unsuccessful lawsuit to claim ownership of the land. Likewise, in Slimbridge there is a thousand-acre meadow known as New Grounds or Dumballs, which was fully formed of silt deposited by the river by the early 17th century. Again Charles I claimed its ownership.[14] On the opposite bank upstream near Rodley, Lower and Upper Dumball also formed in the 17th century, continuing to the 18th century, as a sand bar inside the old sea wall had started growing grass by 1785.[15] Throughout this period the Severn estuary accumulated more silt than it shifted. It has been calculated that since Roman times the estuary bed has risen by 1.7 metres.[16]

In extreme cases meanders can become cut off and the old section of river bed dries up. This is measurable in places where it has affected human activity, namely the

The tendency of rivers to meander is well seen in the section of the river below Leighton in Shropshire.

important towns. Archaeological evidence has shown how the waterfront at Gloucester shifted westwards after Roman times as the river found a new course, and the position of medieval quays buried under later buildings shows how this same channel eventually silted up in the Middle Ages. By the 11th century the river had shifted 36 metres westward of the Roman quayside, so if there was a bridge in Roman times it would have been rendered redundant by the shifting course. This shift was only partly natural, as it was aided by reclamation and landfill.[17] Gloucester's first medieval bridge was built across this channel in 1119, but already in 1370 it was called 'Little Severn' and it has been known as 'Old Severn' since at least 1529.[18] After the residual stream was culverted in the 18th century there was no longer any sign that the river had ever flowed there. Similar processes have been observed on a smaller scale in Shrewsbury, where channels upstream and downstream of the town's bridges, as well as Coleham Island by the English Bridge, all slowly silted up in the latter Middle Ages.

Upstream of Shrewsbury is an old course of the river, cut off 5,000 years ago to form a classic oxbow lake. Cutting into the banks of a large loop in the river, the waters eventually broke through and left the old loop dry, or nearly dry. The old river bed is a large loop around Coton Hill, part of which is now a nature reserve. During flooding in 2003 I remember watching the old river bed quickly fill with water, as did the adjacent sports field just beyond our house. It was a shocking moment because it was so unexpected, and a reminder that even where the river channel has developed, the subtle gradient of the old course is still remembered by the river.

Left to nature, some stretches of the river would dry up in a severe drought. To guard against this possibility Llyn Clywedog, completed in 1967, was built to maintain a flow

Islands of shingle occur naturally at several places along the river and are often found on the downstream side of bridges, like this one at Caerhowel Bridge.

Below Stourport the river level has been regulated by locks since the mid 19th century. This is the lock at Holt Fleet.

of water as far downstream as Bewdley. In 1976 the water authority released close to the maximum permitted levels of water, mainly to supply water for abstraction lower downstream. This is a vital function of the natural river. The Severn provides water to six million people, but there are other points of abstraction, notably Ironbridge power station, and water diverted to the Gloucester and Sharpness Canal, which is diverted back into the river lower downstream. Farmers also use river water to irrigate their fields. If the river flowed naturally, without any regulation or abstraction, it would look very different. Regulation is only really effective at topping up the river at low water, and the influence of the reservoirs decreases further downstream, where the flow is affected by an increasing number of tributary rivers. The relatively stable image we have of the river is therefore artificially constructed to suit our practical requirements and aesthetic expectations.

Other schemes to regulate the flow of the river were undertaken in the 19th century. The bed of the river, dredged and artificially deepened, has changed much more than the direction of the channel, and it was done largely to aid navigation and optimise the river's commercial potential. The irony is that the most comprehensive schemes for improving the channel for commercial vessels came in the 19th century, when the river trade was already in decline. For centuries, and even in its 18th-century heyday, Severn trows and barges navigated the river in its natural state. A Severn improvement scheme was begun in 1835 and over the next nine years the natural river was altered in an attempt to rescue the ailing commercial waterway. Locks were built at Holt, at Lincomb and at Diglis below Worcester. The completion of the latter in 1844, with weir and locks just below the junction with the Worcester and Birmingham Canal, meant that Worcester was no longer influenced by tidal waters. The chief engineer was Sir William Corbett and his supervising engineer was Edward Leader Williams, father of the artist Benjamin Williams Leader, whose romantic landscape paintings, such as *Smooth Severn Stream* (1886), would later portray the Severn as if such meddling had never happened.

ꙮ 2 ꙮ
Plynlimon

If you begin your river journey at the mouth and travel upstream, it is generally easy enough, when two rivers join, to differentiate the main channel from the tributary. On the Severn this remains true at least as far upstream as the confluence with the Vyrnwy, and arguably as far as the river's first main tributary, the Clywedog, which joins the Severn at Llanidloes. The flow of the Clywedog is now managed by the reservoir upstream, but in its former natural state it was said that the Clywedog contributed more water to the river than the so-called main channel;[1] and from the confluence the Clywedog has a course three miles further than that of the Severn. But the Clywedog was never considered to be the main river. Even though it rises on the edge of Plynlimon only a mile and a half to the north of the Severn, it is at an altitude over 100 metres lower. The source of the Severn is the highest point at which streams rise.

Plynlimon has been regarded as the source of the Severn for as long as the issue has concerned topographers of Wales, beginning with Giraldus Cambrensis, writing in the early 12th century. William Worcestre, writing in the 1470s, relied on his Salopian correspondent Sir Roger Kynaston to place the river's source in the distant Cambrian Mountains.[2] John Leland, antiquary to Henry VIII, noted something that no subsequent writer has been able to resist repeating: that the two greatest rivers of Wales, the Severn and Wye, rise on Plynlimon not two miles from each other, and fall into the same estuary.[3]

Plynlimon – *Pumlumon* (five peaks) – is the mountainous region of western Powys, south of Machynlleth, and was also once known, and known to Giraldus Cambrensis in the 12th century, as Elenid (both names are found in the *Mabinogion*). The name Plynlimon is rather loosely applied, meaning both a group of hills and the single hill – *Pumlumon Fawr* – which is the highest of the group. Several more rivers have their source on Plynlimon, notably the Rheidol and its tributaries Hyddgen and Hengwm, which drain to the west coast of Wales.

If the Severn rises in a mountainous wilderness, Plynlimon is a typically British form of wilderness. It is a forbidding landscape of peaty moorland and deep glaciated cwms, but hardly a trackless waste. Every place along the Severn bears a human imprint and

Plynlimon is no exception. The Ordnance Survey has been mapping Plynlimon since the early 19th century and it shows by the naming of each *nant, esgair, bryn, carreg, cwm* – stream, ridge, hill, outcrop and valley – that this is a place that has been intimately known. It continues to be so now in the name of science. Two generations of river gauging stations monitor the flow of the river like the heartbeat of a newborn child, every change in the volume of water recorded.

From the area around the source, prehistoric cairns can be made out on the hill tops at Carnfachbugeilyn, Carn Biga and Carn Fawr. A group of cairns at Pen Pumlumon Arwystli stands between the Severn and Wye, testifying to the crossing of the Cambrian Mountains by semi-nomadic Neolithic and Bronze Age communities, and perhaps even to a settled community around the prehistoric copper mine at Nant yr Eira below Pumlumon Pen Arwystli. Just to the north of the Severn is the valley of Hengwm, which is overlooked by many seemingly related cairns, suggesting that the valley was an important route across the mountains. Cairns occupy the highest and most visible points, conscious imprints of human presence on the landscape. Carreg Wen – the white stone – is a small Bronze Age standing stone that would overlook the Upper Severn valley were it not enveloped by trees. It is on lower ground than the cairns, but is special in another way – it is a large block of quartz. Quartz stones and boulders are found regularly scattered across the open hillside, but the material was never used in the building of the cairns. What special properties could have been invested in this stone standing near the head of the river?

There are ruined stone sheepfolds, and ruined 19th-century farmsteads in the sheltered valleys on Plynlimon, relics of a time when there was a living to be had on the

The river is now very much monitored.
A series of monitoring stations on Plynlimon plot its volume and rate of flow.

uplands. Two miles north of the Severn is a 19th-century farmstead at Bugeilyn, which was probably the site of a much earlier farm. The name Bugeilyn, which is also given to the adjacent lake, is probably derived from *bugeiliaid*, which originally meant 'herdsmen', although in modern Welsh it is taken to mean only shepherds. Cattle were probably herded on these mountain pastures in medieval times, perhaps in permanent farms, but the dominant theme in the history of upland farming in Wales is of seasonal habitation only, the tradition of the *lluest* or shepherding station.

A *lluest* is smaller than a farmstead, comprising only a cottage, with few ancillary buildings. There were once two such *lluestau* beside the Severn, both now lost to forestry, a sad loss of precious relics of life on the hills, the value of which has only been recognised relatively recently. Rhyd-y-benwch is three miles below the source, Blaen Hafren only a mile below. Just north of Blaen Hafren was Cwm Biga Uchaf, of a similar char-

The quartz standing stone known as Carreg Wen is now separated visually from the river by forestry. Originally it overlooked the headwaters of the Severn, although its builders must have had a very different sense of the river than our modern understanding of it.

acter, all once the home of shepherds. Blaen Hafren offered shelter to walkers when the route to the source gained some popularity as a walking destination in the 19th century.[4] There were valuable sheepwalks on the hills, to which the sheep migrated in late spring and returned at the end of the grain harvest, although some hardy breeds were kept on the mountain over winter.[5] Peat was dug from here until cheaper coal was imported by the railway to Llanidloes that opened in 1859. It was a landscape of 'coarse grass, with occasional patches of loose stones and bogs', which render Plynlimon 'very dreary and unattractive'.[6]

In the Middle Ages the uplands were the property of Strata Florida and Strata Marcella abbeys, seized by the crown at their Dissolution in 1536 and then partially sold to private landowners. Boundary stones put up in 1865 divide ownership of the moors between its subsequent owners, the crown estate and the estate of Watkin Williams Wynn, a division which is a serious matter on land where there are profitable shooting and mineral rights. Grouse shooting was popular in the 19th century, as was fishing in Plynlimon's lakes, but neither have left any trace on the ground. By contrast, shafts, adits and spoil heaps are the remains of several centuries of mining, which seems always to have happened in fits and starts.

Copper was probably mined from Plynlimon in prehistory. When, in 1858, Captain Reynolds of Llanidloes discovered a source of lead ore at Nant yr Eira, between the sources of the Severn and Wye, he found opencast pits there of great antiquity. Mining tools, ore and charcoal have been found there, and the charcoal has been radiocarbon dated to the Bronze Age. For a few years in the 18th and again in the 19th century the upland waste was once more peopled with miners, who drove an adit and sunk a shaft, but in just over 20 years the 'Snowbrook (Plynlimon) Silver-Lead Mining Company' had won little more than 200 tons of ore. It was typical of the over-optimistic mining schemes of the 19th century, when more resources went into the mines than ever came out. At Geufron, some five miles below the source, evidence of early mining can still be seen on the ground: the remains of pits, adits, a drift mine and a shaft of a lead and copper mine. Below the Severn-break-its-neck waterfall is a rib of white calcite in the river bed which would have alerted a practised eye to the presence of winnable ores in the area. Copper was mined just above here at Nantricket in the later 19th century – 209 tons to be precise, in the 40 years after 1868 in an area that is now covered in trees.[7]

Small-scale mining remains often cease to be an eyesore when nature is allowed to take its course, and ever since the miners accepted defeat in the late 19th century, Plynlimon has settled back into remote wildness with ease. A.G. Bradley wrote in 1920 that Plynlimon was 'cradled among cloudy solitudes rarely trodden by human foot, watched over by brooding mountain tops amid a silence that is rarely broken'.[8] But the scene was not as timeless as the author liked to think and was less an undiscovered landscape than an abandoned one.

One definition of a wilderness seems to be a fragile landscape under threat. Once the threat was mining waste; these days the wilderness of Wales is threatened by forests, reservoirs and wind farms. Nant-y-Moch reservoir now occupies the headwaters of the Rheidol, including Afon Hyddgen, and was completed in 1964 as part of the Rheidol hydro-electricity scheme. It has less impact on the landscape than other recent innovations. Forests were planted in the 20th century on farmland that was no longer viable or needed as agricultural land, of which Wales has more than its fair share. Wind farms are quite another matter and have become the new pine trees of upland landscapes. Secured to the ground by massive formations, they are a good deal more conspicuous than anything that has ever appeared on the hills before, and because they harness a relatively small amount of power, they have become increasingly resented by local communities.

On Plynlimon it is not as yet wind turbines but another familiar sight – upland forestry – that dominates the pilgrim's final ascent to the source of the Severn. Hafren Forest is an ancient-sounding name but it is a recent creation, part of the 20th-century afforestation of formerly marginal farmland that included Blaen Hafren, Cwm Biga Uchaf and Rhyd-y-Benwch. Ever since the creation of the Severn Way footpath, improvements have been made to this most rugged section of the river's course. A three-mile walk from Rhyd-y-Benwch is on hardcore track or boardwalk through the forest, while excellent forest roads mean that vehicles can be seen less than a mile from the source. The landscape is thus very different to that experienced by 19th-century and earlier visitors. The small farmstead of Blaen Hafren is no longer visible, but for a small stone-lined structure that may have been a sheepfold. I met no native farmers there, only fellow walkers, most of whom were local.

The official source is marked by a wooden post, mounted on a paved platform that ensures that no one need get their feet wet. It is set in inhospitable eroded peatlands at just over 600 metres above sea level, and the post marks the spot where the multitude of streamlets and oozings coalesce into a single channel, which very quickly starts to carve out a distinctive V-shaped valley. The beginning is inauspicious and indistinct, collecting water from a wide area almost as far as the boundary with Ceredigion, which is 400 metres west of the official source. When George Borrow visited in the mid 19th century he was told that the exact source of the Severn was disputed, but whichever spring was esteemed with that title, he thought it seemed 'rather a shabby source for so noble a stream'.[9] Borrow was not wrong. There is nothing neat or decisive about the source, which yields peat-stained water rather than a bubbling spring of clear liquid.

Few people have found picturesque qualities on Plynlimon that are worthy of praise. Benjamin Heath Malkin made strenuous efforts to visit the sources of several major Welsh rivers on his tour of the southern half of Wales in 1803. Although he admired Plynlimon as a vast bed of mountains, 'the ruggedness and inhospitality of its environs is in general so unrelieved, that it affords little for the picturesque enthusiasm'. Plynlimon

The source is unspectacular, just the place where streams and oozings coalesce into a single channel on the eroded peatlands of Plynlimon.

The mountain river soon forms into a steep-sided valley,
where it enters Hafren Forest.

is clearly a different proposition close-up. 'It is the most dangerous mountain in Wales, on account of the frequent bogs, which hold out no warning, concealed as they are under a smooth and apparently firm turf.'[10] Malkin's advice was to employ a guide.

Plynlimon was not one of the highlights of the Celtic Grand Tour of the late 18th and early 19th century because it does not have dramatic scenery and is not on a route to or from such scenic thrills. Thomas

This idealised image of the source appeared in Edward Pugh's *Cambria Depicta*, published in 1816, one of the few books of Picturesque views of Wales that included Plynlimon.

Pennant, for example, did not visit Plynlimon because he was told that 'it was an uninteresting object, the base most extensive, the top boggy, and the view from it over a dreary and almost uninhabited country'.[11] His informant had a point, as anyone who has walked on extensive Welsh moorland on a grey day could testify. George Borrow did visit it, and had to admit that Plynlimon 'does not look much of a hill'. Instead 'a mountainous wilderness extended on every side, a waste of russet coloured hills, with here and there a black, craggy summit … The scene would have been cheerless in the extreme had not a bright sun lighted up the landscape.'[12] In 1870 the bishop of Gloucester made a pilgrimage to the source with a companion, who related the bishop's enthusiasm for the place. About a mile below the source the stream 'defied the bishop's attempts, more than once, to jump over it'.[13] John Randall, who wrote about the Severn for the *Shrewsbury Chronicle*, found the upper stretches of the river as wild as any New World frontier. Indeed he remarked that although the English language had conquered the Australian and North American continents it had yet to penetrate 'the mountain fastness of Plynlimon'.[14]

The symbolic importance of Plynlimon should not be underestimated. Mountains are a key element in Welsh national identity, and can be seen as inalienable repositories of Welshness, safe from outside influence and a part of Wales that has never really been conquered by outsiders, either military generals or mine captains. Attachment to specific places, even unvisited places that retain an overwhelming presence, is the essence of Welshness in the industrial valleys of the south and in the mountains of the north. Gwyn Jones was born in industrial south Wales in 1907, but the mountains of mid and north Wales were his adult inspiration. He could see Plynlimon from the hill above his home near Aberystwyth, and wrote of it in the 1940s at the same time as he was working on his translation of the *Mabinogion*. From a distance Plynlimon was 'a score of rosy lumps, divagated by green valleys, black woodlands, the silver ribbons of rivers, its fields brown, grey, pink, emerald, until the blunted tops of the five mountains are lost in purple distance half-way to the English border. All this is Wales.'[15] To be Welsh is to live among mountains, and Plynlimon is a quintessentially Welsh mountain range.

Plynlimon gained a place in national mythology as a result of Owain Glyndwr's rebellion in the early 15th century. Plynlimon was a stronghold of Glyndwr in the early, invincible part of his rebellion. On Mynydd Hyddgen in 1401 he led a small Welsh force to victory over a superior army. The success of the battle was as much political as military – considerable support was attracted to the winning side, who now had access to support from south Wales. The significance accorded to Owain Glyndwr's exploits on Plynlimon can be measured by the legends that have attached to the place. Early histories recorded only 120 Welshmen against 1,500 English and Flemish forces. Glyndwr was supposed to have slept, or perhaps sought refuge, in a cave, possibly the cleft in the rock near Hyddgen known as Siambr Traws Fynydd. Craig y March (Rock of the Horse) is supposed to bear the hoofprints of Glyndwr's horse Llwyd y Bacsie; Cwm Gwarchae (Valley of the Siege) was supposed to have been so-named because Glyndwr fought there. Cerrig Cyfamod Owain Glyndwr (Stone of Owain Glyndwr's Treaty) is apparently where Glyndwr and Hugh Mortimer agreed to end hostilities; Y Stablau are caves where Glyndwr's horses were stabled.[16]

The source of the Severn almost exactly marks the boundary between Montgomeryshire and Ceredigion, east and west Wales, and is at the heart of the Cambrian Mountains between north and south Wales. Plynlimon is also the hill from which three of the great Welsh rivers flow – Wye, Severn and Rheidol – and it has been imagined as the fountain-head of Wales by many writers, beginning with the poet Lewis Glyn Cothi who, by chance, lived as an outlaw on the eastern slopes of Plynlimon after his involvement on the losing side in the battle of Mortimer's Cross in 1461, a battle in the Wars of the Roses in which the majority of the blood shed was that of Welshmen. He was one of a generation of Welsh poets living in the aftermath of the Glyndwr uprising and acutely aware of his nation's status, or lack of it:

> From high Plynlimon's shaggy side
> Three streams in three directions glide;
> To thousands at their mouth who tarry,
> Honey, gold and mead they carry.
> Flow also from Plynlimon high
> Three streams of generosity;
> The first a noble stream indeed
> Like rills of Mona runs with mead;
> The second bears from vineyards thick
> Wine to the feeble and the sick;
> The third till time shall be no more
> Mingled with gold shall silver pour.

George Borrow, who can hardly be accused of failing to immerse himself in the native culture, sang this song of nationalist pride when he visited Plynlimon and drank from each of the three rivers. In the long run, as we will see, the greatest influence of these lines would be on English authors. In the tale in the *Mabinogion* called *How Culhwch won Olwen*, Cai and Bedwyr sit on the outcrop Garn Gwylathr (the name has not survived) on Plynlimon, which is exposed to 'the strongest wind in the world'.[17] This shows the special status of Plynlimon as a mountain of the mind. In reality it is far from the highest mountain in Wales, peaking at only 752 metres, well below the summit of Snowdon at 1,085 metres and other high mountains like Cadair Idris and the Arans. But its imagined pre-eminent loftiness is also well expressed by Michael Drayton in his very different search for the *genius loci*, in which he deified the landscape with female rivers and patriarchal mountains. Plynlimon is eulogised as the source of the great Welsh rivers:

> What once the *Druids* told, how great those floods should bee
> That here (most mightie Hill) derive themselves from thee.
> The Bards with furie rapt, the *British* youth among,
> Unto the charming Harpe thy future honor sang
> In brave and loftie straines; …
> That all the *Cambrian* hills, which high'st their heads doe beare
> With most obsequious showes of lowe subjected feare,
> Should to thy greatnes stoupe: and all the Brooks that be,
> Doe homage to those Floods that issued out of thee:
> To princelie *Severne* first; next to her sister *Wye*,
> Which to her elders Court her course doth still apply.
> But *Rydoll*, young'st, and least, and for the others pride
> Not finding fitteth roomth upon the rising side,
> Alone unto the West directlie takes her way.
> So all the neighbouring hills *Plynillimmon* obey.[18]

Michael Drayton, whose *Poly-Olbion* was published in 1613 and is subtitled 'England's [sic] great variety', was one of the first authors to perceive the Severn as a natural expression of British nationhood, only a few decades after the Union of England and Wales in 1536. The idea is developed as he describes the course of the river downstream. In his view, to cut a barrier across the Severn was therefore not merely unjust but against nature, and that is precisely what happened when the Mercian king Offa raised his dyke 'athwart the Cambrian wast' at Buttington. Severn therefore

> … sees the wrong thus offered her,
> Though by injurious Time deprived of that place
> Which anciently shee held: yet loth that her disgrace
> Should on the *Britains* light …[19]

Drayton's riposte is a lengthy description of the island's great history, but the point is surely the unnaturalness of the old division between England and Wales. Such mythologised histories inevitably lead to the justification of the present. In the case of the Severn it should be noted that the authors who have sought to emphasise Plynlimon as a fountain-head of Britishness have been English rather than Welsh. The Reverend Luke Booker is a good example. In his narrative poem *The Springs of Plynlimmon* of 1834 he raised a Union flag on Plynlimon when he wrote of the Severn and Wye:

> Twin rivers – none more beauteous seen
> In rocky dell or meadow green,
> Effusing, as with joy, to crown
> The Union (mark'd for high renown)
> Of Cambria grand, and Anglia fair, –
> On Earth's vast chart the loveliest pair
> Of nations, blended now in one, –
> More fine, – more brave – Earth boasted none.[20]

Francis Brett Young wrote his patriotic narrative poem *The Island* during the Second World War. Less self-satisfied and more defiant than Booker, Young personified the river's story, in which Plynlimon stands for the world in a state of nature:

> Severn is born of the sodden mosses
> Where smooth Plynlimon's dome is bowed
> Under the rain the West Wind tosses
> From tattered fleeces of sea-born cloud;
> Where the sour-grass moors lie wet and wan,
> And the mawn pool's mirror is misted glass,
> And the skirts of the sky's pavilion
> Daggle the lint-white cotton grass;
> Where wild the curlew whinnies and cries
> And whimbrels wheel in windy weather
> And buzzards peck at the glazing eyes
> Of sick lambs lost in the rain-lodged heather.
> Only the carrion wings rejoice
> Screaming above the smell of slaughter;
> For the mountain's voice is but the voice
> Of wind-stripped grasses and welling water …[21]

In the poem, the river's journey is from savagery to civilisation, which is achieved by the pacification and harnessing of nature. It is hardly an original formula, but Young's is a rare voice that makes a poetic virtue out of the cruelty of nature. Plynlimon, and the Severn in general, have more often been celebrated in literature and art as a benign presence, expressing the purity of nature rather than its cruelty. On the Severn this has been made easier because it can be written about through the medium of a goddess: Sabrina.

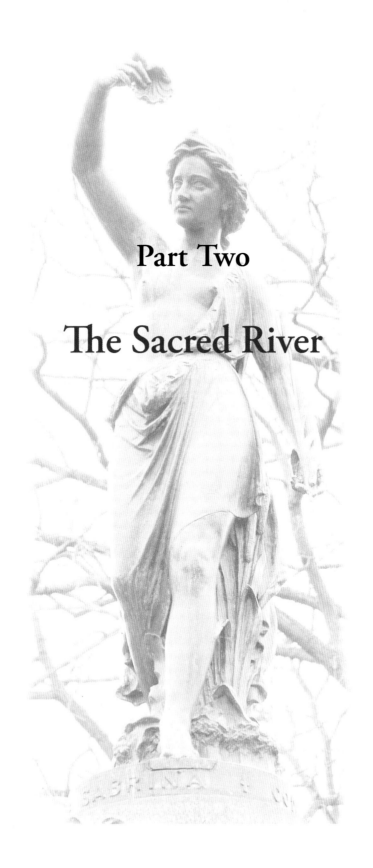

Part Two

The Sacred River

৩ 3 ৫
Sabrina

There is a story of five sister water spirits on Plynlimon, who one night agreed that, the next morning, they would make separate journeys to visit their father the Ocean. Vaga (the river Wye) was first to wake and make her way southwards. Sabrina woke next and headed eastwards to take a more leisurely route to the sea, and she did not divert southwards until she was warned by a small bird that Vaga was well ahead of her. Rhydiol (Rheidol), Llyfriant and Mynac (Mynach) all woke late and, realising that Sabrina and Vaga had started out before them, took shorter, westward routes to the sea. Some elements of this story are at least as old as the Middle Ages, but this version was copied from the window of the Phoenix Gallery in Llanidloes. According to William Harrison, writing in the 16th century, the three rivers on Plynlimon (Wye, Severn, Rheidol) were 'commonlie called the three sisters', although none of the ancient authors – chiefly Nennius, Geoffrey of Monmouth, and the various authors of the *Mabinogion* – mention it.[1] Michael Drayton deified the rivers with nymphs when he published *Poly-Olbion* in 1613, but did not refer to three or five sisters. The inclusion of five instead of three rivers was, as we shall see, current by the 18th century, but seems to have been based upon a mistranslation of *Pumlumon* as 'five rivers'. The revival of such stories in the 21st century shows a society still hungry for river myths and for celebrating the spiritual side of nature.

Many ancient authors wrote of Sabrina. Whether she was a Celtic goddess is a matter of speculation – she is not mentioned as a goddess directly in any pre-Christian context, but the idea was brought into the debate about pre-Roman culture by Anne Ross, pioneer of pagan Celtic studies in the 1960s, supported by the possible pre-Christian origin of the legend that Geoffrey of Monmouth recounted in the 12th century. The myths of Sabrina may therefore be an echo of the Celtic divinity, but she is a goddess in a more tangible sense: an idealisation that can be moulded to suit whatever we want her to be. The Sabrina of literature has been used to represent nationhood, freedom, martyrdom, family, chastity, purity of the human spirit and purity of nature. All of these myths were consciously made by their authors; there is no reason to think that there was ever a Sabrina that was not manufactured to meet the needs of contemporary society.

The earliest known version of Sabrina's story, in which the protagonist is known as Hafren or Habren, appears in Geoffrey of Monmouth's *History of the Kings of Britain*, which was written in Latin and completed in about 1136.[2] As a work of national myth it has remained powerful, and has given us characters such as King Lear and Cymbeline. As a work of history, Geoffrey remained authoritative well beyond the Middle Ages and was so popular that the story of Hafren survived to be retold by Spenser, Milton, and many later, lesser writers. Not that everybody has been impressed by it. William Camden, refusing to suspend his disbelief, sneered that it was 'only a Fable of Jeffry's invention'.[3]

Geoffrey's tale draws upon national foundation myths. As a Welshman, he was keen to put the Celtic side of the story, and to him the Severn was an important frontier and perhaps a national symbol. Brutus, grandson of the Trojan Aeneas, was the founder of Britain, an island that is divided among the three sons who succeeded him – Locrinus, king of England, Kamber, king of the land west of the Severn and Albanactus, king of Scotland. Another Trojan, Corineus the brother of Brutus, was king of Cornwall. When Britain was invaded by the king of the Huns, Locrinus assembled an army and defeated the invading force, although the king of the Huns escaped and lived like a wild man until he was drowned, giving the river Humber its name. Meanwhile Locrinus fell in love with Humber's concubine Estrildis, daughter of the king of Germany, who had been captured by the Huns in an earlier victory. The romance of Locrinus and Estrildis irked Corineus, who browbeat Locrinus into accepting his daughter Gwendolen in marriage. But Locrinus continued to see Estrildis in secret after his marriage, and Estrildis bore a daughter, Hafren. Once the feared Corineus had died, Locrinus gave up the charade of married life to live with his Germanic rather than his Celtic family. Gwendolen sought revenge and assembled an army of Cornishmen that met Locrinus just beyond the Severn at a point by the Stour. Locrinus was slain by an arrow and, with his son still too young to be crowned king, Gwendolen assumed the throne of England. She ordered Estrildis and Hafren to be cast into the river, but with a twinge of sympathy, ordered that the river be named after the blameless daughter. For Geoffrey, Hafren is therefore a permanent reminder of the tragic union of Celt and Saxon.

Was this all a product of Geoffrey's imagination? William of Newburgh commented sourly in 1190 that Geoffrey wrote to satisfy his 'inordinate love of lying, or for the sake of pleasing the Britons'.[4] This might be jealousy, or counter-chauvinism, but at least indicates to us that he was not merely repeating commonly held beliefs about the past. Geoffrey's claim that his source was an ancient Welsh manuscript is tantalising. It is true that, in the context of Geoffrey's narrative, the story of Hafren and the river is an unnecessary diversion. It seems plausible, therefore, that Geoffrey was determined to insert an old story gleaned from an earlier manuscript source, even though it added little to the overall story. But the meaning invested in it is surely Geoffrey's. The story associates the innocence and purity of Hafren with the river, a notion that has been exploited in different guises ever since. Sabrina's death could easily be rewritten as martyrdom, and a play on just such lines was said to have been performed in the Dingle beside the river at Shrewsbury in 1516.[5] Furthermore, the story of the early British kings and Sabrina's death became part of the nation's official mythology. Geoffrey was clearly the main source for the chronicle of British kings given in Spenser's *Faerie Queene* of 1596, in which the unlucky offspring of the 'lewd love' between Locrine and Estrild,

> ... the sad virgin innocent of all
> Adowne the rolling river she did poure,
> Which of her name now *Severne* men do call.[6]

The subject matter also found its way on to the London stage in *The Lamentable Tragedie of Locrine*, which was printed in London in 1595, overseen and corrected by 'W.S.', for which reason it was once attributed to Shakespeare. The play broadly follows the plot set out by Geoffrey, with some embellishment. Estrildis and her daughter are kept in secret in an alternative palace on the bank of the river Lea at Deucolitum (St Albans?). But geography plays only a minor role until the final scene, 'Nigh to the great river of Mertia' where, in a riverside cave, the defeated Locrine takes his own life, followed by Estrildis. Gwendoline wanted revenge and felt thwarted until Sabren was discovered:

> And not a common death shall Sabren die,
> But after strange and greevous punishments
> Shortly inflicted upon thy bastards head,
> Thou shalt be cast into the cursed streames,
> And feede the fishes with thy tender flesh.[7]

Only because Sabren eluded her and jumped headlong into the river did Gwendoline check her feelings. Forced to concede the young girl's bravery, Gwendoline declared that the river should be named after her. Locrine's tragedy is one of 'lawless treacherie, of usurpation and ambitious pride', caused by his pursuit of private desires over public duty.[8] It was this play that Algernon Swinburne used as the model for his own verse drama *Locrine*, written and published in 1887.

Swinburne seems to have treated Geoffrey's story of Sabrina as history rather than myth. As he wrote on New Year's Day in 1887, Locrine 'came to grief through imprudently marrying two wives and ... [his] young daughter Sabrina became (and is now) the goddess of the river Severn ... in which she was drowned'.[9] In this love story, Swinburne made use of its geographical potential, if in very conventional ways. The court, where Locrinus follows empty protocols of married life, is contrasted with the woody idyll by the river Lea where Estrild and Sabrina live in secret. So the falsehood, treachery and vacuous social conventions of the court – Gwendolen scolds Locrinus as 'traitor born and liar, false-faced, false tongued' – are contrasted with the purity, honesty and poverty of the riverbank, which is in a deeper sense infinitely richer. As Estrild says:

> Have we not enough here of diadems
> Hung high round portals pillared smooth with stems
> More fair than marble?[10]

'Flowers are serious things, but towers are toys,' Sabrina adds. Not until the final scene does the action shift to the bank of the Severn, where the opposing armies of Locrine and Gwendolen settle their scores. Here Swinburne allows Locrine to die with his real and proper family – Estrild and Sabrina – rather than the one that society recognizes. Sabrina drowns herself, but the river is purified rather than polluted by the body of the drowned girl. Her half-brother Madan watches as

> … The water whirls
> Down out of sight her tender face, and hurls
> Her soft light limbs to deathward.[11]

In *Poly-Olbion* Michael Drayton also portrayed Sabrina as the purifying spirit of the river, and for him the river's youthful upstream stretches seem to have personified the Severn. The river may be the watery grave of Elstred and Sabrine, but

> In a deadlie dreame
> Your corses were dissolv'd into that crystal streame,
> Your curles to curled waves, which plainlie still appeare
> The same in water now, that once in locks they were:
> And, as you wont to clip each others neck before,
> Yee now with liquid armes embrace the wandering shore.[12]

Drayton's Sabrina is a way of revitalising our sense of the river as a living thing, but his invocation of a presiding deity – think of Isis and the Thames – is a classicizing one and not the continuity of Celtic lore. Drayton was an Englishman writing in a Renaissance tradition; he had no direct knowledge of pre-Christian deities.

John Milton's version of the story appears in the masque *Comus* and has a strong religious context. His allusion to the Severn was appropriate, given that *Comus* was first performed at Ludlow Castle in 1634 to accompany the inauguration of the earl of Bridgewater as Lord President of Wales. The parts were played by the earl's children, except for Sabrina, who was probably played by a commoner. In the masque a Lady tries to resist the advances of Comus, the superficially suave lothario whose inner corruption only appears as events unfold. The Lady and Comus argue about soul and body, the struggle between rationality and libido, virtue versus vice, moral rectitude versus immoral depravity. But the Lady cannot resist Comus without the help of a guardian angel and divine grace, the latter represented by Sabrina. To free the Lady from Comus, her brothers seek the help of the Attendant Spirit, who, disguised as a shepherd, epitomising humility and simplicity, raises Sabrina with a song. Sabrina is able to help the Lady because she is virtuous and a virgin. Here Sabrina represents divine intervention. Where people had once invoked the saints to intercede on their behalf, now Milton can call on Sabrina, a Protestant re-incarnation of the Virgin Mary.

> There is a gentle Nymph not far from hence,
> That with moist curb sways the smooth Severn stream;

> Sabrina is her name, a virgin pure;
> Whilom she was the daughter of Locrine,
> That had the sceptre from his father Brute.
> She, guiltless dame, flying the mad pursuit
> Of her enraged stepdame Guendolen,
> Commended her fair innocence to the flood
> That stayed her flight with his cross-flowing course;
> That water nymphs that in the bottom played
> Held up her pearled wrists and took her in.[13]

Taking pity on her innocence, the nymphs, directed by the god Nereus, the Old Man of the Sea,

> … through the porch and inlet of each sense
> Dropped in ambrosial oils, till she revived
> And underwent a quick immortal change,
> Made goddess of the river. Still she retains
> Her maiden gentleness …[14]

Henceforth Sabrina lives in a pastoral idyll where the shepherds throw garlands of pansies and daffodils, and sits 'under the glassy, cool, translucent wave'. The allusions are classical but they merely dress up Christian morality:

> For maidenhood she loves, and will be swift
> To aid a virgin such as was herself
> In hard-besetting need.[15]

Morality is a cornerstone of the fairy tale, and one that embeds it deep in native culture. In the Reverend Luke Booker's 1834 poem *The Springs of Plynlimmon* Sabrina was a 'Cambrian Maid' pure in heart, but her stepmother had other ideas. Booker altered the plot of the traditional story by adding another villain, Beredith. When Sabrina was courted by the wealthy Beredith her stepmother saw an opportunity of ridding herself of an unwanted stepdaughter. Alas,

> … base was this high suitors flame,
> Dishonouring love's delightsome name.
> Yet tho' Sabrina him despis'd
> He, by her step-dame, much was priz'd
> A ruthless, worthless dame was she.[16]

Stepmothers were always the villains of fairy tales, usurpers of the true family. With the stepmother's blessing, Beredith maintained his pursuit of Sabrina and followed her to her favourite spot on the river:

He strove to seize her flowing hair;
When – nerv'd by Terror and Despair –
She, from a rock that girt the shore,
Sprung – and deep sank to rise no more!
Aghast, look'd down from where he stood,
Her vile pursuer, as the flood
Enclos'd within its cold embrace,
The purest – fairest of her race![17]

The most tantalising and interesting aspect of this episode is that, according to Booker, the event of Sabrina's drowning was commemorated every year:

And the annual Day,
That took the virtuous maid away,
Pictur'd a mournful, moving sight –
All deck'd in vests of purest white –
A lovely, pensive, virgin train,
Link'd arm in arm across the plain,
Each with a lily and a rose,
Emblem of Her that woke their woes.[18]

This pageant, also mentioned by Milton in the 17th century, was described by John Dyer in the mid 18th century as a custom prevalent between the Wrekin and Dolforwyn. By the end of the 19th century it had disappeared and was interpreted as another example of a declining rural culture.[19]

The 18th-century poets introduced a new agenda, appropriate to an emerging mercantile, industrial and imperial nation. John Dyer's allusion to Sabrina appears in his poem *The Fleece*, published in 1757, an unlikely poetical discourse on sheep rearing and a vindication of English breeds. This is pastoral verse in the stylised manner that pre-dated the Romantics, in which the shepherds are 'swains', one of whom climbs up Breidden Hill and compares the noble scene set out below against the 'gardens black with smoke in dusty towns'. Swains and nymphs pay homage to Sabrina, 'guardian of the crystal flood' who 'shall bless our cares' as a protectress of the flocks. Sabrina, reclining with her sisters in 'hoar caves, around Plynlimon's brow', mingles seeds and herbs with

… the divided torrents, ere they burst
Thro' the dark clouds, & down the mountain roll.
Not taint worm shall infect the yeaning herds,
Nor penny-grass, nor spearwort's pois'nous leaf.

From the Wrekin to Dolforwyn the swains declare their gratitude:

> ... o'er the dimpled stream a thousand flow'rs,
> Pale lilies, roses, violets and pinks,
> Mix'd with the greens of burnet, mint, and thyme,
> And trefoil, sprinkled with their sportive arms.[20]

This is an idyll better suited to the limpid waters of the upper river than the bustling, commercialised and silted lower river. But in Dyer's poem the river is not a real river at all. In an unlikely final image a 'trading bark with low contracting sail' lingers among the reeds, listening and watching as the rustics spread flowers and settle down on the riverbank to feast on early fruits and 'dulcet cream'. Dyer's image is of a landscape blessed by its river, written in the classical pastoral style but transported from the Mediterranean to the temperate climate of the Atlantic seaboard.

Whenever Sabrina has been used to represent purity she has always migrated upstream. In the version known to the 20th-century author Brian Waters, Hafren is said to have fled from her father's Dolforwyn Castle, which overlooks the Severn below Newtown.[21] Waters may have learned this from John Dyer, who described Dolforwyn as 'Sabrina's early haunt'; or from Thomas Pennant, who interpreted Dolforwyn as 'Meadow of the Maiden'.[22] In the mid 19th century John Randall added a further twist, when he was told by the locals at Caersws of a nearby place called Rhos-ddiarbedd, the 'field of no quarter', which was a rival to the Meadow of the Maiden. Caersws was thought to have been a city founded by Locrinus, and the accompanying story he learned clearly echoes Geoffrey of Monmouth's version, with the same elements of a jealous stepmother and virginity finding a watery grave.[23]

Dyer's gentle move in the direction of national pride was taken further by the Reverend Luke Booker, vicar of Dudley, who was able to invoke a sense of nationhood with a good deal of self-satisfaction by the 1830s. *The Springs of Plynlimmon* is structured around the medieval tale of the three river deities on Plynlimon, but now increased to five. (John Dyer had also referred to five rivers, in his case adding the Clywedog and Ystwyth to the trio of Severn, Wye and Rheidol.) By adopting an allegorical tone, Booker made Britain's greatness seem pre-ordained as soon as its great rivers found their routes across the land and conferred their blessings upon it. As these highways of destiny reach the sea, the logical extension is that Britain's destiny is to sail out into the Severn Sea and onwards to the world. The story, therefore, is a new British creation myth that begins on Plynlimon, which is here depicted as a father figure who urges his five water spirits to seek out 'their great Sire, the Sea'. Off go the Wye (Vaga) and Severn (Sabrina), and the minor spirits the Rheidol, Mynach and Ystwyth to

> ... bless the vales thro' which ye stray:
> The grateful vales their flow'rs shall bring
> And waving fields shall laugh and sing.[24]

The similarity between the rivers of Plynlimon and the four rivers flowing out of Eden was not lost on Booker. His geography, however, was not as well informed as his

The sculpture of Sabrina in the Castle Gardens at Bridgnorth proclaims her as the Goddess of the Severn.

bible reading. The Ystwyth and Mynach do not rise on Plynlimon.

Of the five rivers Sabrina takes the most circuitous route to the sea, as if initially unsure of herself and losing her bearings. She takes a meandering course, turning any which way she pleases, as if to maximise her fluvial benevolence. As she travels east she passes the Breidden Hills, where in future years a pillar would be raised to commemorate the naval triumphs of Lord Rodney and the British navy over the French in the West Indies, in ships built from Powysland oaks floated down the river Severn. These glories were still fresh in the mind of Booker's generation, when martial prowess went a long way to defining Britain as a nation. At Shrewsbury Sabrina circles round to form a crescent and then ordains that

> A city, on that spot shall rise;
> Which (as my waves increase) shall claim
> Distinctive honours to its Name.[25]

Commerce would shed its 'wealth-creating smile' on Shrewsbury, and downstream the wonder of the Iron Bridge is anticipated as a triumph of genius, art and commerce. And so on, to Bewdley, Stourport, the cathedral at Worcester (Vigornia), and the Vale of Evesham. Sabrina may have flowed through scenes 'destitute of man's abode' but they were destined to host living and thriving communities, as if the river was nourishing the land into existence.

> In prospect, too, thro' Evesham's vale,
> Commerce, she knew, would spread its sail,
> And Nature such luxuriance give,
> That, there, in plenty all may live –
> The vale a Garden – fruit and flow'rs,
> Nurtur'd by genial warmth and show'rs.[26]

Disruption of this pre-ordained land of the blessed is sensed as Sabrina flows past the future battlefield of Tewkesbury. When the river turns red with the blood of Britons fighting each other, it is an affront to nature, but the river will win because it has the power to purify:

> Sabrina knew that level plain
> Wou'd drink the blood of thousands slain;
> And need her waves to wash away
> The carnage-horrors of the fray.[27]

And so on. Patriotism can take many forms, however, and Sabrina was revived in the 20th century in a less triumphalist manner as the patron goddess of the river and a symbol of local and regional culture. If you consulted a list of vessels navigating the Severn in the 18th and 19th centuries you would be hard pressed to find any of them named Sabrina – an ironic exception being the steam launch *Sabrina* built in 1871 for the engineers and directors of the Gloucester and Sharpness Canal. The Royal Navy's use of the name reflected the martial outlook of Booker and his contemporaries. The first HMS *Sabrina* was an 18-gun sloop launched in 1806, but decommissioned in 1816 during the peace following Waterloo. HMS *Sabrina*, an M-class Destroyer, was built for the Royal

Sabrina in the Quarry Park at Shrewsbury, sculpted by Peter Hollins in 1846. The classical nymph was originally made for Weston Park, Staffordshire, but was moved to her present position in 1985.

Navy in 1916 and saw active service in World War I, although she was scrapped with the rest of her class after only a decade of service. Six barges, named *Sabrina 1-6*, were built by Charles Hill & Sons in Bristol in 1944 at the behest of the Ministry of War Transport for service on the Severn navigation, and the Ministry's self-conscious reference to the region's heritage at such a time is hardly coincidence. Now Sabrina is everywhere, lending her name to river boats and bridges, as well as riverside streets and housing developments in Bridgnorth, Bewdley, Shrewsbury and Worcester; Shrewsbury even has a Sabrina Brass Band. In Worcester the late 20th-century footbridge named after the nymph of the Severn is just upstream of the same mythical figure carved on John Gwynn's 18th-century Worcester Bridge.

Sabrina's transition from Celtic goddess to classical water nymph was achieved by the English poets such as Drayton and Milton. The next phase, her transition from

This mermaid-like figure of Sabrina is in the park at Llanidloes.

a classical nymph of polite culture to today's goddess of popular heritage, is best seen in the small number of public sculptures depicting Sabrina. For sculptors commissioned to make likenesses of Sabrina in the 19th century, the prototype was the classical water nymph, naked above the waist, her lower half draped in classical robes, bulrushes in her hair. Such was the design made by John Bacon for the sculpture at Croome Park, cast in Coade stone in 1802.[28] The bronze statue of Sabrina at Amherst College in Massachusetts is also a scantily-clad nymph. The version carved in 1846 by Peter Hollins was originally made for Weston Park in Staffordshire, but was given to the town of Shrewsbury in 1879 and has been in the Quarry Park by the riverside ever since, although it was only placed in its present position by an ornamental pool in the Dingle in 1985.[29] James Milo ap Griffith's 1881 sculpture in Bridgnorth, now in the Castle Grounds, is broadly in the same vein; the semi-naked nymph, proclaimed as Goddess of the Severn, stands above a drinking fountain, holding a clam shell and bulrushes. The most recent representation of Sabrina is a sculpture by Sue Thornton and Neil Reeves in the riverside park at Llanidloes. Having no unique visual reference points, the artists sought a familiar and accessible image for a democratic age and chose a mermaid. The wooden sculpture of Sabrina made as part of a 'Circle of Legends' at Tintern Old Station in 2002 is also a mermaid.

Behind this Sabrina-mermaid revival is the desire to re-imagine the river Severn and to bring back a sense of mystery and wonder in a utilitarian, institutionalised landscape. It is surely part of a wider unease about a world that we are increasingly covering with concrete and tarmac. Sabrina comes out of this modern version like the *genius loci*, or presiding deity of the river, with a decidedly prelapsarian air. At the legend's root is a timeless notion of purity, water as pure as mountain springs, unsullied by the grime of life, and Sabrina's story is one of innocence betrayed, which takes us a long way from the idea of a mere Celtic goddess and is the fruit of centuries of conscious myth making. The cumulative effect is to ensure that Sabrina today is just as alive as she has ever been.

❧ 4 ❧
A River of Churches

It is said that the tall spire of Worcester St Andrew was once the favourite perch of a cormorant. From the height of 245½ feet, it could swoop down into the river and fly back to its perch in less than a minute, usually with an eel in its beak.[1] The eels have gone and, but for its spire, so has the church of St Andrew, which stood behind the South Quay. But churches still command the skyline at Worcester, not least in the form of its riverside cathedral, and throughout its course churches are among the major landmarks of the river.

Before the churches there were pagan worshippers, but the extent to which they paid special reverence to the river is difficult to pin down. If what follows seems impressionistic, perhaps that is because there has been no systematic study of rivers as sacred places. Rivers, especially rivers with islands in them, belong with other natural features like caves, mountains and springs, as places that assumed a sacred character throughout prehistoric Europe. They play a significant role in many creation myths and their association with fertility is obvious. One of the most potent notions about rivers is that they are the boundary between the living and the dead, a feature of prehistoric societies that has been discovered from the southern to the northern tip of Europe.[2] Their mysterious qualities must have prompted questions: Where does the river flow from? Was it divinely sent? Where does it flow to? What gods or ancestors live there? What is surprising is not how many sacred sites are close to the river, but how few of them we have been able to recover.

The Broadstone, a Bronze Age standing stone on the floodplain near Tidenham, was surely focused on the river, even if it is now cruelly out of sight of the Severn behind the railway embankment. The most exciting groups of riverside prehistoric monuments have been found between Welshpool and Newtown. Near Berriew is a cluster of Neolithic and Bronze Age sites that testify to the ritual importance over many centuries of this place, which might have acquired its original significance because it is close to the Dyffryn ford.[3] The earliest feature is probably a Neolithic long barrow, raised in the early 4th millennium BC, the earliest phase of which was a cairn of river-borne boulders.[4] Several hundred years later, probably in the early 3rd millennium BC, a henge,

The cathedral and the spire of St Andrew in Worcester (the rest of the church has been taken down) are among the unforgettable sights on the Severn skyline.

or ritual enclosure, was built, to the south-west of which is the stone known as Maen Beuno. The standing stone might be associated with the henge (like the Heel Stone at Stonehenge over which the midsummer sun rises), even though it was later associated with the 6th-century monk St Beuno. The henge probably had a stone circle within it. Henges were commonly built close to sources of water, including Stonehenge, where the earthworth avenue leads toward the river Avon.[5] Later on, round barrows were built close to the henge and, eventually, on top of it. The henge appears to have been the focus of activity, the centre of a riverside ritual landscape as Stonehenge was, albeit on a larger scale.

Another ritual landscape has been discovered at Sarn-y-bryn-caled, to the south of Welshpool, part of which was excavated in the early 1990s before it was disturbed by the building of a Welshpool bypass. Although the main sites are now approximately one kilometre from the river, the course of the Severn in prehistoric times ran much closer to them, although we do not know precisely the exact course or courses of the old meanders. In the early 4th millennium BC a long linear earthwork, known as a cursus, was constructed. One end of it may have terminated at the riverbank, or perhaps it was oriented parallel to the river. Either way, the river appears to have been a significant factor in its location. Several hundred years later the importance of this place was re-emphasised by the building of other ritual structures and enclosures. They include three round ditched enclosures, one of which may have been a henge monument similar to the one described above, and in c.2000 BC a circle of timber posts was erected.[6]

On the hill above Lydney is the Roman temple dedicated to the god Nodens which was established in the 3rd century, although the surviving structures date from rebuilding in AD 364 and later. The temple was never washed by the river's floodwaters or tides, as it stands at a safe distance on the hill above the floodplain, but it over-looks the lower section of the river and estuary. The site was a healing sanctuary, while Nodens was probably associated with the sea, and was perhaps the god of the estuary. A mosaic within the temple, destroyed in the 19th century, depicted dolphins, fish and sea monsters, while various bronze artefacts recovered by excavation showed a sea god driving a chariot, fishermen and tritons.[7]

No temple has been discovered that is known to have been dedicated to Sabrina; her supposed Celtic divine status rests to a large extent upon the association of other Celtic rivers with deities.[8] This association was sometimes marked by casting prestige objects into the river – this was common in British rivers such as the Trent, the Thames, and the Witham – and sometimes rivers were associated with particular divinities. For example, in Gaul, Matrona (mother) was goddess of the Marne, Sequana of the Seine, Souconna of the Saone, and in England Verbeia was goddess of the river Wharfe – we know this because an altar was set up in her honour at Ilkley. In English the Dee derives from 'Deva', or goddess; in Welsh Dyfrdwy is 'water of a deity'. But there is no comparable evidence for the Severn. True, the Severn has always been regarded as feminine (Sabrina is a feminine form in Latin), but no altars set up in her name, nor any inscriptions to her, have been discovered. It remains a curious and unexplained fact that rivers flowing east to west – like the Thames and the Trent – have yielded enormous quantities of offerings ranging from human skulls to valuable ceremonial metalwork (most Iron Age metalwork recovered by archaeologists originally found its way into the river in the form of offerings thrown into the water), but north-south flowing rivers such as the Severn and Wye have yielded very little.

So when churches were sited along the Severn, they were not built in a landscape purged of history; the notion that some places in the landscape are closer to the divine than others remained prevalent through the Middle Ages. But there were many other reasons why churches succumbed to the gravitational pull of the river. Their sites were sometimes chosen to be close to crossings, to serve the inhabitants of towns, villages and castles, or simply because the land was cheap, or wasteland.

Christianity had reached the Severn as early as the 4th century, assuming that the building excavated at Wroxeter that looks like a church really was one. It had an aisled 'nave', an apse at the east end and a portico at the west end, so in plan it clearly resem-bles the basilican form adopted in early Christian architecture. There were probably also Christians in Worcester. A bronze cross with a chi-rho monogram has been discovered there, and just within the walls of the Roman town is the church of St Helen, dedicated to the mother of Constantine, the first Christian Roman emperor. St Helen's church may have been continuously a place of worship since Roman times – which would explain why Worcester was chosen as the see, or religious centre, of the kingdom of the Hwicce in 680. St Helen had been the primary church of the region and may have been the seat of a British bishop.[9] Its counterpart in Gloucester is St Mary de Lode, which is

St Mary de Lode is Gloucester's oldest church and has outlived the channel of the river that flowed on its north-west side.

probably the city's oldest church. Excavation there uncovered an earlier building of the 5th or 6th century, with burials oriented east-west in the Christian fashion, which was either a church or a mausoleum.[10]

The Severn may have washed clean the souls of our Celtic and Saxon ancestors, as the Jordan cleansed the soul of Jesus when he was baptised by John. Until fonts were made for riverside churches – and none of the surviving fonts of Severn churches is earlier than the late 11th century – the river was the ideal place to perform a fundamental Christian rite of passage.

The river was also, by tradition at least, a boundary in early Christianity between the Christian Celts and the pagan Anglo-Saxons. In a 14th-century *Life of St Beuno*, the saint is said to have established a monastic community at Berriew, and was walking by the river when he heard the voice of an Englishman on the opposite bank. Immediately he uprooted the community and retreated to north Wales, leaving only a disciple, Rithwlint, to live as a solitary by the river.[11] The Lower Severn valley may have retained its Christian culture in an unbroken tradition from the Romans. There is a marked absence of pagan Saxon burials in the area around Gloucester. Worcester probably never lost its Christian community.

The Severn was possibly also the place where the Celtic bishops reconnected with the Latin church. Augustine, sent by the pope on a mission to convert England in AD 602, met the Welsh bishops, ending their sense of isolation as a Christian community. Bede describes a place that was known as Augustine's oak, but there were several such places in later history, one of them near Bewdley.[12] A more likely location is at Aust Cliff, from which the M48 motorway now enters on to the Severn Bridge, since Bede describes it as the border between the Hwicce and West Saxon kingdoms.[13] If so the Welsh bishops crossed the river to meet the pope's envoy, signifying, if you wish, their homage to the pope and acknowledging his authority. Augustine urged the archbishop and seven bishops of Wales that the Celtic church should celebrate Easter on the same day as the Roman church. He even performed a miracle – restoring the sight of a blind man – to help persuade them. At a subsequent meeting, however, the Welsh refused to shift from their own tradition, having sought the counsel of a hermit. According to later folklore (i.e. not in Bede's original account), the hermit lived at Blackstone near Bewdley.[14]

There really were hermits by the river, as attested in several places. Numerous medieval references to chapels at Tidenham and Beachley show that there was a cluster of hermitages at the mouth of the river, although not every reference necessarily refers to a different chapel. For example, there was a chapel of St Ewen by a passage ferry house at Beachley in 1573, but it had been demolished by 1779, and close by was a chapel of St Margaret in the 15th century. The 'hermit of St Nicholas' mentioned in 1270 and 'Patrick the chaplain of St Nicholas' mentioned in 1273 seem to indicate yet another chapel. The hermitage on Chapel Rock at Beachley is mentioned in several sources from the 13th century onwards. It was only accessible at low tide across the muddy foreshore and is the only chapel known to have been built in the river rather than on its banks or bridges.[15] It was probably dedicated originally to St Tecla, the 8th-century nun who aided Boniface in his missionary work in Germany. In 1290 the chapel was referred to as St Tryak de Betesley, and later St Tryacle or St Treacle, but since 1830 it has been dedicated to St Twrog.[16] In the 1940s a navigational light was placed beside the ruin,

The ruins of St Tecla's chapel on Chapel Rock below Beachley.
It is possible that the hermit provided a navigational light or acted as a ferryman.

which perhaps honours the original function of the chapel, and around the ruins is a minute island of grass. On the opposite bank there was a medieval chapel on the sea wall at Oldbury; the building has now metamorphosed into Chapel House. Nearby was a holy thorn that was said to bloom at Christmas, similar to the one at Glastonbury and also fancifully claimed to have been planted by Joseph of Arimathea.[17]

Hermits operated the ferry at Redstone Rock near Stourport, where they eked out a meagre existence living in caves. Or at least they did in theory. The Brethren of the Redstone became the stuff of local legend. According to Bishop Latimer, writing in 1538, the caves were anything but a solitary retreat, having room for about 500 men, and nor were the hermits prone to asceticism, given that they had a reputation for harbouring thieves and traitors. The 12th-century monk Layamon, chronicler of British history in his poem *Brut*, is supposed to have lived there. The catacombs at the foot of Redstone Rock could certainly house a community, but not one of 500. Thomas Habington visited the site in the 1630s, when it may still have been frequented by Catholics as a sacred place. It comprised a chapel and other rooms, with an altar hewn from the rock. Above the altar was a painting showing an archbishop saying Mass, perhaps St Thomas Becket, with attendant symbols of the Passion, and a defaced legend that appeared to offer indulgences to those who prayed there. But Habington heard nothing to link the hermits with 'Radston's Ferry', which was still in operation at that time. He learned from a local man that 'many who trafficked on thys river gave as they passed by in theyre barges somewhat of theyre commodityes in charity to this Hermyte'.[18] The place is said subsequently to have been a cottage, a school and a riverside public house, but it had been abandoned by the early 19th century.[19]

You can still see lines of joist holes of 19th-century buildings built against the natural cliff, which belonged perhaps to the alehouse frequented by watermen. All the cavities

The ferry at Redstone Rock near Stourport was operated by hermits known as the Brethren of the Redstone. Their riverside cave dwellings, once incorporating a chapel, were subsequently put to other uses and remained occupied until the 19th century.

have the roundness and smoothness produced by time, adorned with several layers of graffiti and protected by a fence with fresh rolls of barbed wire, in the name, presumably, of health and safety. This once holy place lies just beyond the edge of a riverside caravan park and a housing estate which, despite adopting the names Hermitage Way and Redstone Way, seems to have turned its back on what looks now to be an unappreciated part of the local heritage. There is a good path, but no sign, and the caves have remained the marginal place they always were.

A little further upstream was another hermitage, at Blackstone Rock, which may also have been inhabited by a ferryman, although it is set well back from the river.[20] The most complete record of it was made in the early 18th century by William Stukeley, who reported that it consisted of a subterranean chapel and cell. This lonely riverside spot on a quiet stretch of the river seems to have inspired Stukeley to portray it as a perfect romantic ruin: 'Near it is a pretty rock upon the edge of the water, cover'd with nature's beautiful canopy of oaks and many curious plants. Near the water upon the rock, liverwort grows plentifully.'[21] Nearly a century later the peace had been shattered and the sacred aura was defiled. By the first decade of the 19th century it had been converted to 'a cyder-mill and cellar' and little more than a decade later it was 'a kind of farming repository' used to store 'potatoes, cheese and agricultural implements'.[22]

There was a hermitage at Shrewsbury near the confluence of the Rea brook; by tradition there was also one at Tewkesbury (the hermit was a Northumbrian named Theoc) at the confluence of Severn and Avon, and one at Melverley at the confluence of Severn and Vyrnwy.[23] The other well-known ancient Severn-valley hermitage was high up in the cliffs above Bridgnorth, said to have been inhabited first by Athelstan's brother in the 10th century, an apocryphal story probably derived from a 15th-century verse romance, *Athelston*.[24] It is a wooded rather than a riverside location, but it was once claimed that

Caves at Blackstone Rock are, by tradition, said to have been the dwelling of a medieval hermit, and perhaps one who was engaged in helping travellers cross the river.

The present ruins of St Oswald's Priory give no indication that it once stood by
Gloucester's quay, let alone near the river which has long since dried up.
The church contained the relics of the Northumbrian saint Oswald.

from the hermitage a tunnel leading to buried treasure went under the Severn to the
friary or the castle, depending which version you heard. In the 1880s, when such sayings
were treated more seriously than they are now, an excavation was begun in the hermitage
floor, but it found no trap door and no buried treasure. Other tunnels dug beneath the
Severn in Shrewsbury were said to link the Austin Friars, the abbey and St Mary's parish
church.[25]

Celtic and Saxon Christians were drawn to the river in equal measure, but although
the Celtic church is older, the earlier dated foundations are all on the English section
of the river. Some have Romano-British origins. The earliest English churches come
into the category of what would later be called monasteries, with priests living in closed
communities, or minsters, staffed by priests charged with spreading the Christian
message and offering guidance to new converts. Many of them are by the river. Early
post-Roman churches at Wroxeter, where the church was built partly from masonry
salvaged from the Roman city, and at Worcester were probably monastic sites, and in
each case the Roman tradition, as well as the river, determined its location. Likewise,
at Gloucester, where Wulfhere son of Penda was the first Christian king (675-84), a
minster was founded c.679 that later became St Peter's Abbey and later still the cathedral. It stands in the city rather than by the river, but the relationship of church to river
in Gloucester is obscure, the old channel of the Severn having silted up and been built
over long ago. St Oswald's Priory stood outside the walls of the Roman town, near the
old eastern arm of the Severn. It was one of Gloucester's earliest and most important
churches, founded as a minster in the late 9th century by Aethelred and Aethelflaed,

daughter of King Alfred, who were subsequently buried in the church's mausoleum, alongside the relics of St Oswald, which had been brought to the church in 909. The church was re-founded as a house of Augustinian Canons in 1153.[26] Until the 15th century Gloucester's principal wharf was St Oswald's Quay.

Deerhurst was originally a minster church, and has some of the finest Anglo-Saxon architecture in England, testifying that it was an important religious centre in the kingdom of the Hwicce. It is first mentioned in 804 when Athelfric gave it land. There was a ford near the church which may well have influenced its location, and also another Saxon church close by, which has survived as Odda's Chapel, even though it was later converted to a house. The presence of two substantial churches may have been related to the division of lordship here just before the Norman Conquest. Odda's chapel can be dated precisely to 1056 by an inscribed stone. In translation it reads 'Earl Odda ordered this royal chapel to be constructed and dedicated in honour of the Holy Trinity for the soul of his brother Aelfric ...'. Minsterworth church was rebuilt in 1870 but its name is suggestive of an early foundation. Kempsey church stands close to the river. It was probably also the site of a Saxon minster – the present church is Norman in origin – and the bishops of Worcester had a palace close to the church from Saxon times until it was demolished in 1695.

Comfortably the most impressive church on the banks of the Severn is Worcester Cathedral, which has similarly early origins. It is best viewed across the river from the west. The east view is compromised by unflattering 20th-century developments, but the cathedral has perhaps always been seen to its best effect from the riverside; the open space of the river provides clarity to the view, and the cathedral has a commanding presence. The present building has many layers of history beneath it. The site was determined by Roman and Iron Age settlements, which in turn were determined by the

Worcester Cathedral from the river Severn, painted here by William Marlowe c.1760, is a classic view both of the river and of the cathedral.
(Image from Worcester City Museum collection)

Llandinam, as viewed here by Samuel Ireland in the late 18th century,
was originally a Celtic *clas*. The church is prominently sited on the hill above the river.

Newtown church was founded in the 13th century as the chapel of Llanfair-yng-Cedewain,
beside which Newtown was begun in 1279.
Floods in 1852 eventually drove the parishioners away to a new church.

nearby ford. The cathedral site was established early as a regional spiritual centre. When the see was created in 680 a new minster church was built, to which another was added in 983. For a century the two Saxon churches stood side by side, and then Bishop Wulfstan began the present cathedral building in 1084. The small space between the cathedral and the river was taken up with the infirmary, the monks' dormitory and the infirmary chapel. What stands now is the accumulation of spiritual and secular power over many centuries.

In Wales the *clas* is the equivalent to the early monastery and minster, and two existed at Llandinam and Istrat Hafren, now known in its English form as Tidenham. *Llan* sites are the consecrated enclosures in which the Christians buried their dead and which later became associated with saints. They are found in several places along the Welsh section of the river, at Llandrinio, Llanllwchaiarn, Llandinam, Llanidloes and Llanfair-yng-Cedewain (Newtown). Llandinam's church is on a slight rise above the river. It was the mother church of the Upper Severn valley and in the 12th century its abbot was Dolffyn ap Rhiwallon, a direct descendant of Bleddyn ap Cynfyn and thus a member of the Powys royal family.[27] Llandinam retained an abbot until the end of the 13th century. Llandrinio is a rare example of Norman architecture in Wales and is close to the bridge at which there was probably an earlier crossing point. Llanidloes church is almost on the river's bank, and is opposite the confluence of the Severn's first major tributary, the Clywedog.

Arguably the most imposing churches on the riverbanks were the monasteries that emerged with the revival of monasticism between the 11th and 13th centuries.

Sailing upriver, Llanthony Secunda was the first of the great abbey churches that watermen passed on the Severn, here shown in ruins in the late 18th century.

Monasteries had a powerful riverside presence, not just for their landmark buildings. Their fish weirs were found along the English section of the Severn, and their estates built quays and operated their own trading vessels on the river. As they travelled upriver the first monastery that rivermen would have seen was Llanthony Secunda, the Augustinian priory founded at Gloucester in 1136 after its mother house in Wales was captured by the Welsh. Llanthony became the richest Augustinian house in England, although it owed its prosperity to the city rather than the river, and attracted royal visitors on account of its proximity to Gloucester Castle – Henry II came in 1241, Edward II in 1327 and Henry VII in 1501.

Buildwas Abbey was founded on the bank of the Severn in 1135 by a colony of monks from Savigny in Normandy, which had been absorbed into the powerful Cistercian order by 1147. The site was remote enough for them to live in austere simplicity, but had good enough communications for them to gain access to their various estates on both sides of the river. Buildwas was probably already a crossing point – there was a bridge there by 1318, probably built by the abbey – which may have been the decisive factor in choosing the site. The monks transported timber and stone by river from Shirlett and Broseley.

Strata Marcella, near Welshpool, was founded in 1170 on the bank of the Severn, part of the colonisation of Wales by the Latin church following Welsh acceptance of the authority of Rome. It was a Cistercian house, one of the descendants of Whitland in Carmarthenshire. Answerable to the abbot of Citeaux in France, it was the least

The romantic ruins of Buildwas Abbey, viewed here in the late 18th century, when such buildings were attracting antiquarian interest.

'imperialist' of the monastic orders and was popular with local Welsh rulers. The abbey maintained its Welshness, providing traditional hospitality to poets like Tudur Aled, who reciprocated by singing the traditional praises of its abbot, Dafydd ab Owain. In the late 1320s Edward III tried to persuade the Cistercian authorities to put Strata Marcella under the control of Buildwas, suspicious of its role in conspiracy against English rule. Imperial ambition was clearly at work here, but in the event the abbot of Buildwas was appointed only a temporary visitor of Strata Marcella.[28] The buildings were entirely dismantled at the Reformation and it is now only possible to see the outline of the abbey from the air. The most treasured, or useful, of its architectural fragments were snapped up by local parish churches; the font in Buttington church, carved with early-13th-century stiff leaf, is said to have been the capital of the central pier in the Strata Marcella chapter house. Interestingly, the church close to the bridge is otherwise of the 15th century – whether there was an earlier church on the site is unknown.

Shrewsbury Abbey stood just outside the medieval town, beside the river near its confluence with the Rea and close to a ford that was to be replaced by the Stone Bridge. Before the monastery was founded in 1083, there was on the site a hermit's wooden chapel dedicated to St Peter, and it was here that Bishop Wulfstan kept vigil and prayed on his visitations to Shrewsbury in the early 1070s. The townspeople apparently thought it odd that he should choose to worship at such a humble chapel outside the town, but Wulfstan predicted that it would 'in time become the most glorious place in Shrewsbury', a prophecy amply fulfilled.[29] The precincts of the abbey extended to the waterside, or, to put in another way, the river was once wider at this point than it is now. One of the few surviving buildings of the abbey precinct is called the 'old infirmary' (although it was probably not an infirmary), which stood at the water's edge, beside a channel of the river that was already nearly dried up by the 16th century when John Leland visited Shrewsbury. The railway line to Hereford passes over it now.

Shrewsbury Abbey has flooded many times over the centuries, as has Tewkesbury Abbey, dramatically and unexpectedly in 2007 when it was an island in the floodwaters. The origin of Tewkesbury Abbey is obscure, made so partly by the mythologizing of its monks in the later Middle Ages. The Benedictine abbey was founded at the confluence of the Avon and the Severn in 1087 by Robert Fitzhamon and was to enjoy a succession of wealthy patrons, including Robert Fitzroy, illegitimate son of Henry I, and the powerful de Clare family of Marcher lords, which explains why it is such an outstanding work of architecture.

Hospitals provided charitable homes for the elderly and infirm in exchange for offering intercessory prayers. They were often built on main roads and had a direct association with bridges. The hospital of St George at Shrewsbury was founded in the 12th century close to the Welsh Bridge – although a charter of 1121 calls it St George's Bridge, raising the possibility that bridge and hospital were linked. The hospital closed in the 13th century but its chapel survived, absorbed into the adjacent hospital of St John the Baptist, which by the end of the Middle Ages was no more than an almshouse. Today it is the site of the Theatre Severn. In Gloucester the hospital of St Bartholomew began as a house built close to Westgate Bridge by the bridge founders, Nicholas Walred

The only surviving building of the Franciscan friary at Shrewsbury is this range built in the 1520s, probably originally part of the refectory, now converted to cottages.

and William Myparty, in which they and the bridge workmen lived with a community of the infirm. After the founders' deaths it was governed by a hermit priest before it was recognised officially as a hospital by Henry III in 1229. In 1333 it supported 90 sick, lame and blind people. The original hospital and its chapel were replaced in the late 18th century by the present Gothick almshouses.[30]

The new mendicant orders, known as friars, that emerged in the 13th century vowed to live a simple life and to contribute to the local community, unlike the monks who lived in closed communities. Friars therefore sought the bustle of the town rather than the isolation of the wild, which drew them to the fringes of towns and, in Shrewsbury and Bridgnorth, to the riverside, where the friaries had a powerful presence. Shropshire's first community of Franciscans, or Greyfriars, had established themselves by the Severn at Bridgnorth in 1244. The friars became the chaplains of the chapel on Bridgnorth Bridge, but they did not always endear themselves to the town. In 1272 they were accused of piling up stones on the bank to reclaim a piece of ground from the river 150 feet long and 50 feet wide. This altered the natural flow of the river causing 'water to pound upon King's Mills [upstream at Pendlestone], the damage whereto is 5 merks per annum'. Friary buildings remained until they made way for a carpet factory in the 19th century, although the Reverend Bellett remembered the former refectory 'with its oak-panelled ceiling and stone fireplace' standing beside the factory.[31] Token remains of the medieval buildings stand in front of the late 20th-century residential development, enough to commemorate the riverside spot as a former holy place. Shrewsbury's Greyfriars arrived in 1245 and settled inside the loop of the river but outside the town walls, in a place that befitted their humble outlook. The land was probably cheap but the site was prone to flooding and in 1420 water is said to have risen over eight feet deep (2.4 metres) inside the Greyfriars church. A single domestic range, built by the Greyfriars in the 1520s, still stands beside the river, next to Greyfriars Bridge. There is an apocryphal story that the magnificent Jesse window in St Mary's church in the centre of the town was brought from the friary after it was closed down.

The Dominicans, or Blackfriars, also established their church and living quarters outside Shrewsbury's town walls, and on the riverbank downstream of the Stone Bridge. No trace remains of their friary, which was near St Mary's Water Lane. The Austin Friars came to Shrewsbury in the 13th century, by the end of which they had settled by the Welsh Bridge. The friary has gone but the name lingers in Priory Road and the former Priory School, now Shrewsbury Sixth Form College.

Crossing points attracted churches for the practical reason that they were accessible, but also because it made them conspicuous. Churches were the landmark buildings of the

Upton church was built in the 14th century but was mostly demolished in 1937, except for the tower with its 18th-century pepperpot top. A new church had been built in 1877 away from the river.

Middle Ages and it is understandable that for this reason many of them are by the river. Atcham has an early Norman church, first mentioned in 1075 when Orderic Vitalis (1075-1142), monk and the author of the *Historia Ecclesiastica*, was baptised there. It is nice to think that he could have been baptised in the river but there is no proof of that. The font in the church is 17th-century. The church is built partly from masonry salvaged from Wroxeter and stood by a crossing point on the river, where the ferry was replaced by a bridge by 1221. Another ancient ferry site is just upstream at Uffington, where the medieval riverside church was rebuilt in the 19th century. Upton-upon-Severn's old stone church also stood by the medieval timber bridge. The 14th-century tower, which must once have acted as a beacon for travellers, remains, but the rest was demolished in 1937, some time after Sir Arthur Blomfield opted for a new site on Old Street further back from the river. Unlikely as it seems, the Elizabethan magus Dr John Dee was made rector of the church in 1553, even though he had no other connection with the town.

St Mary de Lode was also built close to the river, standing near the site of the medieval quay on the now-vanished eastern arm of the Severn.[32]

Quatford was the site of a collegiate church, staffed by priests living in a strict religious discipline, founded in 1084 by Roger, earl of Shrewsbury. According to legend, his second wife, Lady Adeliza, was crossing from France to meet her new husband for the first time when a priest had a dream. He told her that she should found a church on the very spot that she first set eyes on her husband. Quatford was said to be part of Roger's favourite hunting ground, and it was here that she first saw him, beside an oak tree.[33] This presupposes that Quatford was forsaken wilderness, but surely it must have been the river, not an oak tree, that determined the site of the church. Foundation of a collegiate church, whose consecration was attended by bishops from Worcester and Hereford, was surely intended to complement a riverside town, which Roger's son, Robert de Belleme, was soon to give up in favour of the high sandstone cliffs of Bridgnorth. At Quatford the church stands on a sandstone cliff just above the river and the road, where few drivers are lucky enough to notice it. Despite the immediate plentiful supply of building stone, the 12th-century fabric is built of imported tufa, shipped here on the Severn from perhaps as far afield as Dursley in Gloucestershire, from where stone could have been delivered to the wharf at Berkeley.

In Worcester, St Clement's church was built close to Worcester Bridge, although the parish it served was on the opposite bank. The common myth is that the parish had tried to build the church on one side of the river but the devil kept removing the stones to the opposite bank over night until the builders gave up and decided to live with the anomaly.[34] In fact, St Clements had begun life as a free chapel, only later being required to serve a parish. The 12th-century church was damaged in the Civil War and demolished in 1823 so that a new one could be built in a more convenient place.[35] Its dedication is significant. Clement was martyred by being thrown into the sea with an anchor around his neck, and his symbol was an anchor, so the dedication suggests a concentration of maritime occupations close to the bridge. There were tenements on the west bank owned by watermen as early as the 11th century.[36] Like perhaps St Mary de Lode in Gloucester, it was probably one of the first watermen's churches.

Other riverside churches owe their location to associated defended sites or castles. Shrawardine castle and church were destroyed in the Civil War but the rebuilt church has retained its Norman font. Holt is a richly decorated Norman church, originally a private chapel standing next to a castle that was begun in 1086, but the village shifted away from its original focus after Holt Fleet Bridge was opened in 1828. Roger, earl of Shrewsbury, also raised a castle at Quatford. Ashleworth church, above Gloucester, is of Norman origin, but is now largely a late-medieval church with 15th-century manor house and tithe barn nearby – a Gothic and picturesque English manorial ensemble on an older template. Berwick, close to the river near Shrewsbury, combines house, chapel and almshouses, a combination that seems earlier than its actual 17th-century origin.

The shifting course of the Severn has meant that some former riverside churches no longer appear so. The high tide may once have lapped against the wall of Slimbridge churchyard, but it is now two miles from the river, set back from the Severn behind the New Grounds thrown up after land in Awre parish was washed away. The volatility of the tidal river often made it impractical to build a church on the banks (but see Minsterworth below). Lydney church is well away from the river but stands by The Cut above the harbour, from which a ship was once launched.[37] If a church does not stand by the river, sometimes the river goes to the church. There is a flood mark on the door of Tirley church, even though it is more than half a mile from the river. Frampton-on-Severn church stands in the field away from the river, set back behind the Gloucester and Sharpness Canal. The present building was consecrated in 1315, but there was an older church intimately associated with the river. Its font, like that of Tidenham on the opposite bank, is made of lead, one of several manufactured in the Bristol region in the 12th century, which could only have been imported by river.

Ribbesford is the mother church of Bewdley, but also in essence a Severn church. The fabric is Norman in origin and incorporates a carved tympanum over the north doorway that has aroused a good deal of debate among antiquaries. According to a local tradition it was said to depict a folk hero called Horsehill John, 'Who shot a buck near Severn's useful stream / And killed a salmon when he did the same'.[38] The carving was once therefore thought to represent John killing a salmon, but not everybody was convinced. It was pointed out that the tympanum 'is so uncouthly carved, and has been so bedaubed with paint and plaster, that it is difficult to trace even the outline of the figures'.[39] Since Frederick Preedy restored the church in the 1870s the carving has become more legible and the myth has been exposed: the carving shows a hunter, perhaps a centaur, shooting at an animal.

There is a distinction worth making between riverside churches and the churches of riverside communities. Ribbesford stands well back from the river, but was the last resting place of many Severn watermen. John Burton, the 19th-century historian of Bewdley, recorded many of the epitaphs on the gravestones in Ribbesford churchyard, not all of which are now legible. John Robinson made his life 'through Severn's dangerous course' and enjoyed 'full forty years in friendship's trusty Bark' (he was 54 when he died in 1821). Use of improbably lofty language was the order of the day, as in the epitaph dedicated to the Severn waterman John Oakes, who also died in 1821, a mariner tossed to and fro by 'Boreas's blast and Neptune's waves'. In the Ironbridge Gorge, Benthall is the church of a riverside community, although it stands well above the river. Like nearby Broseley, it has cast-iron ledgers (gravestones) of watermen, who can often be distinguished by the sign of an anchor.

Watermen had their own chapels in the 19th century, or at least were deemed to need spiritual guidance and had chapels provided for them. In Worcester a retired trow named *Albion* was converted into a chapel at some time after 1816 by the Reverend John Davies, vicar of St Clement's, who became known as the Apostle of the Watermen. Even though the *Albion* sank in the 1860s all was not lost, as it was salvaged and put ashore in the churchyard of Old St Clement's, where it continued to serve the watermen for several years. It was destroyed in 1947. Davies was also involved with the building of the Mariners' church in Gloucester Docks, which opened in 1849.

Gloucester's Mariners' church was built in 1849. It is in the heart of the docks and ministered to the needs of the watermen on the Gloucester and Sharpness Canal as well as the Severn navigation.

Aside from practical considerations, were there spiritual reasons why so many churches were built so close to the river? Were hermits attracted there because such places were at the mercy of natural forces, as testing as the Biblical desert? Or was there thought to be a special virtue in places where two bodies of water joined? The significance of running water to Christianity is well known, with its associations of purity and cleansing. It is thought usually to find expression in holy wells, but rivers might have been viewed in the same terms, especially given the role of the river Jordan in the life of Jesus. The placing of several churches in relation to the river is at least suggestive of such a link, even in the case of churches like Llandinam and Quatford, which overlook the river in the same way that the Roman temple at Lydney overlooks the estuary. In practice it is difficult to disentangle all the reasons why the site of a church was chosen. Churches were often built by roads that crossed the river, like at Upton and St Bartholomew in Gloucester, but the crossing becomes less significant in the upstream stretches where the river could be crossed in many places. Some churches were perhaps sited away from the riverbank for practical reasons. Tewkesbury Abbey is set on slightly higher ground, and a wall was constructed to protect its precincts from the waterlogged ham by the river. In a similar manner Frampton-on-Severn and Tirley churches are set well back from the river, not that that has safeguarded the latter from floods.

Atcham church stands right on the riverbank, but thanks to the protection afforded by one and in more recent times two bridges, it has never flooded. Melverley church, close to the Severn on the bank of its tributary, the Vyrnwy, is even closer to the water. Melverley is the finest of the timber-framed churches of the borderland, but it is first

Atcham's riverbank church was built close to a crossing point of the river.
It is protected from floods by the two Atcham bridges just upstream.

recorded in 1558, with no evidence that it is an ancient foundation, or close to a crossing point. Newtown's medieval church was also close, too close, to the river. Richard Fenton passed through the town in 1804 and noted the tower with timber-framed belfry, the arcades with wooden arches, and the rood screen, 'which, as to carving, gilding and painting, is perhaps the most perfect thing of the kind in the kingdom'.[40] Alas, the river drove the parishioners out after it flooded in 1852, although luckily a new church had already been built for the expanding town in 1847. They took their precious screen and some wall monuments with them. The ruined old church, retaining its (restored) timber-framed tower, marks the ancient settlement of Llanfair-yng-Cedewain and the relationship with the river.

Another victim of the 1852 floods was Minsterworth church. The church, which contained fabric of the 12th century, had probably been built close to a crossing point and was reached down steps. When the church was reluctantly taken down in 1869 Henry Woodyer built a replacement that is reached up steps and consequently less likely to be flooded. According to a commemorative tablet in the chancel of the old church: 'in great floods it was to be entered by the waters of the river Severn which in 1852 overflowed the nave to a depth of 18 inches and at all other times damp and unhealthy, its floors being below high water mark. The old edifice seemed in its decay to have reached a state which precluded all attempts at repair'. The new church floor was four feet (1.2 metres) higher than the old floor level. The parish commissioned the Belgian glazier Capronnier to make a stained glass window for the new church, and appropriately enough, it shows Christ walking on water. Newnham-on-Severn had a riverbank church by 1018 but it was badly damaged by floods soon after 1360. A new church, built partly from masonry salvaged from the old church, was built on higher ground in 1366, on land given by Humphry de Bohun. The earthworks next to the church are the remains of a castle built in the 12th century, where Henry II assembled his forces before launching a campaign in Ireland in 1171.[41]

These churches are not just places of worship serving riverside settlements, but embody many aspects of riverside life. Awre church has a chest, perhaps dating from as far back as the 13th century, which was reputedly used for laying out cadavers recovered from the Severn. Tidenham's church tower was used as a navigational beacon. Anglo-Saxon Deerhurst, Early-English Slimbridge, and Tudor-Gothic Newtown all testify to the wealth and power residing by the river, even away from its main trading and strategic centres. Gloucester's strategic importance on the Severn earned its abbey royal associations and was one reason why Henry VIII elevated the abbey to cathedral status in 1541. But at Atcham, one of the quieter stretches of the river, the gravestones extend to the edge of the bank, and there is only the gentle sound of the water flowing, a fitting reminder of eternity.

Part Three

The River as Frontier

∽ 5 ∾
Fords and Ferries

Crossing points have always been key places on the river, and the earliest of them were fords and ferries. The cities, towns and villages on the Severn are often where they are as the consequence of a crossing point, a layer of Severn history that is largely overlain by later bridges. Upstream there are so many places where the river can be crossed that a crossing point in itself is not always the clinching factor in the location of settlements, but on the lower river it becomes more important, and determined the foundation of both Worcester and Gloucester. Many fords must once have existed on the Severn whose names and locations have been lost, either through disuse, or because the river bed has shifted, or because it has been dredged. Other fording places have been forgotten because the bridges that replaced them are themselves now ancient.

Early fording points are sometimes recorded in place names, such as Rhyd-y-benwch, Rhydyronnen, Rhyd-esgyn, Rhydwhyman and Rhyd-y-Groes in Wales. *Rhyd* place names also occur in England just downstream of Worcester, and near Bewdley. The English equivalent, 'ford', does not necessarily imply a place where the river was crossed, because it was also used to describe shallow water. Nevertheless Forden in Montgomeryshire, Montford, Robertsford, Danesford and Quatford in Shropshire and Ribbesford in Worcestershire may all be places where the river was once crossed in dry seasons. Naturally, examples decrease as you continue downstream and the river widens.

Roman roads crossed the Severn at several places – Arlingham, Gloucester, Wroxeter, Forden Gaer, and further west towards Caersws – initially probably all at fords. When Richard Fenton spent a summer's day in 1804 tracing the line of the Roman road in Wales he claimed that sections of it had been eroded by the river and were exposed in its banks, proof that the river had altered its course since Roman times. Even so the road appeared to have crossed the river at least three times between Caersws and Newtown, and twice at the small township of Penstrowed near Newtown.[1] Some fords were not on important routeways, but belong instead to local history. At Llanllwchaiarn, the ancient settlement superseded in the 13th century by Newtown, there was a ford where a ferry also operated, but where no bridge was ever built. Three old fords within two miles of

Llandinam were still known in the 19th century. They are near farms – including Lower Gwerneirin and Craigfryn – and perhaps were used only by local farmers.

Despite the breadth of the river, its frequent shallows and seasonal variation (which has largely disappeared since the flow has been regulated by locks, reservoirs and dredging of the river bed) allowed the lower river to be fordable in places during low water. It was said that the river remained fordable in summer at Worcester from the old Worcester Bridge down to Diglis.[2] This stretch of the river had a tidal range of six feet (1.8 metres) until Diglis Lock was constructed in 1844.[3] The last of the great fords to survive was probably the crossing between Arlingham and Newnham, which was also the lowest point at which the river could be forded. Perhaps when in AD 43 the invading Roman legions turned their attention to the conquest of the Silures tribe of south Wales, they crossed over this ford, which was on a Roman road to south Wales. Wagons and travellers on horseback still apparently used the mile-long ford in the 18th century, although not always safely.[4] The crossing was safe if travellers employed a guide who knew where to follow a rocky ridge that usually remained submerged.[5] It has been said that the ford remained serviceable until 1802 and that the last man to cross the river here was John Smith, then the new tenant of Overton Farm on the left bank of the river. His entire stock of cattle, sheep, wagons and household goods, as well as his family, all crossed safely via Newnham from his home in Littledean.[6] The stone ridge was connected to the shore by a section of firm sandbank, but when the river changed course and washed the sandbank away the ford was no longer passable.

We tend to think of river crossings merely in practical terms, but there is a forgotten history of superstition and veneration associated with fords, as well as political and military symbolism. When a river is a national boundary, as was the case for the stretch of river between Berriew and Buttington that formed the border between medieval Wales and the Lordship of Montgomery, fords had a heightened significance. Such was the case with the two most famous Severn fords of the Middle Ages, Rhydwhyman and Rhyd-y-Groes, which can hardly have been more than a few miles apart (assuming that they were not the same place). Both have an important place in Welsh history.

Rhydwhyman is probably the 'horseford' mentioned in the Domesday Book of 1086, and its Welsh name is derived from *rhyd chwima*, or swift ford. Now it is an inconspicuous and unvisited spot. The water still riffles over the shallows with the same swiftness but it would only be fordable when the river level is very low. The place is easy to identify because it is at the end of the lane that leads down the hill from the medieval stronghold of Hen Domen. It was this crossing that the Ffridd Faldwyn Iron Age fort overlooked, that the Roman army defended with its nearby Forden Gaer fort, and that was defended on the English side by the Normans at Hen Domen. The ford was on the boundary between Powys and the lordship of Montgomeryshire, and thus had both Welsh and English names. Strictly speaking we only know the Latin version of the latter, *vadum aquae de Mungumery* – the ford of Montgomery.

The ford was a royal meeting place during the rise and fall of Llywelyn ap Gruffudd. From 1256 Llywelyn had swept through Wales from his Gwynedd power base and asserted increasing authority over north and mid Wales, threatening the interests of

Henry III and the Marcher lords. Envoys of Llywelyn and Henry met at the ford to negotiate truces on several occasions between 1258 and 1267. Rhydwhyman was chosen probably because, notwithstanding that a meeting was impractical in mid stream, it could be seen symbolically as a neutral place on the border between the two territories. Negotiations culminated with the Treaty of Montgomery in 1267, which was concluded at the ford in the presence of Llywelyn, Henry III and the papal legate Ottobuono (the future pope Adrian V). When Llywelyn crossed back over the Severn he did so for the first time as the acknowledged prince of Wales but, perhaps more importantly, having secured recognition for Wales as a nation state.[7] Two years later Llywelyn met Prince Edward at Rhydwhyman on amicable terms, but events would soon turn in favour of the young heir to the English throne. The last meeting at the ford was in 1274, convened to discuss breaches of the Treaty.[8] Three years later King Edward abandoned diplomacy and the ford in favour of an all-out invasion. But the significance of the ford was not quite over. In 1288 Bishop Richard Swinfield of Hereford rode his horse to the middle of the stream in order to stake his claim that the Severn between the fords of Rhydwhyman and Shrawardine near Shrewsbury was to be the boundary of Hereford and St Asaph dioceses.[9]

Rhyd-y-Groes has a place in Welsh culture as a symbolic threshold between Wales and Mercia or England, for it was there that Gruffudd ap Llywelyn, prince of Powys and Gwynedd and for a brief period the only Welsh prince to have ruled over Wales in its

Samuel Ireland's view of Montgomery shows the Dyffryn ferry on this relatively quiet stretch of river between Welshpool and Newtown. John Byng crossed here in 1784 and described this place in the 'luxuriant country' of the Severn vale as a 'happy turn of the river'. The ferry may be the one that replaced the ford known as Rhyd-y-Groes.

entirety, defeated the forces of Leofric, earl of Mercia, in 1039. The precise location of Rhyd-y-Groes has exercised historians, but there is no agreed conclusion. The site must be close to the border, but on the Welsh side. It could be the place known in English as Buttington, where a combined Mercian and Welsh force overcame a Danish incursion in 893.[10] Alternatively, it could have been on the river near Forden. There is a farm near Forden named Rhyd-y-Groes, although it is over two miles from the river. Lady Charlotte Guest, whose translation into English of the *Mabinogion* (completed in 1849) brought it to a wide audience, made her own enquiries, and learned that below the confluence of the Rhiw and Severn at Berriew there was an old crossing still known as 'Rhyd y Groes ar Havren', but replaced by a ferry in her day.[11] If, as is implied, the crossing point was an important one, it would have been defended. The most likely candidate would therefore be the ford by Dyffryn farm, which is likely to have been a medieval crossing because it was protected by the motte at Lower Munlyn. The Ordnance Survey marked the ferry on its 19th-century maps but unfortunately did not name it.

'Rhonabwy's Dream' is the latest of the tales that make up the *Mabinogion*, and it confirms the association of the river and the ford with personal transformation. The tale satirises the Arthurian narrative tradition and is therefore a reliable guide to its conventions and commonplace meanings. Written in Powys in the 12th or 13th century, the scene of the story is the Severn at Rhyd-y-Groes, or the 'ford of the cross'. Arthur's forces assemble at the ford and cross it to fight the battle of Badon. By passing across the river Arthur crosses an important symbolic threshold, and assumes a warlike mode. Many other rivers have been thought of as similarly liminal places where transformations occur, so 'Rhonabwy's Dream' can be seen as part of a wider European tradition. Arthur's fording of the Severn to Badon is comparable to Julius Caesar's crossing of the Rubicon on his march to power in Rome, or Aeneas's crossing of the Styx from the land of the living to the land of the dead (which was only possible at the behest of the ferryman) in the *Aeneid*. Respect must be paid to the river and its gods. In Herodotus' account of the Persian invasion of Greece in the 5th century BC the downfall of the Persian emperor Xerxes was brought about by hubris – instead of ferrying his army across the Hellespont, the narrow strait in north-west Turkey dividing Europe from Asia Minor, he defied the gods and built a bridge of boats instead.

Some vestige of these ancient superstitions was carried over into Christianity, in which holy men had a spiritual role in passage across the river. There are two saints associated with river crossings. St Christopher, still popular as the patron saint of travellers, is often shown in medieval church wall paintings carrying the child Christ across a stream. (Christopher derives from 'Christ-bearer'.) St Julian the Hospitaller, a mythical character, became a ferryman as penance for his sins. Christian holy men were found at river crossings in the specifically Christian context of charity. They were humble men engaged in the worthy task of assisting travellers across dangerous waters by maintaining roads and bridges, and piloting ferries.

There are several references to chapels near the mouth of the estuary that were associated with hermits, some or all of whom may have operated ferries or navigational lights. The ruins on Chapel Rock are the remains of the former chapel of St Twrog, from where the Aust-Beachley ferry may once have been operated. Hermits operated a ferry at Redstone Rocks near Stourport. In 1770s the river was still fordable here at what had become known as Redstone Rapids, where wagons ploughed through the river at low tide, but no one crosses the river there now.[12] The occupant of the hermitage at Blackstone Rock near Bewdley may also have operated a ferry, if only on an occasional basis, although there is otherwise no evidence of a ferry there.

The Severn had many more ferries than hermitages, however, and few of them can have been operated by holy men. Bridges have superseded the important Severn ferries, although references to many of them are found scattered in medieval and later documents. The word 'lode' is unique to the Severn and is often an indicator of a ferry, although the word can mean any embarkation point, whether for trading vessels or ferries, or a road leading to the river. The ambiguity is inevitable since some ferrying points clearly did also carry river cargo. In 1540, for example, there was an old barge and a stock boat at Upper Lode ferry near Tewkesbury.[13]

Clevelode is mentioned in 1086, and is probably the oldest reference to a Severn ferry. The ferry at Wulmerslode (or Upper Lode) is mentioned in 1248, Lower Lode in 1300. In 1480, property at Apley in Shropshire is described as the weir and 'the loode' with a house and close, and in 1494 the ferry was described as 'the fery other whyles called the loode of Apley with the were [weir] to the same fery or lode belonging'. Hampton Loade is first mentioned in 1594 as 'Hamptons Lood'.[14] Other crossing points include Saxon's Lode near Upton, and Framilode, which had taken its name by the 7th century.[15] The 'passage de Overlode' near Gloucester is first named as such in 1300, but probably refers to the causeway over the marshy ground of what is now Alney Island. Abloads in Gloucester was a road that led north of the town over marshy ground.

Most of the towns had associated older ferry crossings, but not all of them. As late as 1313 there seems to have been no passage over the Severn at Bewdley, only the ford at the end of Lax Lane, downstream of the later bridge. A Bewdley ferry is first mentioned in

The Lower Lode Inn below Tewkesbury

1336; it made a profit of £2 in 1381, when a market was granted to the town, and more than double that by 1424.[16] The passage at the Haw near Tirley is first mentioned in 1248 and by the 19th century could also take carriages, although a local man, Jeremiah Hawkins (d.1835), was famous for swimming his horse across the Severn here.[17] Even as late as the 19th century the river had more ferry crossings than bridges. The story of Severn fords and ferries, however, is often of their replacement by bridges. Most of the Severn bridges cross the river at places where there were older fords or ferries, rights to which were acquired before the bridges were built. Llandrinio, Ironbridge, Holt, Haw and Mythe are all well-documented examples. When Mythe Bridge was built, the builders purchased the Upper Lode Ferry for £1,650.[18] When Holt Fleet was completed, further downstream from the old passage, the village shifted with it.

Ecclesiastical association with ferries was often more practical than spiritual. Tewkesbury Abbey owned the Upper Lode ferry, where the tenant of the adjoining farmland was required to ferry passengers across the river.[19] It also owned the Lower Lode ferry, which provided access to the abbey's estates on the west bank of the river.[20] Since the Middle Ages ferries have been associated with inns rather than hermitages, however, partly because ferryman was not a viable single occupation and most of them were also inn keepers. Many of the inns remain standing by the riverbank – the Old Ferry Inn at Beachley, Old Passage Inn at Arlingham, Lower Lode Inn near Tewkesbury, Boat Inn at Coalport among them. The Harwood family of Shrewsbury were ferrymen, but also owned and built barges, built and rented out pleasure boats, and owned a warehouse in addition to the Boathouse Inn. Just downstream, the Quarry ferry was owned

This view of Tewkesbury by Samuel Ireland shows the Upper Lode ferry, where the Mythe Bridge was later built. The ferry is first recorded in 1248.

The Boat Inn at Coalport was the passage house of the Coalport Ferry that took workers from the well-populated village of Jackfield across the river to work, especially at the Coalport Chinaworks.

in the 19th century by Richard Williams, who had a net and basket-making business and hired out boats to fishermen; he was succeeded by Richard Ellis, a Shrewsbury boat builder. Next downstream was the Cann Office ferry, operated by the Burr family who had a factory manufacturing lead pipes on the opposite bank to the town.[21] Such a diversity of interests was possible in a large town like Shrewsbury, and in the industrialised Ironbridge Gorge, where the Crumpton family operated a ferry from the Dog and Duck at Jackfield, and also operated coal barges. One of their ferries bore the inscription AMC 1654 (Adam and Mary Crumpton).[22] At Quatford the ferryman had less opportunity for a supplementary business, but when John Randall went there in the 1850s he found a ferryman who was also a fisherman for roach, dace, perch, gudgeon and the occasional salmon.[23]

Most ferries were large rowing boats, some of them large enough to carry carts and carriages. Others carried horses, especially after a towpath had been established on the upper river which required the occasional change of banks, and/or farm animals. At Arley, John Randall saw a ferry used for transporting cattle in 1860.[24] By the 19th century, rope ferries were used because they prevented the boat being swept away by a strong current, as at the horse ferry at Hampton Loade. The boat was moored to the middle of the river and the ferryman punted the vessel from one bank to other, in a swinging motion.[25] This must have been similar to the arrangement at Coalport ferry that was observed by Joshua Field in 1821, and was perhaps an improvement made after the disastrous loss of the ferry boat in 1799. 'The ferry boats are decked a foot below the gunwale. They have an anchor up the stream and a chain … fixed from the anchor to the top of a short mast, then by the rudder and the man can steer the boat across the river without any trouble'.[26] Ferries moored to a cable across the river, like the modern ferry at Hampton Loade, are a later innovation, introduced after the river was no longer navigated by masted vessels.

This view of Shrewsbury by Samuel and Nathaniel Buck shows,
downstream of the Welsh Bridge, a small ferry and the Boathouse Inn.

The Boathouse Inn, Shrewsbury, today, with the footbridge that replaced the ferry in 1922.

Ferries remained important even into the 20th century, although they declined rapidly with the rise of motor transport. The ferry between Newnham and Arlingham, first recorded in 1238, was apparently the lowest point at which ferries could cross regardless of the tide.[27] By the 19th century it could take carriages as well as foot passengers. Despite the inconvenience – at low tide passengers on the jetty-less Arlingham side had to be carried to the shore on the crew's backs – the ferry continued to the mid 20th century. For over 50 years after its opening in 1851, Arlingham cattle were ferried to Newnham railway station.[28]

Once a towpath was created on the upper section of the navigation in the early 19th century, horse ferries were needed where the towpath switched banks (the teams of bow-haulers that hauled vessels upstream, by contrast, had a right of way along either bank). One of the horse ferries, at Underdale near Shrewsbury, operated until the 1880s when it was replaced by a new ferry a few hundred yards upstream that connected the new suburb of Cherry Orchard with the town. The ferry lasted only 28 years and in its latter stages charged a halfpenny toll for bicycles, before it was replaced by a bridge in 1910.[29] In the Ironbridge Gorge the Coalport ferry continued to operate until the Jackfield and Coalport Memorial Bridge was built in 1922. The ferry was valued by local people as the alternatives, Coalport Bridge or the Iron Bridge, involved quite a detour. The bridges also charged tolls, to avoid which some workmen at Jackfield bought their own coracles.[30] In Worcester the ferry from the cathedral's Watergate to the Chapter Meadows continued until the 1950s, and was revived in 1983 as a summer attraction.

The sites of the two lowest Severn ferries are now occupied by its two largest bridges – the Severn Bridge from Aust to Beachley (the Old Passage), and the Severn Second

The pedestrian ferry at Hampton Loade has been in operation since at least the end of the 15th century.

Crossing from Redwick to Portskewett (the New Passage). The most famous of all Severn ferries was the one that plied the Old Passage. At just over one mile, the Old Passage is the shortest distance across the mouth of the Severn and must have been an important crossing ever since sailors were brave enough to put out on its often turbulent waters. In popular imagination, this was another place where Ostorius Scapula and his army crossed into the territory of the Silures in AD 43 during the Roman invasion of Britain. In keeping with the river's reputation as the frontier between England and Wales, it was also, by tradition, the venue for a meeting between Edward I and Llywelyn ap Gruffudd in the 1270s. They arrived on opposite shores, not knowing who should cross. Llywelyn hesitated, Edward embarked and, recognising the danger of psychological defeat (as seen through English eyes), Llywelyn walked waist-high into the water to meet the English king, carried him ashore on his shoulders, paid due homage and launched into a fulsome tribute: 'Most wise king, your condescension has overcome my pride, and your wisdom triumphed over my folly.'[31] All very silly and no doubt apocryphal, but it does reveal that the symbolic significance of a ferry crossing in royal protocol, which evidence of the ford at Montgomery demonstrates was not a fiction, was remembered when Thomas Harral wrote about it in the 19th century.

The passage from Aust to Beachley is the best documented ferry crossing on the Severn. As early as 1131 Winebold de Bolan granted right of free passage to the abbot and monks of Tintern. By 1652 the ferry was operated from Aust by 12 men and the ferry rights were hereditary. The New Passage was owned by the Lewis family of St Pierre

This view of Newnham by Samuel Ireland shows the Newnham-Arlingham ferry, which was later used to transport cattle for market.

(on the Welsh bank) before the Civil War, but it was suppressed by Cromwell during the Commonwealth because its owners had been Royalists. When it was revived in 1718, the Lewis family re-established its right to it.[32] Rights to the Old Passage were owned by the duke of Beaufort but leased out. The Whitchurch family leased it from 1765 until they sold it in 1845 to the South Wales Union Ferry, whose company wanted the rights to profit from an important mail route.

In 1725 Daniel Defoe thought little of 'the ugly, dangerous and very inconvenient ferry over the Severn' at the Old Passage: 'the sea was so broad, the fame of the bore of the tide so formidable, the wind also made the water so rough, and which was worse, the Boats to carry over both man and horse appeared … so very mean, that in short none of us car'd to venture'.[33] John Wesley waited five hours at the New Passage but the boatmen refused to cross it during stormy conditions and he had to cross by the Old Passage the next day. In fact the crossing could only be made in certain favourable conditions. When the tide and the wind went in the same direction there were no crossings. In other words, when the wind was southerly or westerly – the direction of the prevailing wind here – a crossing could only be made on the ebb tide. If the wind was northerly, only the flood tide afforded safe passage.[34] If conditions were right, the passage was smooth and quick. Henry Penruddocke Wyndham arrived at the ferry house in Beachley on his return from a tour through Wales in 1777, 'from whence the boat, with a strong wind, wafted us over the Severn to Aust, within the short space of nine minutes'.[35]

Defoe was right to be cautious, though. The sailing packet *Jane* sank in September 1839, with the loss of its crew, Mr Whitchurch and his son, and its passengers, including William Crawshay III of the south Wales ironworking dynasty. The passage was then taken over by Mr Whitchurch's other son, James Whitchurch, but he too perished when the new sailing packet *Dispatch* sank in March 1844 in stormy conditions.[36] Contemporary newspapers reported that accidents such as these happened in full view of passengers waiting at the passage houses. A second *Dispatch* sank in 1855 when it hit wooden piles, and seven people were drowned.[37]

Both ferries were on important mail routes, for which reason Thomas Telford proposed radical improvements in the 1820s. The New Passage was on the Bristol-to-Milford Haven route but he dismissed it as 'one of the most forbidding places at which an important ferry was ever established – a succession of violent cataracts formed in a rocky channel exposed to the rapid rush of a tide which has scarcely an equal upon any other coast'. He suggested a new ferry route much further west, which would land at Sully Island, just off the coast near Cardiff. For the Old Passage he proposed for the London-Chepstow mail route a suspension bridge from Aust to Beachley.[38] A local man, Thomas Fulljames, also made proposals for a road and rail crossing and a Severn barrage in place of the Old Passage.

But this was the beginning of the steamboat era on the Severn when considerable investment was made in the ferry services. The *St Pierre*, named after the manor that owned the ferry rights, was brought into service in 1825, the first paddle steamer added to the fleet at the New Passage. The Old Passage followed suit, building a 486 foot (148 metres) pier at Aust and ordering a steamboat from Bristol, which was named *Worcester* and began service in 1827. This ferry burned to the waterline in 1832 and was replaced by the *Beaufort* that same year, and a second *Worcester* in 1838. Improvements in the service and the growing popularity of travel brought new expectations. Nicholson's *Cambrian Travellers' Guide* of 1840 was less than impressed with the Old Passage: 'The boatmen are, of course, rude in their manners, indifferent to the accommodation of the passengers and practised in the arts of extortion.' Currents and tidal conditions only added to the discomfort of the passengers: At low tide passengers disembarking at Beachley 'will have to disembark at a short distance from the usual landing place and be subjected to a very slippery walk over the surface of rock covered with confervae, fuce and other marine plants'.[39]

In 1864, railway branches were built to the New Passage terminals, but this was only ever a temporary state of affairs, and when the Severn Tunnel opened in 1886, the ferries were no longer viable and ceased trading. The passage boats *Chepstow* and *Christopher Thomas* began offering excursions from the New Passage terminals, but they were sold off in 1890. An unexpected reprieve for the ferries came with the rise of the motor car. From 1909 the Great Western Railway operated a car-transporting service through the Severn Tunnel, but it was a cumbersome exercise and no better than a car ferry, although it continued until the Severn Bridge was built.[40] A competing private venture was started by Enoch Williams, whose new motor launch ferry first operated from Aust in 1926, only to founder two years later when the pier was badly damaged. Enoch Williams was, however, a determined man, and having bought the ferry rights from the duke of Beaufort, he revived the service in 1931 and decided to compete directly with the railway company by carrying cars. A year later nearly 6,000 cars had crossed the Old Passage. The duke of Beaufort agreed to renew the lease in 1945 for a further 21 years, an agreement that would determine when the Severn Bridge was completed and opened.[41] The service operated three vessels, the *Severn Queen* of 1934, *Severn King* of 1935 and *Severn Princess* of 1959. In its latter days the ferry passed beneath the new Severn Bridge.

Having been almost the first ferry to be written about, Aust was the last meaningful ferry on the Severn; the final service crossed on 8 September 1966. Replacement of Severn's ferries and fords had taken less than two millennia, but given the relatively short history of bridges, the fords and ferries were in use for a much greater length of time, and it will be a long time before cars can claim to have crossed the river for as long as coracles did.

❧ 6 ❧
Severn Bridges

When the old Worcester Bridge was taken down in 1781 the workmen had trouble removing the old piers, which were particularly resistant to being broken up. The material was iron slag, the residue of iron smelting that had been dumped on the riverbank in Roman times. Perhaps it was the Romans who recognised the durability of the fused minerals and decided that they would make a lasting core for piers spanning the river, or perhaps the slag was used for core when a new bridge was built in 1313.[1] The problem encapsulates something of the story of Severn bridges, of how river crossings are periodically renewed, and the appearance of the old bridges is quickly forgotten. On the Severn there are bridges that stand, bridges that we know existed and, before that, bridges that we think existed. The present stock of Severn bridges includes some of the celebrated technological landmarks of the past three centuries, but older than that is a forgotten world of bridges as charitable works, and bridges as an arm of the military.

The story of the Severn's bridges seems to begin with imperial Rome. First, superstitions had to be overcome, and who better than the Romans for being utilitarian and unsuperstitious when it suited them? Julius Caesar, campaigning in Germany, had built a bridge across the Rhine in order to defeat its native peoples, and also its native gods.[2] Less than a century later Roman imperial administration came to Britain and in due course began the process of bridging the Severn.

By the mid 15th century there were only 12 bridges on the English section of the river – three at Gloucester, one each at Upton, Worcester, Bewdley, Bridgnorth, Buildwas, Atcham, two at Shrewsbury and one at Montford Bridge. Less is known about bridges in the Welsh section. Baldwin's Bridge, later known as Caerhowel Bridge, was built in the 1250s and may have been the first of them.[3] According to Sir Roger Kynaston, writing in 1478, by then the Welsh section had bridges at Llandrinio, Buttington and Caerhowel, and also possibly at the main settlements of Newtown, Caersws and Llanidloes.[4] That makes only 18 bridges on a 220-mile river. The majority of crossing points on the river continued to be fords and ferries for several centuries yet.

Bridges have a false air of stability and permanence. The Severn has slowly but surely undermined, or in some cases rapidly swept away, most of the bridges that have spanned it, so that the only surviving ancient bridge is the one begun in 1101 at Bridgnorth, and although it has survived, it is so repaired, restored, rebuilt, re-styled and widened that its original form exists only in the imagination. Most references to medieval bridges in contemporary documents refer to their state of disrepair. Bridges could easily become dilapidated enough to become dangerous, as Worcester Bridge was satirised in 1699:

> They say our Bridge is Tumbling Downe
> S'lud I'me Halfe afraid to come to towne.[5]

Until the Iron Bridge was built across the Severn in 1779 it had not been possible to bridge the river in a single span. This was not just an aesthetic consideration. As Thomas Telford remarked, bridge piers built on the river bed or the bylets impound water on the upstream side, and lower the channel on the downstream side, to the detriment of vessels using the river.[6] The effect is exacerbated in times of flood, when localised flooding occurs upstream of the bridges and when piers are vulnerable to flotsam as strange as icebergs and as large as tree trunks. Much was made of the fact that the Iron Bridge withstood the force of the 1795 flood when bridges at Buildwas, Bewdley and Stourport were fatally damaged, but it did not come out of it unscathed and underwent repairs and strengthening of the abutments in the first two decades of the 19th century.[7] Bridges of the Severn are not really single events but an ongoing story of remedial works and improvements. That there are no surviving bridges on the Severn dating from earlier than the mid 18th century is testament to the destructive power of the river.

The oldest Severn bridges that we know about were on Roman roads, built to serve the military and a product of the imperial administration. Apart from Worcester, the Romans built a bridge by the wharf at Gloucester, on a channel of the old Severn that had already silted up by Saxon times.[8] The river was also bridged at Wroxeter, which was first a fort and later a city. The Roman road leads directly to the original riverside fort and, in the typically British way, the route is now a public footpath. Two millennia of floods have washed away all traces of the bridge, but William Camden claimed in the 1580s that bridge foundations had recently been uncovered while a fish weir was being built.[9] In the early 19th century it was claimed that when the river level was very low the stone foundations of bridge piers could still be seen in the river bed.[10]

The tradition of Roman imperial bridge building may have been inherited by the Anglo-Saxon kings, but the half millennium after the Romans is a dark age for documented bridge building, and perhaps also for bridges themselves. After the Romans, the next earliest reference to a possible Severn bridge appears in the *Anglo-Saxon Chronicle* for AD 896, when the Danish army encamped by the Severn at *Cwatbrycge*, modern Quatford near Bridgnorth.[11] But there was not necessarily a bridge there. The Anglo-Saxon word *brycg* seems to have referred to any kind of improvement in the crossing of rivers or marshes, including causeways and fords. Slimbridge, whose name has the same origin, also has never had a bridge.[12] Worcester, being a regional capital of the Hwicce on the Severn, is one city that probably did have a bridge in Saxon times. John of Worcester documents the existence of one in 1088 – possibly the old broken Roman bridge, because before the forces of William II could cross it and attack the rebellious barons it needed repairing.[13] Military campaigns began at Gloucester in 1055 and 1063, suggesting that there was a bridge there by that time, and the causeway across the floodplain that would later link Foreign, Westgate and Over Bridges was in existence by 1086.[14]

From the 12th century onwards there are more reliable references to Severn bridges, partly because more bridges were being built. Bridges were both a cause and a consequence of economic revival in medieval Britain and, not following the Roman precedent of central planning, they were built as a result of local initiative. Shrewsbury's medieval bridges acted as an extension of the castle in fortifying the town. Both were close to fords, and the act of building bridges was instrumental in the subsequent strategic and commercial importance of the town. References in a charter of 1121 suggest that both bridges were in existence by then.[15]

The church often took the initiative in raising money for building and maintaining bridges, which was recognised as an important act of charity. Matthew's Gospel describes how in the Last Judgment those who have given succour to the needy, amongst whom travellers may be counted, will be admitted to the kingdom of heaven.[16] Thomas de Cobham, bishop of Worcester (1317-27), composed a model letter in which he explained that contributing to the construction and repair of bridges was a work of mercy pleasing to God.[17] In William Langland's 14th-century *Piers Plowman*, Truth exhorts the wealthy to 'use their profits to repair the hospitals and to help folk in trouble – to get the bad roads mended quickly and rebuild the broken bridges'.[18] The same impulse inspired pious men to erect hospitals to accommodate the aged and infirm (origin of the later

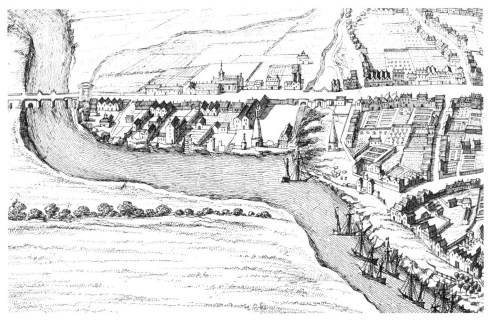

In this early 18th-century bird's eye view of Gloucester the main channel is clearly seen, but it also shows the dwindled old eastern channel and the remnant of Foreign Bridge. Between the bridges is St Bartholomew's Hospital.

almshouses), and many of these refuges were built close to bridges. Hermits who took a vow to follow the rule of St Paul bound themselves to work for others and were frequently engaged in repairing roads and bridges.

In Gloucester, Foreign Bridge, spanning the Old Severn, was begun on 15 May 1119 by Nicholas, a priest at St Nicholas' church. By 1203 the church of St Nicholas was described as the church of Gloucester Bridge (i.e. Foreign Bridge) and the parson was its keeper. Although it was described as *pons magnus Glocestrie* (the great bridge of Gloucester), the river channel it spanned was shrinking. Three centuries later Leland described the bridge as having seven arches of stone, four of which remained visible until the 18th century, after which the dwindling stream was culverted. Four eastern arches were uncovered by excavations in 1973.[19] Gloucester's Westgate Bridge spans what is now known as the east channel, but in medieval times was the Great Severn. It was begun in the 12th century, perhaps also in 1119, by a chaplain, Nicholas Walred, and a former burgess of the town, William Myparty. They are said to have built a house close by in which they lived and which provided workmen's lodgings as well as lodgings for the infirm, thus combining two charitable endeavours. It was later recognised officially as St Bartholomew's Hospital, whose brothers described themselves as the wardens and preachers of the bridge, and therefore administered the funds and organised upkeep of the bridge – in 1264 they donated four oak trees for its repair.[20] There is certainly some confusion around the sources of these two bridges – among the earliest stone bridges to be built in Britain – and perhaps the same Nicholas was involved in both enterprises.

Samuel Ireland's view of Westgate Bridge in Gloucester shows the central timber span, which could be raised to allow passage to masted vessels, but could also act as a drawbridge in times of conflict.

At Atcham (just outside Shrewsbury) a bridge was built by the abbot of Lilleshall by 1221, replacing the ferry, and paid for by the collection of tolls.[21] Buildwas Bridge is first mentioned in 1318 and was probably built by the adjacent monastery.[22]

Individuals also made substantial contributions to bridge building. Maisemore Ham Bridge was not quite a Severn bridge, as it spanned the old river Leadon that was taken in by the new west channel of the Severn at the end of the 15th century, but it was on the causeway leading west out of Gloucester from Westgate Bridge. The bridge was begun in the 13th century by William Anketil, a tenant on the estate of Gloucester Abbey; he erected a cross on the bridge with an accompanying inscription: 'In honour of our Lord Jesus Christ, who was crucified for us, William fitz Anketil of Linton made this cross and thus began the bridge of Maisemore'.[23] Beside the modern Maisemore Bridge, over the west channel of the Severn, which was built in 1956, is a 19th-century cross brought from Gloucester St Michael that commemorates the earlier cross, although the connotations have shifted from charity to a sense of heritage.

Bequests and alms paid for the building of bridges, as did the granting of indulgences. The doctrine of Purgatory – where the sins of the deceased are cleansed – sprouted an industry of prayer and the performance of requiem masses to ease the passage of souls through it. Credit could be built up by performing good works on Earth, reducing the time of suffering afterwards. These 'indulgences' became one of the most effective ways of funding good causes, and flourished from the mid 14th century, given timely relevance by the Black Death of 1348-49. Certificates were issued that specified the number of days by which the time spent in Purgatory would be reduced in exchange for performing specific good works. When Bewdley's first bridge was built in the 1440s, John Carpenter, bishop of Worcester, offered an indulgence of 40 days to anyone who contributed to the work.

The association of bridges with prayers and good works is why some medieval bridges had chapels. In most cases the chaplain or warden of the bridge acted as cashier and administrator of bridge funds and repair works. When priests are said to have built bridges, as in the case of Nicholas Walred in Gloucester (or Peter Colechurch in London), it does not mean that they were in charge of the stone masons. In the case of Westgate Bridge and Foreign Bridge in Gloucester, it is clear that clerical responsibility for the bridge was supplementary to the clerics' main responsibilities at hospital and parish church respectively.

But bridge chapels must surely hark back to an earlier culture of superstition, of river gods that must be placated. Bridges are also fertile metaphors – Christ is the bridge between men and God, souls bridged the treacherous waters of life to pass from mortality to immortality – and this must have helped to strengthen the notion of bridge building as holy work. The idea of bridge chapels was probably imported into England in the late 12th century at Old London Bridge, following earlier examples in France, notably the famous bridge in Avignon. An even earlier bridge, the 6th-century bridge over the river Sangarius (Sakarya) in north-west Turkey, has a votive arch dedicated to the emperor Justinian, and a bridge chapel, and the slightly earlier Karamagara Bridge in Cappadocia (modern eastern Turkey) has a pointed arch with letters on each voussoir spelling out

Bridgnorth Bridge was begun in 1101
and in this late 18th-century view still retained its gatehouse.

the text of Psalm 20, verse 8.[24] Swedish bridges incorporate pagan runic inscriptions, and there are examples showing scenes from the legend of Sigurd the dragon slayer and Christian crosses.[25] When Ancus Martius built the *pons Sublicus* in Rome *c.*600 BC it was placed in the care of a high priest, or *pontifex* (Roman emperors later adopted the title *pontifex maximus* and it is the origin of the word Pontiff).[26] The bridge chapel adapted ancient superstitions to the needs of medieval life and religion.

The Severn had at least two specific bridge chapels. The chapel on Bridgnorth's bridge was dedicated to St Sitha, who was invoked by housewives and household servants, especially when they were in danger from rivers or crossing bridges. The chapel contained an image of the saint whose decoration, according to an inventory made in the later Middle Ages, included jet and amber beads, a silver pilgrim shell and silver rings, all gifts of suppliant pilgrims.[27] The wardens of the bridge were the brethren of the nearby Franciscan friary. Bridge chapels were not necessarily sited on the bridge; Bewdley chapel, first mentioned when a new bridge was built in 1483, stood close to the bridge above the Mersour Tavern.[28] Walter Rode, who in 1483 was the first bridge and chapel warden, received a donation of 20 marks (£13 6s 8d) from Richard III.

Another possible bridge chapel was on Shrewsbury's Stone Bridge. The local antiquary Thomas Phillips, who witnessed workmen taking down the Stone Bridge in the late 1760s prior to the construction of the English Bridge, noticed that when it had been made good after flood damage in 1545 the gatehouse appeared to have been 'repaired out of the ruins of some religious place'. The chief component was three Gothic niches, in which figures remained intact. They showed a mitred abbot, a man holding in his arms the Lamb of God and, in the centre, a woman holding a book, probably St Winefride.[29] The main centres of Winefride's cult were Shrewsbury and Holywell in Flintshire. Her relics had been at Shrewsbury Abbey since 1138 and Robert, the prior of Shrewsbury, was her hagiographer. Her cult became popular in the 15th century, and shrines were set up on the pilgrimage route from Shrewsbury Abbey to Holywell, of which that on the Stone Bridge must have been the first. In 1416 Henry V made the pilgrimage on foot and Edward IV (1461-70 and 1471-83) is reputed to have done the same.[30]

Charity was not always enough to keep a bridge in good repair. Upkeep of bridges was often, and in some cases still is, paid for by the collection of tolls, but for most of the medieval period they could only be levied under a special licence known as pontage. In the early 13th century in the wake of Magna Carta, crown lawyers were able to broaden the definition of the king's highway to mean any common way, which was important because the king guaranteed free passage on the highway. Private tolls were therefore no longer allowed. Instead, pontage grants were issued by the Crown for a limited period, usually of between three and five years, to carry out specific works. The first such grant for a Severn bridge was awarded to the town of Shrewsbury in 1259, and most of the English Severn bridges received pontage grants on more than one occasion in the 13th and 14th centuries. Atcham received its first grant in 1315, Buildwas in 1318 (the earliest documented reference to the bridge), while Shrewsbury received five separate pontage grants between 1336 and 1351 and Bridgnorth four between 1324 and 1337. The people of Worcester were granted pontage in 1272 for six years in order to repair the bridge badly damaged by Prince Edward – soon to be Edward I – during the baronial wars that culminated in the defeat of Simon de Montfort at the battle of Evesham.[31] Bridge-breaking was a common strategy in wars in which the Severn acted as a defensive barrier, because it was like raising a drawbridge over a moat.

Montford Bridge, upstream of Shrewsbury, received its first grant in 1285 when a list of tolls was drawn up. All goods crossing the bridge were subject to tolls, from a farthing for ten fleeces of wool to fourpence for each tun of wine. Passengers crossed freely, except for Jews who were charged a penny if they were on horseback, a halfpenny on foot. Jews can have constituted only a minuscule proportion of people crossing Montford Bridge, but they were routinely singled out in pontage grants during the years of persecution leading up to their expulsion from England in 1290. Tariffs were applied more or less uniformly across the country and were periodically reviewed to take account of new commodities – for example, in a pontage grant of 1412 for Montford Bridge, wrought iron, sea coals, charcoal, herrings and roof tiles had been added to the list.[32] Pontage was applied to goods crossing bridges rather than passing under them, despite the fact that damage to bridges was often caused by river-borne vessels. Pontage grants for Montford Bridge do, however, included clauses adapted specifically to the Severn navigation. Floats of timber passing under Montford Bridge were subject to toll payments, and fines were levied when they struck and damaged the bridge. Later, the city of Worcester successfully took a case to the Star Chamber in 1503 protesting that they should be allowed to charge a toll on Bewdley vessels, which were responsible for damaging what was an important route between England and Wales.[33]

What did these bridges look like? Timber remained a mainstay of bridge construction in the Middle Ages, but Gloucester, Worcester, Bridgnorth and Shrewsbury all had stone bridges by the 14th century. In Gloucester, Foreign Bridge, begun in 1119, was one of the first stone bridges in Britain, while Westgate Bridge retained at least one timber span into the 19th century; this may have been common, not least because it allowed a drawbridge to be constructed. In the 13th century timber had been donated for the repair of the bridge from royal forests, as also for Worcester and Bridgnorth bridges, which must also have been partly of timber at that time.[34] Over Bridge, built over the new west channel near Gloucester and still unfinished in 1543, was part timber, part stone in the 17th century, despite being described as a stone bridge by Leland.[35] The bridge opposite Gloucester Castle was of timber when it was repaired in the 1220s and presumably also in 1264, when it was burned down during the Barons' War.[36] A timber bridge replaced a ferry in the 15th century at Upton-upon-Severn. The second Bewdley Bridge was also of timber, built after the original bridge was destroyed in 1459, and it remained in use until Richard III granted money for a replacement in 1483. On the Welsh section of the river all of the bridges were of timber until the final quarter of the 18th century.

Bridges mirror the societies that build them. Stone bridges were among the highest achievements in medieval technology, comparable to and borrowing from the technology of stone vaulting in churches. On the English stretch of the river the principal stone bridges were fortress-like, with stout stone piers and cutwaters buttressed against the current. Bridge piers were constructed during the summer months when the river was low and the foundations could be protected by a small coffer dam. Shrewsbury's two bridges, Bridgnorth's bridge and Foreign Bridge in Gloucester all had round arches; the later Worcester bridge built in 1313 and the bridges at Bewdley and Buildwas had pointed arches.[37] In the towns, defensible gatehouses were built on the bridges to intimidate unwelcome visitors. Gates could be shut, allowing whole towns to close up at night. Worcester Bridge, Gloucester's Westgate Bridge and the new Bewdley Bridge, built from 1483, both had gatehouses, but fortified bridges *par excellence* were to be found in Shrewsbury.

As its name implies, the Welsh Bridge was the entrance to Shrewsbury from Wales. Its drawbridge and fortified gatehouse sent a message to visitors from the Welsh March and the self-governing parts of Wales, or *Pura Walia*, of the power vested in the town. Visitors were greeted by a figure above the gatehouse, now identified by consensus as Edward, Prince of Wales, popularly known as the Black Prince (who died in 1376), but in the 18th century identified in the popular imagination as a variety of individuals, including Richard, duke of York (father of Edward IV), Llywelyn the Great and Dafydd ap Gruffudd, who was tried and executed for treason at Shrewsbury in 1283. The statue is all that survived when the Welsh Bridge was taken down – 'to the regret of every person of taste and every lover of antiquities' – and can still be seen on the wall of the Old Market House in the town centre.[38] The bridge on the corresponding English side, known as Stone Bridge, also incorporated a drawbridge and gatehouse, but was less martial than the Welsh side. It spanned the main channel of the river between the town and the former Coleham Island, the now vanished island that stood at the confluence of the Severn and Rea brook. The bridge over the smaller eastern channel, which had silted up by the 16th century, was known as Monk's Bridge or Abbey Bridge because the Benedictine abbey stood on the far bank. Town and church quarrelled over jurisdiction and responsibility for the bridge.[39]

In the towns a medieval bridge was not just a river crossing but also a street. Buildings on bridges yielded rents that helped fund the maintenance of the bridge, a system that followed French precedent. By 1285 there were four shops on Foreign Bridge in Gloucester, as well as an unspecified number of houses; there were ten properties on the bridge in 1455.[40] Bridgnorth Bridge had several houses as well as its chapel. The gatehouse on Bewdley Bridge was also the home of the toll-gatherer. In Shrewsbury the presence of houses on the bridges long outlived the need to fund the bridge repairs that determined the economic conditions of their creation. In 1370 a glover named John the Child was allowed to put down a ladder from his house on the Stone Bridge onto an island of stones and immerse his lambskins and goatskins in the river. In 1586 George Trevenant was said to have obstructed the passage under the English Bridge because the fish traps he had laid under his house impounded the water on the upstream side.[41]

Building a house on the bridge was a precarious business. So as not to obstruct the highway these buildings projected from the parapets on timber struts. Two houses on the Shrewsbury Stone Bridge collapsed and fell into the river on Christmas Day 1752, the timber struts supporting them having rotted.[42] Not that this put people off; as late as 1752 a lease was signed for building three houses on the Welsh Bridge.[43] A survey of

Thomas Phillips' view shows the last days of the Welsh Bridge, as viewed from Frankwell Quay. It shows the gatehouse and, on the left, a short row of cottages that projected from the parapet. (Courtesy of Shrewsbury Museums and Art Gallery)

the Stone Bridge made by Thomas Farnolls Pritchard in 1765 showed two dwellings on the upstream side, but eleven on the safer downstream side, including a tenement of six dwellings above the waterwheel, as well as the Bridge House.[44]

Another of the functions of bridges, now forgotten, was to act as lock-ups. Shrewsbury's prisons were housed in the upper storeys of the gate towers. It seems a fitting place for a prison, in limbo on the river, but it was also a place where you could easily be forgotten (prisoners relied on family or friends to feed them). Bewdley's lock-up was the Bridge House on the town side of the bridge. The Bewdley chapel-and-bridge wardens were also responsible for the goom-stool, or ducking stool, used to punish scolds. Women were ducked to quench the fire in their heads and presumably to be reborn as more virtuous souls, a grotesque caricature of Christian baptism. Worcester had its goom-stool, which appears to have been set up in various places, including the riverside. In 1660 four witches – a woman, her two daughters and a male associate – were brought to Worcester from Kidderminster. 'Many charges against them and little proved', was Henry Townshend's verdict, but 'they were put to ducking in the river and they would not sink but swam aloft'.[45] Worcester Bridge was one of the focal points of the city where stocks were set up.[46]

There was little bridge building on the Severn in the 16th and 17th centuries, although Atcham Bridge was rebuilt about 1550.[47] Surviving stone bridges of the Severn belong to the 18th century and later, beginning with a period of renewal that owed as much to economic development as to the dilapidation of earlier crossings. The medieval systems of funding had gone, not simply because the religious assumptions that underpinned them had been repudiated. No longer were alms collected for repair work, and after Henry VIII's Statute of Bridges of 1530 the county became the

John Gwynn's finest surviving work on the Severn is the bridge at Atcham, completed in 1771. It was on an important route from London to Holyhead, which may explain the splendour unusual in a rural bridge.

default institution responsible for the upkeep of bridges, unless the responsibility had previously been invested in another specific institution or individual. An exception to the rule was the bridge at Upton, funded by a charity established in 1576 by Edward Hall to be responsible for the repair of the bridge and church (the charity is still active as a general charity in the parish). A new stone bridge was completed there in 1593.[48] Bridges were part of the renewal of towns and economic life in the 18th century. Because it has been overshadowed by the Victorian railway boom, it is often forgotten that the 18th century was a period of change driven by economic growth and improved communications in the form of canals, turnpikes and bridges. Nowhere was this more apparent than in Shrewsbury. Its two old bridges were narrow, made narrower and cramped by the houses on the bridges. Moreover the gatehouses impeded traffic, which suited the defensive-minded Middle Ages, but no longer suited the more progressive, business-like 18th century. It is hardly surprising that plans to replace them both were set in motion.

The replacement of Shrewsbury's Stone Bridge by the English Bridge brought a successful native architect, the London-based John Gwynn (1713-86), back to his home town, but only after a protracted series of events that swung first against him and finally in his favour. Robert Mylne (1733-1811), who had won the competition to design the new Blackfriars Bridge in London, was initially employed as the architect to replace the Stone Bridge, ahead of the local man Thomas Farnolls Pritchard. (Pritchard was nevertheless employed in survey work on the old bridge and was to make his own spectacular contribution to the stock of Severn bridges.) Mylne's scheme for widening the old bridge failed, however, and it allowed John Gwynn a way in to design what we now know as the English Bridge, which was finished in 1774. It led to other Severn commissions. Gwynn

Llandrinio Bridge, a fine red sandstone bridge, was built in the 1770s, probably by John Gwynn.

This early 19th-century view of the English Bridge in Shrewsbury shows its original form, before the deck was made level in the 1920s.

built the new bridge at Atcham, completed in 1771, which like the English Bridge was on the important London-Holyhead road, and he also built Worcester Bridge. The similar but smaller bridge at Llandrinio has also been attributed to him. Llandrinio is the most rugged of the bridges, perhaps because it was not built to complement a town. (Today, at the ends of the bridge there are concrete roadblocks, and just beyond it is a pill box, testament to Llandrinio's unlikely role in the defence of Britain. During World War II the town was the end of the Western Command Stop Line No 1, which extended from here to Tewkesbury.)

The English Bridge hailed a new period in Severn and Shrewsbury history. The new design shrugged off the medieval air of Shrewsbury, of the bridge as a kind of border control, and proclaimed it a modern town open for business. Compared with the old bridge encumbered by houses and tower, the new symmetrical bridge had cleaner, simpler lines and was a thoroughfare open to the sky, giving clarity to the riverscape and a modernising uplift to the river and the town. The English Bridge was altered in the 1920s but because the masonry of Gwynn's bridge was re-used, it retains much of its 18th-century character.

Gwynn's Worcester Bridge, completed in 1780, marked a similar period in the city's history. It was part of a larger urban regeneration, costing £30,000, that transformed the city's relationship with the river. The new bridge was constructed slightly downstream of the medieval bridge. An avenue was laid out on its western approach, beyond the city, where there were two round Doric lodges, and on the city side 'a handsome street' was

John Gwynn's Worcester Bridge has been altered from its original appearance, but retains the original rusticated masonry arches and balustraded parapet that were intended to proclaim the British as the new Romans.

built, 'thus opening an airy and elegant communication with the interior of the city'.[49] This is Bridge Street, where the Georgian terraced houses that were added in the 1790s still form an elegant entrance to the city, even if the modern one-way traffic system works against it. Gwynn also envisaged terraced houses on North and South Parades, but they were never built, and new quays were constructed either side of the bridge instead, giving the riverside a more mercantile character.[50] Keystones on the bridge were carved with figures of Sabrina on the upstream side to symbolise the inland river, and Oceanus on the downstream side to stand for the tidal river, as if to emphasise that this was a pivotal position in the course of the Severn. Gwynn's work on the Severn compensated for his unfulfilled ambition to enhance the riverside in London. His ideas had been set out in 1766 in a pamphlet entitled *London and Westminster Improved*, but they apply equally to Worcester and Shrewsbury: 'The English are now what the Romans were of old … excelling all other nations in commerce and navigation', and so 'let us employ our riches in the encouragement of ingenious labour, by promoting advancement of grandeur and elegance'.[51]

Worcester Bridge is no longer the set piece it once was; the lodges were taken down when the bridge was widened and reconstructed in the early 1930s. The bridges at Llandrinio and Atcham, however, survive in their original form. Atcham is the more stately, and enjoys a rare serenity (at least from the downstream side) because traffic no longer crosses it. The view of the bridge is now obscured on the north side by the road bridge that replaced it in 1929.

Georgian Britain saw the emergence of a new kind of professional, the civil engineer, epitomised by the career of Thomas Telford (1757-1834). Telford had come to Shrewsbury to work for William Pulteney, newly elected as the town's Member of Parliament, who intended to live in Shrewsbury Castle. By 1787 Telford had been appointed Surveyor of Bridges for Shropshire, a post that led to important bridge-building commissions on the Severn in the 1790s. Using John Carline and John Tilley as contractors, Telford replaced the medieval Montford Bridge in 1792 and the contractors built a new Welsh Bridge in Shrewsbury in 1795 to their own design. In both cases a new site was chosen slightly downstream from the original. This had more marked consequences in Shrewsbury because the importance of its main thoroughfare, known as the Mardol, was diminished. Thomas Telford's Bewdley Bridge, built to replace the medieval bridge damaged in the great flood of 1795, was also a stone bridge on a new site. It brought particular satisfaction for Telford and his chief mason John Simpson, who Telford described as 'a treasure of talents and integrity'. As Telford himself wrote, 'The dry season … has enabled us to raise Bewdley Bridge as by enchantment. We have thus raised a magnificent bridge over the river Severn in one season.'[52] In Gloucester the corporation wanted an architect rather than an engineer to replace the medieval Westgate and Over bridges: 'the scientific principles, approved and acted upon by the ancient masters of architecture, and which have stood the test of ages' were preferred to the new iron technology that had been pioneered on the Severn. Westgate Bridge (1813-16) was by the architect Robert Smirke, and Over Bridge, crossing the

This rustic bridge on the Severn, drawn by Samuel Ireland, is labelled 'near Llanidloes' and was perhaps at Felindre.

Maisemore channel, was by Thomas Telford (1825) and has the longest masonry span of a bridge in England.

Thomas Telford's counterpart in Montgomeryshire was Thomas Penson (1790-1859). He built bridges in Felindre and Caersws in 1821 and the Long Bridges in Newtown and Llanidloes in 1826. The older bridges had been built of timber, in the case of Llanidloes only in 1741. It was 'much decayed' by the 1820s, although it was apparently only used in winter – in the summer, the river was usually fordable here.[53]

Timber might seem a flimsy material with which to build a permanent crossing over a formidable river, but it was still used for bridge building into the 19th century. Thomas Telford's wooden trestle bridge at Cressage was built in 1799-1800 and stood for over a century before it was replaced in 1914. Thomas Pennant remarked that all of the bridges on the Welsh section of the river were of timber, until Llandrinio Bridge was built in the 1770s.[54] The others all survived, or at least continued to be repaired using timber, into the 19th century. Richard Fenton, visiting Newtown in 1804, crossed a wooden bridge which, 'seemingly old and infirm, yet stood', when others had been destroyed by the flood of 1795.[55] The bridges at Brynderwen and Caerhowel were replaced after being damaged in the flood of 1852. In the case of the former, all the woodwork was swept away by the river, leaving only the stone abutments. In 1860 the wooden railway bridge at Caersws was replaced after a flood had washed away the embankment. The pine-wood trestle bridge built in 1859 across the river at Mofordion near Llanidloes for the Llanidloes and Newtown Railway has outlived the line it served. But we should keep this in perspective. Maisemore Bridge was described in 1710 as 'being made of timber', but had 'severall times within this 40 years last past been carried away by inundations of water in the river of Severne, and by the often repaireing of it the timber [of the manor] was much diminished'.[56] A new masonry bridge was begun there in 1710.

In the English section of the river in the 18th century, the natural successor to timber was not stone but iron. Preens Eddy was a wooden bridge built in 1780 at the downstream

Coalport Bridge changed gradually from the wooden bridge built in 1780 to the iron bridge that stands today, completed in 1818 when the parapet was cast by John Onions of Broseley.

end of the Ironbridge Gorge, one of two new bridges that serviced the increase in cross-river traffic with the rapid industrial development of the east Shropshire coalfield, which in turn was aided by accessibility to the Severn. Through piecemeal repair and replacement it changed by degrees into an iron bridge, completed in 1818 when local ironmaster John Onions cast extra arches, surface plates and parapet.[57] Its name was changed to Coalport Bridge, but the adjacent pub is still known as the Woodbridge Inn. The other contemporary bridge in the Ironbridge Gorge is, of course, the Iron Bridge itself, notable for its use of carpenters' joints and an ancestry in the timber rather than the stone tradition.

The story of iron bridges does not quite begin in the Ironbridge Gorge, however. The idea of using iron for bridge construction had been around since the mid 18th century, and in 1769 Maurice Tobin built a wrought-iron bridge to span a waterway at Kirklees Hall in Yorkshire. The story of the Severn iron bridges begins with the unlikely figure of Thomas Farnolls Pritchard (1723-77). By the 1770s he was a well-established Shrewsbury architect and surveyor, who enjoyed a busy practice working for a variety of secular clients, as well as receiving some ecclesiastical commissions. One of his buildings, Shrewsbury's Foundling Hospital (now Shrewsbury School), is a prominent landmark above the Severn in Shrewsbury. Pritchard had worked for the Downton estate in south Shropshire, and was possibly the man who designed a single-span bridge over the river Teme at Downton in 1772. Its profile is reminiscent of the Iron Bridge although it is constructed of stone and spans a narrower river than the Severn. Next, Pritchard was engaged in the construction of a bridge over the Severn at Stourport. The bridge was completed in 1775 and was said to have been constructed around an iron frame but, not yet confident enough to reveal itself, it was encased in rusticated masonry. It is not known which foundry cast the iron components. Unfortunately the bridge lasted only 20 years, another victim of the 1795 flood.[58]

Nevertheless, when a proposal was made for a new bridge to span the Severn in the Ironbridge Gorge and Pritchard became involved, he quickly resolved on an iron bridge, and never lacked confidence in the technology. Nor did Abraham Darby III, at whose Coalbrookdale foundry the iron was cast and who was responsible for erecting the bridge and its approach roads. The project was to be funded by shareholders, many of whom had interests in the local iron trade, either as ironmasters like Darby or John Wilkinson, or as investors like Edward Blakeway and William Goodwin. Darby agreed to indemnify the other shareholders against any overspend, which proved his financial undoing. He was a victim of overconfidence, or perhaps of a desperate ambition to match the achievements of his father and grandfather, both of whom had established new successful businesses in the metals trades. A bridge that was supposed to cost £3,250, in the end cost much more – figures of £5,250 and £6,000 were in circulation at the time, but the exact figure is not known.[59]

A lot of ink has been spilled about the building of the Iron Bridge. One of the unfortunate laws of historical enquiry is that great events in history generate uncertainties, opening the door to speculation and pet theories. Such is the case with the Iron Bridge, and arguments about where the bridge was cast have been kept alive unencumbered by supporting evidence. It should be straightforward. An inscription on the bridge helpfully states that it was 'cast in Coalbrookdale', and when in 1785 two visiting Frenchmen, Alexandre and Francois de la Rochefoucauld, asked to visit the place where the bridge was cast, they were taken to the Coalbrookdale foundries.[60] However, it has since been claimed that Coalbrookdale could represent almost anywhere in the east Shropshire coalfield that is close to the river. Such a claim is a sore underestimation of local culture and its intimate sense of place. The argument is largely predicated upon two sources: Phillippe de Loutherbourg's 1801 painting 'Coalbrookdale by Night', a mistitled work that actually shows the riverside ironworks at neighbouring Madeley Wood; and a comment by the Reverend Richard Warner that the bridge was cast 'upon the spot'. But de Loutherbourg lived in London; Warner lived in Bath. It has also been argued that large cast iron ribs could not have been transported just over a mile from the Coalbrookdale works to the riverside and that the ribs must therefore have been cast closer to the river. This is another specious argument with no evidence behind it. No one has suggested that the Coalbrookdale foundries were unable to deliver large bridge components to Buildwas in 1796, which is two miles upstream. Following the flood of 1795 the company was also invited to replace the old bridge at Bewdley with a cast

This view of the Iron Bridge by William Williams was commissioned by Abraham Darby III in 1780. (© Ironbridge Gorge Museum Trust)

iron structure; it declined the invitation only because it could not expedite the masonry abutments and approach roads. The only local foundry capable of casting items over five tons in weight – which could only have been achieved by using multiple melting, or 'air', furnaces – was the Coalbrookdale works, where the tradition of iron casting continues. The wooden patterns for the castings remained at the works until they were burnt in 1902-3.

The bridge was already a talking point before it was completed. John Wesley was a frequent visitor to Madeley parish, which nurtured one of the most dedicated of Methodist communities, and noted in his journal that he saw the iron ribs laid out on the riverbank awaiting erection. But the bridge's fame was largely the result of vigorous promotion by Abraham Darby, who issued an engraving of the new bridge in the summer of 1780, six months before it officially opened. A succession of views by commercial artists followed, and these alerted artists like J.M.W. Turner, Phillippe de Loutherbourg and John Sell Cotman to the dramatic scenery of the Ironbridge Gorge. Oddly, none of these illustrious artists actually painted the bridge, but it became a must-see *en route* to Snowdonia and its many attractions, a journey that came to be known as

Victoria Bridge at Arley was built in 1862 for the Severn Valley Railway to the design of John Fowler, and cast at the Coalbrookdale Ironworks.

The Mythe Bridge near Tewkesbury, completed in 1826,
is perhaps Thomas Telford's finest Severn bridge.
The ironwork was cast by William Hazeldine's Coleham Foundry in Shrewsbury.

Caerhowel Bridge was built in 1858 by Montgomeryshire county surveyor Thomas Penson,
after an earlier iron bridge had failed after only six years.

the Celtic Grand Tour. This was the end of the 18th century, the Age of Enlightenment, and the Iron Bridge was a potent symbol of how technological progress could create a better world. Replicas of the bridge were built at Raincy near Paris and in Prussia, while Thomas Jefferson obtained an engraving of this bridge over an obscure stretch of the river Severn and hung it in the White House.

The bridge bears out Robert Southey's claim that 'of all the works of man, there is not any one which unites so well with natural scenery, and so heightens its beauty, as a bridge'. Samuel Butler, writing in 1782, expressed the sentiments of many: 'The Bridge itself makes a light & elegant appearance tho' apparently no ways deficient in strength. In viewing it either up or down water it resembles an elegant Arch in some elegant Cathedral.'[61] Its slightly raked profile, gaining height to allow masted vessels to sail beneath it, together with the circles in the arch spandrels, belong to the 18th century, but its repetitive arched ribs belong to the rhythm of industrial architecture and look forward to the 19th century, the age in which iron fulfilled its potential as a bridge-building material.

Having established the suitability of cast iron for engineering works, the Coalbrookdale Company quickly learned from its first efforts, and cast parts for several more small iron bridges in the late 18th century. Its next major commission was for Buildwas Bridge two miles upstream of Coalbrookdale, the medieval bridge having been partially destroyed in 1795. Designed by Thomas Telford, the bridge weighed a mere 178 tons, compared to 378 tons for the earlier Iron Bridge, even though it had a slightly wider span of 130 feet (40 metres).[62] The Coalbrookdale Company was still not able to make a profit on it, however, losing over £700 on the project. Bridge building never became the core of its business, but the company continued to cast iron bridges in the 19th century. Among the best of them are the Severn railway bridges at Belvidere, on the Shrewsbury & Birmingham Railway (1849), and the very similar bridges at Buildwas on the Wenlock Railway (1864) and Victoria Bridge on the Severn Valley Railway (1862) at Upper Arley.

Thomas Telford – the Colossus of Roads, as poet-laureate Robert Southey called him – was the dominant figure in iron bridge construction in Shropshire and elsewhere by the beginning of the 19th century. For most of his bridge work he was supplied by the Shropshire ironmaster William Hazledine, who established a foundry and engineering works on the riverside at Coleham in Shrewsbury in the 1790s, and later he was briefly supplied with pig iron from his own riverside blast furnaces at Calcutts in the Ironbridge Gorge. The Coleham foundry cast components for some landmark buildings, not least the ironwork for Ditherington flax mill in Shrewsbury, built in 1796, and it was here in the 1820s that iron chains for Telford's Menai and Conwy suspension bridges were tested for their tensile strength, before being shipped to north Wales. Parts for the bridges at Mythe and Holt Fleet were cast there; by the 1820s these had become standard components that had already been proved on bridges in Scotland. The longest of Telford's cast iron arches was for Mythe Bridge near Tewkesbury, which was completed in 1826, followed a year later by the bridge upstream at Holt Fleet, which opened on New Year's Day in 1828 and was said to have cost £8,300.[63] The functional aesthetic of these bridges was enhanced by ancillary structures, in the case of Mythe by the Gothic land arches of the approach, and a picturesque lodge.

The replacement of the timber bridges in Montgomeryshire occurred when iron construction was economical and well established. Thomas Penson built his first iron bridge at Llandinam in 1846. He also built the iron bridges of Brynderwen (Abermule) and Caerhowel to replace timber bridges damaged in 1852. Caerhowel initially had a suspension bridge by James Dredge but very soon it failed under the weight of three wagon loads of lime.[64] Penson replaced it with a less ambitious iron bridge design in 1858. Buttington Bridge was also replaced by a cast-iron bridge by Penson's successor, W.N. Swettenham, in 1872, by which time this mode of construction was no longer novel.

Ironwork is especially associated with railway crossings. Railway bridges subtly altered the experience of crossing rivers, not least because travellers now experienced the crossing from the relative comfort of a carriage. Railway bridges are not built for stopping on, unlike medieval bridges, which even incorporated refuges on the parapet to accommodate loiterers. To cross a road bridge you have to descend to the riverbank, but railway bridges, which need flat decks, quite often cross whole valleys. The supreme example on the Severn is Stephen Ballard's Hereford and Worcester Railway bridge at Worcester, which soars over the Severn and its flood plain by means of 68 arches and two iron spans.

Railways brought new types of bridges and, eventually, bridges on a much larger scale. Belvidere Bridge in Shrewsbury is a conventional arched iron bridge, little different from a Georgian road bridge. Longer spans required new solutions, however, like girders

The reinforced concrete road bridge at Atcham was built in 1929, and its existence has ensured the preservation of the earlier Atcham bridge.

and bowstring trusses. The Hereford and Worcester Railway was built in 1860 and its Severn bridge at Worcester, mentioned above, has central iron spans. The original cast iron arches were replaced in 1904 by lattice girders. The Tenbury and Bewdley Railway bridge at Dowles was built in 1863-64 by William Clarke and had lattice-girder spans from the outset, but they have been removed and only the stone piers they rested on still stand.

The greatest technological achievement in iron railway bridges was the Severn Railway Bridge below Gloucester, a bridge that is remembered for several reasons.[65] This ambitious crossing, built by Keeling & Wells in 1875-79, had 21 spans, all with novel bowstring trusses, and a swing bridge over the Gloucester and Sharpness Canal. One man is said to have fallen from a pier during construction and landed, seemingly dead, in the sand, only to recover consciousness while his body was being carried away in a sack. The bridge was opened with great optimism in 1879, a hundred years after the Iron Bridge, and on the same day that excavations for the Severn Tunnel were inundated with water (from natural springs rather than the Severn).[66] Unfortunately the bridge was conceived only as a branch line to connect the Severn and Wye Railway with the main line railway between Bristol and Gloucester. Talk of combining the railway with a roadway came to nothing. Dr Beeching would probably have axed the line had not disaster already struck in October 1960. Seven minutes after a train had crossed the bridge it was struck by the petrol barge *Wastdale*, with the loss of five lives and destruction of two of the bridge spans. The remainder was in the process of demolition while the new Severn Bridge on the M4 motorway was being opened. Given that during the war Spitfires and Hurricanes were seen diving under the bridge – a game of chicken that presumably is no longer allowed in the RAF – for it to have been struck by something so ponderous seems doubly unfortunate.[67]

The Severn Railway Bridge was the longest railway bridge ever attempted over the Severn, although not the lowest crossing. For the line that crosses further downstream the Great Western Railway engineers decided to eschew a monumental showpiece like the Forth and Tay Bridges, and opted to go under the river rather than over it. But a railway bridge across the Lower Severn had been seriously considered in the 1840s, the ultimate challenge being to bridge the river between Beachley and Aust. In 1845 Thomas Fulljames (1808-74) produced two designs for railway bridges for the Aust Bridge Company, each of them suspension bridges with a double track. The design allowed for piers to be erected on the rocks but also in the deep water channel, which proved an impractical proposition, especially since the central span of one of the bridges would have been 1,100 feet (335 metres), far too long for chains to support a railway. In 1849 Fulljames proposed another, even more ambitious scheme – a freshwater lake behind a Severn barrage in the form of a castellated two-tier viaduct, with double-track railway on the upper deck and single carriageway on the lower deck.[68]

Where iron and steel became the favoured material for railway crossings, reinforced concrete became the road-builders' material of choice. Road bridges are on a decidedly smaller scale and lack the soaring piers of the high-level rail crossings. The pioneering firm of L.G. Mouchel and Partners built several – at Atcham, Cressage and Jackfield – all of which share family traits of segmental arches and vertical ribs in the open spandrels, a style which was borrowed from cast-iron bridges and remained characteristic of the firm for several decades. It has few admirers, but the bold and simple lines are fittingly understated for designers tired of Victorian decorative excess. Civil engineers were still searching for the definitive language of reinforced concrete.

On a completely different scale are the Severn Bridge and the Second Severn Crossing. The Severn Bridge has always seemed like the end of the river and the beginning of the sea. Look north-east from the bridge and the land closes in to narrow the estuary, but look south-west and it opens out broadly into the Bristol Channel. The bridge replaced one of the oldest of the river crossings, the ferry at Aust, and opened in 1966. Designed by Gilbert Roberts, the *Architectural Review* described the bridge as 'almost as far ahead of its forbears as the jet is in advance of the piston engine'.[69] With a central span of 3,240 feet (987 metres) it weighs a third less than the Forth Bridge, which is only 60 feet (18 metres) longer. It was also the first bridge to be built with an aerodynamically shaped deck and inclined hangers. But these are dry, technical claims that are more likely to impress civil engineers than the people who use the bridge.

Design of modern bridges is only credited when it is conspicuously claimed, with a result that the name of the Severn Bridge's designer is unjustly obscure compared with earlier bridge architects like John Gwynn and Thomas Telford. It is the last epic work of civil engineering on the river and it is telling that when the adjoining M4 motorway service station was built, a viewing area was provided for travellers to admire the bridge. It has elegant, simple lines and a lightness of appearance that defies its long span. You can also cross the bridge on foot. This is the best way to appreciate the scale of the whole bridge and its components, and that of the Second Severn Crossing away in the distance. The bridge is painted white like a lighthouse, to reduce thermal stress rather than to make the bridge stand out, and the winds that buffet you are sea breezes. Its only shortcoming is that it was built for two and not three lanes of traffic. The Second Severn Crossing, completed in 1996, is the £300 million solution to that problem. It has approach viaducts with a wide span over the central deep channel, and incorporates an impressive curve, but one which is largely unnoticed when you cross it. In fact you can cross without realising you are passing over an estuary, thanks to the windshields on the deck.

The Severn Bridge is worthy of the river it crosses, but aesthetic aspirations have largely been weeded out of the civil engineering profession. Later bridges have paid less respect to the river, and there have been many of them since 1966. At Gloucester the A40 crosses both channels; the M50 crosses near Ripple; Worcester and Bewdley have bypass bridges; ring roads around Shrewsbury have necessitated four new bridges; and Newtown and Llanidloes both have new bridges to ease congestion from the town centre. On bypasses the new bridges are merely flyovers, and treat the river as if it is just an irritating obstacle that does nothing more than add to the cost of a road. Bridges are now for crossing at speed; if you loiter and look over the parapet, you will look like a suicide candidate. As if in apology, metal signs are put up naming the river that you might not otherwise even notice. Modern bridges remind us that a great age of bridge

The Severn Bridge, opened in 1966, is seen here from the viewing area especially created for travellers to admire this feat of civil engineering.

technology had come to an end by the 1960s, and the scope for new, dynamic and daring designs has dwindled.

The most interesting of the recent Severn bridges from a technical and aesthetic point of view are for pedestrians. The Castle Footbridge in Shrewsbury is distinguished in the technical category. Its long parabolic profile was, in 1951, 'the first bridge in Britain to use pre-stressed, post-tensioned concrete in a cantilever structure'.[70] The cable-stayed bridge design also found favour as early as the 1950s for Festival Bridge upstream of Newtown, on a footpath that hardly anybody ever uses. If a novel solution is required it is now likely to be a cable-stayed bridge with a single pylon, like Sabrina Bridge (1991) and Diglis Bridge (2010) in Worcester and the new Jackfield road bridge (1994). These structures thwart our expectation of symmetry in bridge design, but there have been sound engineering reasons for them. A new bridge was built at Jackfield after the old one, a reinforced concrete construction of 1913, had to be demolished. The problem was not structural but geological. The underlying rocks in the Ironbridge Gorge are shifting like tectonic plates, and if abutments are lined up on each bank, sooner rather than later they will be misaligned and the bridge will fail. The solution was to anchor the bridge on the south side only, to create a bridge with a single pylon that pays tribute, perhaps unintentionally, to the bridge at the end of the river.

Because we conceive of bridges primarily as a point of transit, our experience of them is very different from the way people experienced them two centuries ago. Upton Bridge, for example, was once the principal meeting point in the town, where bargemen

Jackfield Bridge, built in 1994, is an asymmetrical cable-stayed bridge
necessary to counteract geological movements which would cause the bridge to fail
if there were pylons on both banks.

met up when they were waiting for work, and a daytime congregation of watermen gathered, doubtless joined by older men looking for company.[71] As new bridges reflect the increasing pace of modern life, changing as society changes, they also document our declining relationship with the river.

❧ 7 ❧
Castles and Kings

'The slaughter of the Severn and the death of Idris' is the stark entry in the *Welsh Annals* for the year AD 632. The Severn has been a battleground, or has influenced the site of battles, whenever there has been conflict on British soil. The river has flowed red with the blood of its own people, as well as that of invading Romans and Danes. It is the great natural defensive barrier of western Britain (far more effective than Offa's Dyke) and so its crossing points have been heavily defended and fought over. Armies have sought advantage by fording it, swimming across it and building bridges of boats to traverse it.

What we know of conflict on the Severn begins with the Roman imperial army in the first century AD, and perhaps it was the Romans who first recognised the river as the key to defending rich lowland territories. When their legionaries first fought in Britain they found the centres of power on the hilltops rather than by the water's edge; it was the Romans who shifted military focus from the uplands to the river, and the Severn figured significantly in their subjugation of western Britain. Having quickly secured south-east England after the invasion of AD 43, they found in neighbouring tribes a mixture of acquiescence and hostility. Leaving a large part of Britain unconquered soon proved untenable, however, and in AD 47 the new imperial governor, Publius Ostorius Scapula, decided to extend Roman control to the banks of the Severn and the Trent.[1] This brought the tribes of the Severn – Ordovices in Wales, Cornovii in Shropshire, Dobunni in Worcestershire and Gloucestershire – into direct conflict with the Roman army.

The stretch of the Severn in the territory of the Cornovii corresponds with modern-day Shropshire. Here there seems to have been little resistance to the Roman invasion. If any rearguard action was fought it would have been by means of the defensive hillforts, of which there are several in Shropshire. Of these, it is the 'lowland' hillforts like Old Oswestry that seem to have been the most important, whereas those on higher ground – like the Wrekin or Breidden Hill overlooking the Severn – were less important and may not have been inhabited all year round. The only evidence of significant resistance to Rome was at the Wrekin, where the houses were burned and habitation came to an abrupt end. Perhaps the Wrekin was singled out as a symbolic centre of Cornovian territory, or perhaps it was easily attacked and sent a chilling message to other defended places in the territory. The army that attacked it was that of the Roman general Quintus Veranius, and it was probably based at a campaign (or vexillation) fort at Leighton on the bank of the Severn.[2]

Subjugation of the Cornovii was followed by campaigns further west into Wales, where the tribe of Ordovices were led by Caratacus (the Caradog or Caractacus of Welsh legend), the son of Cunobelinus (Cymbeline in legend), who had fled there from southern England to fight a rearguard action. Such was his reputation that the decisive battle of AD 51 was thought worthy of description by the Roman author Tacitus over half a century later. Caratacus selected a site for battle that would give him a territorial advantage, knowing full well that on a level field the well-disciplined Roman army could easily defeat a much greater force of Britons. According to Tacitus the battleground had steep-sided hills all round, on which Caratacus erected earthwork defences. In order to attack, the Romans had to cross the river, and the plan was that, when they faltered, the river would impede their retreat and leave them prey to the British army. Events took a different turn, however. The river was forded easily enough and the Romans were past masters at attacking hilltop defences, using their shields against the hail of missiles thrown at them.[3] The defeated Caratacus was eventually captured and taken to Rome, where he made an impressive speech about the nobility of armed resistance to invaders and was pardoned by Emperor Claudius. Opinions differ as to the place of battle, not helped by the facts that there are several hills known as Caer Caradoc, which are probably all later attributions based on myth, and that it was documented by a historian living a long way away, but it must have taken place in Ordovician territory, where the principal rivers are the Severn and the Vyrnwy. It might have happened in the hills around Caersws, or at Dolforwyn near Newtown, which offers a good defensible position and an amphitheatre of steep hills descending to the flood plain.[4] Dolforwyn was also an important strategic position in the Severn valley, as the river was fordable at Abermule nearby, although the crossing was hardly suitable for an army of perhaps two legions – *legio XIIII Gemina* and *legio XX Valeria* – and some auxiliary forces, up to 25,000 men.

To consolidate its recent gains Rome needed a legionary fortress. Wroxeter was chosen as a military hub because of its strategic position in the centre of Cornovian territory at a point where the Severn could be crossed, and where any river traffic could be controlled effectively. The fortress was built in the AD 50s by *legio XIIII Gemina* and was at the time probably the greatest concentration of people who had ever lived on the riverbank.[5] It is significant that the defeat of the Wrekin hillfort was followed by the establishment of the legionary fortress by the Severn. The shift from the hilltop – inviting a static and defensive form of warfare – to the riverbank is telling. Rome chose a strategic crossing point for mobile forces that could be, and were, used to launch further military offensives.

Wroxeter remained an important military base during the conquest of north Wales. In addition, on the south side of the legionary fortress a smaller fort was built to house a further 500 auxiliary troops. After AD 60 the fortress was occupied by *legio XX Valeria Victrix*. The legion's 5,500 men were probably only all stationed there in the winter months, but such a concentration of men probably encouraged the founding of a civilian settlement, or *vicus*, on the south side of the fortress. By AD 78 the legion was involved in Agricola's military campaigns in the north of England and Scotland, stretching its lines of communication with a home base in the Midlands. The Severn had long since ceased to be a frontier, let alone a key strategic point, and in AD 90 *legio XX* left Wroxeter and took up home in a newly vacated legionary fortress at Chester, which was much better placed as a base for Roman military control of north Wales. Wroxeter's transformation from fortress to Roman city began at this time.

The Silures, one of the most stubbornly resistant of British tribes, were natives of modern south Wales. The first campaign against them was launched under Aulus Plautius, Britain's first Roman governor and based at a legionary fortress which was established on the Severn at Gloucester, where there had already been Roman military sites on the north side of the city in modern Kingsholm. The initial campaign was also partly an amphibious assault on the south Wales coast, using ports as far upstream as Berkeley.[6] A tradition that the Roman army crossed into south Wales from Aust to Beachley has long since disappeared from the textbooks, but they could also have forded the river between Arlingham and Newnham. The Severn was to prove a convenient point of retreat, given the frustrations of trying to bring to heel a people who fought back with guerrilla tactics. The Roman general Ostorius Scapula, feted after his victory over Caratacus, now saw his star wane quickly. It was Julius Frontinus, governor AD 74-8, who finally subdued the tribes in Wales, and after that the Roman army adopted a more defensive role.

Once the campaigning phase was over and the citizen army had moved on from Wroxeter it was left to auxiliary soldiers to safeguard the new territory. Military strategy was now focused upstream in mid Wales, where forts were built along the course of the Severn at Forden Gaer and Caersws. Forden Gaer protected Rhydwhyman ford near Montgomery and superseded the older hillfort at Ffridd Faldwyn, again the riverbank being preferred to the safety of the hilltop. A road led beyond Forden Gaer and continued along the riverside to a fort built at Caersws, at the confluence of the Severn and Carno rivers. Caersws guards the principal route from mid Wales to the coast (the 19th-century railway took the same route) and there was already an old campaign fort nearby at Llwyn-y-brain. Previously the route had been defended by a hillfort at Cefn Carnedd but again the Roman army chose the riverbank instead of the summit.

Forden Gaer and Caersws were probably built in the AD 70s, but unlike other forts in Wales, when the military withdrew under Emperor Hadrian in the 2nd century,[7] they remained occupied for another century, to guard against a hostile native population or, perhaps, to police bandit country or protect routes to the mineral resources of west Wales. At Caersws there was a substantial civilian settlement, or *vicus*, laid out on a grid plan, which incorporated shops, tavern and workshops to service the troops. This was a substantial village that remained occupied after the garrison was withdrawn, but whether it was the town Mediolanum mentioned by Ptolemy, as has been claimed, is not universally accepted.[8]

When Rome abandoned its imperial outpost there followed centuries of uncertainty, but the period is not marked by new fortifications, although for a time some of the old hillforts like Breidden were reoccupied. According to Bede the Lower Severn was a boundary between the kingdoms of Anglo-Saxon Hwicce and Celts. Later, a fixed boundary between Mercia and Wales was established under the Mercian King Offa who reigned between 757 and 796 and according to Bishop Asser, writing over a century later, ordered construction of the massive rampart that bears his name. Offa's Dyke makes use of the Severn as a boundary where it crosses the floodplain at Buttington, and of the Wye at its southern end.

Controlling the territory of Mercia meant controlling the Severn. After the disappearance of Rome the chief threat to the Mercian territory came not from Wales but from the 'devils of the sea'. The partial Viking conquest of England had begun with sea-borne invasions and raids in the mid 9th century. After gaining a solid hold of the east and north of England the Danes turned their attention to Mercia, which resisted with the help of its ally, the kingdom of Wessex. One of the Danish tactics was to weaken native resistance by launching raids into vulnerable territory, usually returning with valuable loot after having set up a defensive camp over winter. By means of the Severn the Danes could penetrate deep into Mercian territory with apparent ease. That the Severn and the Thames were among their more important targets testifies to the rivers' importance in the economic lives of Wessex and Mercia, but also raises the likelihood that these were naval incursions. Danish ships certainly sailed up the river Lea on a raid in 894. The Danes camped at Gloucester in 877, then further upstream at Buttington in 893 and Quatbridge in 895.

The best victory over the Danes was won at Buttington in 893, as described in the *Anglo-Saxon Chronicle*. A raiding party that had set out from Shoeburyness on the Thames estuary was pursued up the Severn by three ealdormen – Ethelhelm of Wiltshire, Ethelred of Mercia and Ethelnoth of Somerset – until they reached the limit of Mercian territory at Buttington, where the Danes were blockaded. An allied Welsh force under Mervyn of Powys joined the blockade on the west side of the river. Given that the Danish camp was 'washed on all sides by the Severn' it has been argued that it was on a now vanished island.[9] A year earlier the Danes had camped at Thorney Island on the river Colne in the face of a siege by the Saxon forces, so their occupation of an island in the Severn is a possibility. Another theory is that the Danes made use of Offa's Dyke, which crosses the Severn at this point and could have formed the eastern side of their camp, with other defensive earthworks forming the south and west sides in what is now Buttington churchyard. According to the *Anglo-Saxon Chronicle* the Danes were camped there for several weeks but the opposing forces prevented their living off the land, and when their provisions ran out they were forced to eat their horses. To escape, the Danish forces needed to break out, which they duly did by attacking the forces on the east side of the river. The slaughter was said to have been great on both sides, and several thegns, including Ordheh, were killed, but several of the Danes escaped to regroup in Essex from where, in the summer, the Danish army launched an attack on Chester, which suggests that the victory at Buttington was hardly a body blow to the invaders.

When digging began in 1838 for the foundations of a new schoolroom at Buttington, three charnel pits were found containing some 400 human skulls, carefully placed in the centre of the pit, with the long bones arranged around the sides. These have always been regarded as the remains of the slain of Buttington, obviously reburied some time later, perhaps when the parish church was built. The battle site, however, is now impossible to identify, partly because the meandering river has changed its course since the 9th century, but also because none of the earthwork traces that were identified in the 19th century are visible today.[10]

In 895 the Danes returned to the Severn valley. This time they encamped for the winter at *Cwatbrycge*, just below modern Bridgnorth, possibly on the former island in the river there, close to the 'Heathen Ditch' by Quatford church. It was the last Danish incursion into Mercia in the 9th century, but there is no evidence that it involved any fighting on the banks of the Severn, or anywhere else. Instead, Alfred of Wessex and Aethelred of Mercia probably met with the Danes on the Severn and agreed to pay them off. The *Anglo-Saxon Chronicle* says that in the following spring the Danes went to East Anglia or Northumberland, where they settled, except for those who had failed to extort sufficient money from the Saxons, who returned across the English Channel to the river Seine.[11]

The Danes were back briefly in 910, and four years later Edward the Elder drove out a 'great naval force' that attacked the Severn Sea from Brittany. By now, however, the Mercians had learned how to defend themselves and had begun to construct fortified towns. The Saxon word for town and fortress was the same – *burh*. An integrated system of burhs was created by the rulers of Wessex and Mercia to counter these Danish incursions. Aethelred issued a charter creating the burh of Worcester in the last decade of the 9th century: 'At the request of Bishop Waerfirth, their friend, Ealdorman Aethelred

Holt Castle, as seen by Samuel Ireland in the late 18th century. The prominent square tower was built by John Beauchamp *c*.1385. A trow sails upstream unaided.

and Aethelflaed ordered the borough of Worcester to be built for the protection of all the people'.[12] In 912 his widow Aethelflaed, known in the *Anglo-Saxon Chronicle* as the 'Lady of the Mercians', built a small burh at *Cwatbrycge* close to Bridgnorth. Shrewsbury, meanwhile, had also emerged as a town by the beginning of the 10th century and had replaced Wroxeter as a regional centre. It is a naturally defensible site formed by a loop in the river, protected on the open side by a high sandstone bluff.

The Severn remained a river of royal and strategic importance after England was unified under a single crown by Athelstan in 925. At Deerhurst, on a small island in the Severn known as Alney, the conflict between the Danish prince Cnut and Edmund Ironside was settled in 1016. The newly crowned Edmund had been defeated at Ashingdon in Essex by Cnut, to whom he was forced to cede the throne. The border between England and Wales remained Offa's Dyke, which crosses the Severn at Buttington. It was near here that the powerful Welsh leader Gruffudd ap Llywelyn defeated Leofric, earl of Mercia, in 1039 at the battle of Rhyd-y-Groes. Gruffudd had his eye on lands on the opposite side of Offa's Dyke.[13]

Shrewsbury, Worcester and Gloucester (and Hereford on the Wye and Chester on the Dee) became chief centres of the borderland. The Norman feudal lords who moved into the area after 1066 consolidated the existing centres of power. The Normans won no long-term victory over the Welsh and to protect their weak western flank set up the semi-autonomous earldoms – the Marcher lordships – that remained in place until England and Wales were officially united in 1536. Normans built the first masonry castles, but many of the smaller fortifications were motte and bailey castles, which had earthwork and

Samuel Ireland's view of Berkeley Castle, and church, in the late 18th century. The masts of a trow or sea-going vessel can be seen moored at Berkeley Pill.

timber defences, and a timber keep built on the mound, or motte. Castles are one of the defining characteristics of the Norman landscape, expressing not only the elite status but also the insecurity of those who built them.

Urse d'Abitot, sheriff of Worcestershire and the most powerful Norman baron in the county, had built a motte and-bailey castle on the bank of the Severn at Worcester, close to Diglis ford, by 1069. A castle was also built at Holt, by an important river crossing, but it had little military significance and by the 13th century was really just a fortified house. The Gloucestershire section of the Severn was also comparatively safe, protected from the Welsh by castles further west at Chepstow and Monmouth. Gloucester Castle was built in the 12th century close to the river, and later was a favoured residence of Henry III (1216-72), but by the 15th century had become a prison and remained so until it was demolished to make way for the purpose-built gaol that was completed in 1791. In 1067 William FitzOsbern, earl of Hereford, built a motte-and-bailey castle at Berkeley. It overlooks the Severn estuary and is above Berkeley Pill, the former Little Avon river, which provided a safe haven for trading vessels. From the time of its rebuilding in stone in the mid 12th century it has been the property of the FitzHarding (or Berkeley) family.

Worcester and Gloucester remained powerful regional centres, even if they were not immediately threatened. Worcester and Shrewsbury were the centres from which England exerted its power over Wales. They became most vulnerable during internal rebellions, such as the reign of Stephen (1135-54); followers of his cousin Matilda, who had a stronghold at Gloucester, sacked and burned Worcester in 1139, and took some of its citizens for ransom, although the town was re-taken and its bridge secured for the

Shrewsbury Castle, begun in 1067 under the instruction of William I, was the headquarters for Edward I's conquest of north Wales in 1277. It was here that Dafydd ap Gruffudd, brother of the prince of Wales, was executed in 1283.

king soon after. The city had also been attacked by King Harthacnut in 1041 – two of his tax collectors had been murdered in the city – and the citizens fled and sought safety on Bevere Island.[14]

The greatest concentration of Norman and medieval castles along the Severn is in Shropshire and Montgomeryshire, from Bridgnorth on the English side to Caersws on the Welsh side, within 30 miles of the border. Fortifications were built close to the river to protect key crossing points, and therefore were intended to control routes through the Severn valley, as well as to safeguard its productive farmland. Castles along the Severn therefore express the importance of the river in these uncertain times, and in some cases they are close to and superseded the Roman forts.

William I recognised the strategic importance of the Severn and ordered the building of Shrewsbury Castle in 1067. Two years later it was besieged by the Welsh, together with rebellious men of Cheshire; they failed to take the castle but burnt the town before they retreated. Among the besiegers was Eadric the Wild, a Saxon nobleman who owned estates downstream at Cressage where, beside the river, there was a motte-and-bailey castle that was largely destroyed when the Severn Valley Railway was built.[15] Shrewsbury Castle was passed to Roger of Montgomery, one of William's great magnates, when he was made earl of Shrewsbury in 1071.

Roger also built a small motte and bailey castle at Quatford, another important crossing point, and the castle originally known as Montgomery but later as Hen Domen. Hen Domen was the *caput* of a Marcher lordship and remained until the 13th century the military, social and judicial centre of a large estate. The castle is close to the Roman fort at Forden Gaer and guards the same river crossing at Rhydwhyman. Although it was only ever a timber castle it was important enough to be named after Roger's birthplace, Montgomerie in Normandy. Ironically for such an important strategic and powerful place, archaeological excavations have never revealed evidence of an aristocratic life there. In Roger's time it was probably only a military garrison. Later it was the home of the de Bouler family, but they lived a life as materially impoverished as that of the people who lived a thousand years earlier at Ffridd Faldwyn hillfort, only a few hundred yards away, and far below the standard of living enjoyed by legionaries at Forden Gaer, or the residents of the later Montgomery Castle. The contrast with Wroxeter is even more stark, even though both were important regional centres. Items found at Wroxeter had a provenance across Europe, including goods traded from the Mediterranean, but the most exotic item found at Hen Domen was a jug from Lincolnshire.[16]

The earldom of Shrewsbury was abolished in 1102 after the failed rebellion against Henry I and the fall of Roger's son and heir, Robert de Belleme. Robert de Belleme was the most wealthy and powerful magnate in the Anglo-Norman world at the beginning of the 12th century, owning several large estates in England and Normandy. He joined the rebellion that planned to put Robert, duke of Normandy, William the Conqueror's eldest son, on the throne of England in place of his younger brother Henry, who succeeded their other brother William Rufus in 1100. The rebellion having failed, Robert de Belleme's estates were confiscated, as were those of his co-conspirators. Henry took back Shrewsbury Castle and thereafter considerable sums were spent on building and maintaining this stronghold of the Severn. During the rebellious years of Stephen's reign it was held for Matilda but when Stephen captured it in 1138, a hundred men of the garrison were hung from its walls.[17] Shrewsbury was attacked by the Welsh in 1215 and again in 1235 when, although the castle withstood the siege the town was burned down. After that, town walls were built to give the town more protection.[18]

Roger de Belleme began the construction of Bridgnorth Castle in 1101 on a naturally defensible site with cliffs on the east side above the Severn. He planned that it would be an impregnable stronghold compared with the small castle just downstream at Quatford. But it was built begun without a royal licence and Henry I must have taken great pleasure in confiscating the unfinished castle in 1102 after the uprising against the new king had failed. After the subsequent anarchy of Stephen's reign a succession of monarchs took firm control, and the castle was expanded first by Henry II and then again in the 13th century, before it gradually fell into decay as its strategic importance diminished.

Lesser castles were built to protect crossings or vulnerable manors. There was once an important ford at Shrawardine, upstream of Montford Bridge, which was guarded by motte and bailey castles on either bank. Shrawardine Castle, destined to be the more important of the two, was rebuilt in the early 12th century, destroyed by the Welsh in 1215 and then rebuilt by John Fitzalan, whose family lived there until 1583. In fact the castle was occupied continuously until the Civil War. The motte of Little Shrawardine on the opposite bank had been built by 1165, and is now the sole reminder of the lost village that it protected.[19] Further upstream, Alberbury Castle was built in the early 13th century by Fulke Fitz Warine but was destroyed during Llywelyn the Great's campaign in 1223, after which it was rebuilt, although a hundred years later it appears to have become redundant.[20] Only Powis Castle, preceded by Domen Castell or Lady's Mount in the 12th century, was transformed in later centuries into a grand country residence. Lower Munlyn is a little downstream of Forden Gaer Roman fort and probably protected the river crossing at Dyffryn, which might have been the ford known as Rhyd-y-Groes.

The Welsh too had built their own fortifications along the Severn. Small motte and bailey castles are found along the river, often close to the bank. Bronfelin Castle and the

Of the medieval castles that protected the Severn Uplands, only Powis Castle was destined to become a grand country residence in later centuries.

small mottes at Moat Farm overlook the Severn near Caersws, and guard the same strategic point in central Wales as did the Roman fort. Brynderwyn motte and bailey is close to a crossing point, opposite which Dolforwyn was built in the 13th century. Other fortifications near Newtown are at Cefn Bryntalch and Gro Tump in Llanllwchaiarn, which were transformed in quieter centuries into farms.

After Llywelyn ap Gruffudd signed the Treaty of Montgomery in 1267 with Henry III, he was recognised by the English crown as the Prince of Wales, and the concept of a Welsh nation was officially recognised. It has been argued that when he started to build (or probably rebuild) a castle at Dolforwyn in 1273 it was to be the capital of his newly conquered domain, at the heart of the fertile Severn valley, and was close enough to the frontier to protect the territory that had been established by treaty. Unfortunately Llywelyn had to placate both the king and the Marcher lords, and it was the latter, especially Roger Mortimer, who objected to Llywelyn's new castle close to his territory of Montgomery. Building work had hardly begun when Llywelyn received a letter from the royal administrators ordering him not to proceed with the work. Llywelyn reckoned that the new king, Edward I, himself could have no knowledge of the letter as he was travelling in France, and therefore replied that the Prince of Wales could build a castle and establish a market wherever he liked within his own territory.[21] The combination of a stronghold so close to the lordship of Montgomery, a commercial centre that might challenge its economic interests, and a Welsh leader growing in confidence was too much for Roger Mortimer. Accordingly, during Edward's invasion of north Wales in 1277, which was precipitated by Llywelyn's delay in paying homage to Edward as his overlord, the unfinished Dolforwyn was besieged by Mortimer and his men, with considerable assistance from the earl of Lincoln and the cavalry of the royal household. The garrison held out for only two weeks before Mortimer took control of it.[22] Llywelyn, meanwhile, was pushed back into mountainous Gwynedd, where the Marcher lords and the king calculated that he would cause less trouble.

Dolforwyn is more hilltop stronghold than palace or market town. Its ruins are very much exposed to the elements, which is why its medieval fabric is protected under layers of modern, sacrificial stonework, which is intended to bear the brunt of the weather and protect the original fabric beneath. It offers a commanding view of the Severn valley towards Newtown – ironically looking west into Wales rather than east to the Marches – but the view to the east, now obscured by trees, was never as clear, the crossing at Abermule being concealed by a low ridge on the south side of the castle. The small township that was built outside the castle walls, just like the *vicus* of a Roman fort, was only small. Roger Mortimer abandoned it and founded a new town on the Severn at Newtown in 1279, accelerating a policy that Llywelyn himself would surely have followed if he had enjoyed more peaceful times. The castle was inhabited until at least the 1320s, after which time there was no need for a hilltop stronghold in the Severn valley.

The ruins of Dolforwyn embody the wrecked ambitions of an independent Welsh state. Despite a mention by Leland and Thomas Pennant, it did not interest the average tourist when they started touring Wales in the 18th century looking for scenic thrills.

Henry Penruddocke Wyndham did look for it when he passed through in 1777, but assumed that it would have been near the valley floor rather than on the hilltop, and so missed it.[23] Dolforwyn's place in Welsh history is largely forgotten and the site is still little visited. Only in 1980 was a decision made to excavate the site and conserve the ruins still standing, and still accessible if you are prepared for an uphill walk. The castle was relatively modest in scale and hardly outstanding in a nation of castles. The fortress walls survive as forlorn stumps, providing shelter for loitering sheep, but its layout is easy enough to follow. Its architecture belongs more to the early 13th century than Llywelyn's own time, raising the likelihood that Dolforwyn was an earlier castle that Llywelyn restored.[24] Its name is something of a mystery. It is usually translated as 'meadow of the maiden' but *dolfor* – big meadow – hardly describes its bleak situation on the summit of a whale-back hill. Perhaps the name originally applied to the small timber castle on the riverbank near Abermule now called Brynderwen, but it can only have been the hilltop castle that was besieged in 1277.

Fearing Edward I's imperial ambitions towards Wales, Llywelyn decided to resist him. His brother Dafydd, formerly loyal to Edward, attacked the English garrison at Hawarden in Flintshire on Palm Sunday, 1282. Llywelyn broke out of Snowdonia but he was killed in a skirmish in December 1282 and his head was taken to Edward as proof. The king ordered the trophy to be displayed on a stake outside the Tower of London. The conflict was brought to a close when Dafydd was brought to Shrewsbury Castle in 1283. Edward I had made the castle a seat of government during his Welsh campaigns and it was here that Dafydd ap Gruffudd was tried and executed in 1283. Even by medieval standards Dafydd's execution was savage. Edward had been incensed by his perceived treachery, and the accused was handed down a fourfold punishment. For his treachery he was dragged to the scaffold at the horse's tail. For homicide he was hanged alive. For attacking the king's forces during Lent, thus violating Christ's Passion, he was disembowelled and his entrails were burned. As sentence for plotting the king's death his body was then quartered and dispatched to the four corners of the kingdom. It is said that Londoners and Yorkshiremen fought over the best body parts – except for his head, which was displayed, alongside that of his brother, outside the Tower of London.[25]

Dolforwyn Castle was a key stronghold of Llywelyn ap Gruffudd overlooking the Severn valley. Despite its important place in the history of Wales, it is little visited.

This ugly but decisive end to a chapter in the history of Wales also ended a chapter in Shrewsbury's history as the king's principal stronghold on the Upper Severn.

Dolforwyn was never recaptured by the Welsh. When the next rebellion began in Wales under Owain Glyndwr the castle was already ruinous and strategically super-fluous. Glyndwr's rebellion began in 1400. He won an early skirmish at Hyddgen on Plynlimon in 1401 and in 1405 entered an alliance with the Percy and Mortimer fami-lies. (Edmund Mortimer was Owain's son-in-law.) Their power bases were the Welsh and Scottish borders, which explains their ambition to divide the kingdom of England into three, giving Wales and the border counties to Owain, with the boundary marked by the river Severn.

Owain Glyndwr was involved on the periphery of the battle of Shrewsbury in 1403, intending to march his men in support of the army led by Henry Percy (Harry Hotspur). Henry IV arrived in Shrewsbury in time to prevent Hotspur from taking the town, and Hotspur retreated to the riverbank upstream at Berwick, where his forces were encamped briefly. But there is no easy crossing point except further west at Montford Bridge, and in any case the Welsh contingent never arrived. The armies moved east and faced up to each other on the north side of the town, near the road to Whitchurch and well away from the river, where the king's forces won the day.

Events in the Wars of the Roses, in which the Houses of Lancaster and York fought over the succession to the throne, largely passed the Severn by. Bewdley was captured by Lancastrians in 1459 and its first bridge was dismantled. The stones were sent to Worcester to repair the city walls and its own bridge.[26] The townspeople of Bewdley built a new timber bridge, which was replaced in stone at the expense of Richard III in 1483.

The Severn influenced the site of the battle of Tewkesbury in 1471 and had conse-quences for the losing side. The Lancastrian forces were led by Queen Margaret of Anjou, who landed in Weymouth from France, hoping either to restore her husband, the deposed Henry VI, to the throne, or to see her son crowned king. The Yorkist Edward IV, who had regained the throne that he had held in the 1460s, immediately summoned his forces to head off the Lancastrians. The Lancastrians successfully reached Bristol, availing themselves of the city's artillery and stores, and then headed towards Gloucester, intending to cross the Severn and seek support in Wales. But Edward foresaw the plan and sent a message to the city that its gates should be closed to the Lancastrians, denying them access to the bridges. And so the army marched further north until it reached the Lower Lode ferry, south of Tewkesbury. However, crossing the river by ferry was deemed too slow and instead defensive positions were prepared. This is where the battle took place and the weaker Lancastrian force was defeated. It is said that the Severn claimed a number of lives as the losers fled the battlefield towards Severn Ham and drowned trying to cross it.[27] The battle of Tewkesbury, in which the Lancastrians sought refuge behind the defensive barrier of the Severn, only to end up trapped and perishing on the wrong side of the river, was a foretaste of the bitter battles fought on the banks of the Severn in the Civil Wars nearly two hundred years later.

8

The Civil Wars

The first and last battles of the English Civil Wars were fought beside the Severn. In both battles the river was a determining factor in where the confrontations took place, and in the last one the river influenced the course of the battle and the consequences for the losers. Throughout the Civil Wars the river played a significant role in the national strategies of both parties, largely because it provided a natural barrier and was difficult for an army to cross. There remained still only a handful of bridges between Shrewsbury and the sea, so the river was an effective line of defence, in theory at least, and the bridges were crucial pressure points. Upton Bridge is said to have endured more skirmishes than any other place in England.[1] Among the more audacious strategies adopted in the Civil Wars was the construction of temporary bridges across the Severn: in 1645, for example, over 3,000 Royalist cavalry under Major-General Pointz crossed the Severn near Tewkesbury on a temporary bridge, constructed of a line of boats lashed together, on which planks were laid.[2] The Civil Wars were fought largely in the provinces. Charles I fled London in 1642 after failing to agree with Parliament about control of the army, leaving the capital under the control of Parliament. Charles needed to look elsewhere to create a power base from which he could restore his authority, and he chose the west of Britain, where he relied heavily on Wales for recruitment and other resources, and as a relatively safe haven behind the defensive line of the Severn.

The Shropshire section of the Severn began the Civil Wars in Royalist hands. Local grandees mobilised quickly enough for Charles to use Shrewsbury as a safe headquarters in 1642. In September Charles famously addressed the local gentry on Gay Meadow by the river, where the Royalist army was encamped. Control of the town, and of the river, was extended in each direction by establishing garrisons that secured the bridges at Montford Bridge and Atcham. At Bridgnorth Thomas Corbett had mustered a local militia in support of the king by 1642. Basil Brooke, the prominent Catholic and Royalist, owned the manor of Madeley, which was also garrisoned for the king. The other important strategic crossing point was at Buildwas, where at the outbreak of hostilities James Lacon was ordered to build a spiked turnstile on the bridge to prevent its use by cavalrymen, or at least those hostile to the king.[3]

Bewdley Bridge was a crucial defensive position for the Royalists in the Civil War because Severn bridges were scarce and Bewdley's was near impregnable with its gatehouse.

Charles I addressing his troops at Gay Meadow in Shrewsbury in 1642.

Once Charles had raised his own army, largely by enlisting volunteers from the north of England, the Midlands, Wales and the southwest, he assembled them at Shrewsbury. The town was chosen because it was a convenient place for the northern and Welsh contingents of his army to join forces, and was also well positioned for a retreat into Wales should the Parliamentary forces push them back.

Parliament's forces shadowed every movement of Charles and his new army. They were fully aware that while based at Shrewsbury, Charles sent a regiment of dragoons, under Sir John Byron, to retrieve some valuable plate from the university at Oxford. Charles had established a mint at Shrewsbury and intended to melt down the plate, mint it into coins and thus pay his troops. The returning convoy reached Worcester safely, but knew that Parliament's men were in pursuit. Byron's plan was simple: to cross the Severn at Worcester and proceed to Shrewsbury on the protected west bank of the river. The opposition tactics were therefore obvious. Parliament sent a detachment of cavalry under Colonel Nathaniel Fiennes which crossed the river, either by riding as far south as Upton, or by crossing one of the fords between Upton and Worcester, at Pixham, Clevelode or Rhydd – it was September so the river level may have been low. Once they had established themselves on the west bank Fiennes' men needed only to wait for the main body of the Parliamentary army to reach Worcester, threaten Byron's convoy, and then block the convoy's escape across Worcester Bridge to leave the Royalists trapped.

What Fiennes appears not to have known is that Byron had signalled to Charles that he was in difficulty, and that Charles had sent his lieutenant Prince Rupert to help him. Prince Rupert and his cavalry rode down the west bank of the Severn, reaching the outskirts of Worcester on 23 September. Fiennes, meanwhile, was further south at Powick, on the river Teme near its confluence with the Severn. This appears to have been common knowledge, and several folk from the city are said to have walked along the river bank to Powick out of curiosity to see the dragoons.

For organised armies bridges can form fatal bottlenecks, but instead of trapping the Royalists at Worcester Bridge the Parliamentary forces found that the tables had been turned on them. In order to take up a position nearer to Worcester Bridge they crossed the Teme at the narrow Powick Bridge. According to the Parliamentarian John Corbet, the Parliamentary cavalry was ambushed after it had crossed the bridge, within the confines of a narrow lane that prevented it from fanning outwards and forming an effective defensive line.[4] The bottleneck of Powick Bridge behind them prevented an easy retreat. The lane was later known as 'Cut Throat Lane'.[5] An alternative version is that the two armies ran into each other by accident and that the Royalist cavalry reacted more quickly and decisively.

This was the Civil War's first military engagement of any consequence. It is known as the battle of Powick Bridge, but it took place over a mile further north at Wickefield. It was hardly a full-scale battle, a mere cavalry skirmish that would have been forgotten had it not been the first military engagement of the war. It also delivered an important propaganda victory for the Royalist cause. According to Edward Hyde, close advisor of the king, 'this re-encounter proved of great advantage and benefit to the king, for it being the first action his horse had been brought to, and that party of the enemy being the most picked and choice men, it gave his troops great courage, and rendered the name of Prince Rupert very terrible'.[6] Powick Bridge certainly established the reputation as a cavalry commander of Prince Rupert (1619-82), the king's young nephew who had been brought up in the Netherlands, and had in his teens been involved in military campaigns on the Continent before he came to England to aid Charles.

The people of Worcester seem to have paid the battle little heed, but a day later the earl of Essex, commander of the Parliamentary forces, marched his army into the city unopposed and accused the mayor of helping the Royalist cause. The mayor's house was relieved of its valuables, and the city paid for Gascoyne wine and sugar loaves for Essex and his men, at a cost of £8.[7] It was a sign of things to come.

While at Worcester, Essex deployed infantry regiments to secure the Lower Severn towns, of which Gloucester and Upton were the most important because of their bridges. By this means the Parliamentary army prevented Charles from receiving reinforcements from south Wales by the most direct route. Gloucester remained in control of Parliament throughout the Civil War, under its governor, a young Londoner called Edward Massey (1619-74). (Massey later changed sides and supported Charles' son, but was killed before the battle of Worcester while trying to secure Upton Bridge.) Meanwhile Charles assembled his additional forces from north Wales and marched out of Shrewsbury, heading south. On 12 October the mayor of Shrewsbury requested the help of 'three able and sufficient trowmen to carry a hundred men by water to Bridgnorth', the men clearly being foot soldiers.[8] But from Bridgnorth the king moved eastwards away from the Severn towards Oxford, which prevented the first major battle of the war from taking place along the Severn between Shrewsbury and Worcester. In the event the Parliamentary army also moved eastwards, and the cat-and-mouse game ended in the battle of Edge Hill in Worcestershire.

By 1643 events had turned in favour of the Royalists, who were in the ascendant in the Severn valley. They now controlled the bridge at Upton and appeared confident of threatening Gloucester. Lord Herbert had raised a brigade of infantry from Monmouthshire and Glamorgan for the king, and they overran the Forest of Dean and set up camp on the west bank of the Severn at Highnam, only two miles from Gloucester. Although the force was too small to take Gloucester it was able to disrupt supplies to the town from the west side of the city, being protected from attack by the safety of the river.

Parliament's counter-attack was led by Sir William Waller, who was made major-general in charge of Parliamentary forces in western England, including the Severn valley, with his headquarters at Bristol. Waller had the advantage of surprise because the Parliamentary forces did not cross the bridge at Gloucester, where they would have been spotted by the enemy. Instead, on 24 March 1643 they crossed the river at Framilode, using flat-bottomed boats that had been hauled from London to ferry men and horses across.[9] Defeat of the encampment at Highnam was swift, and the following morning the Royalists were persuaded to surrender. The river that they had hoped would guarantee their safety had served to trap them. There was little hope of relief from the nearest significant Royalist forces, billeted in Cirencester, since they would have had to make a 50-mile march via the bridge at Upton, an impossible task within the timescale.

A period of skirmishing followed in which the Royalists troops, reinforced with cavalry and dragoons under the command of Prince Maurice (1620-52), younger brother of the more illustrious Rupert, seized control of Tewkesbury and then built a bridge of boats in order to speed up an attack on Waller's men. In the Forest of Dean, Maurice pinned Waller's forces back to the confluence of the Severn and Wye. Waller found that he was unable to extricate himself without a fight but was determined to avoid a battle. He therefore packed his foot soldiers and equipment over the Severn on the Old Passage ferry from Beachley to Aust. The cavalry, meanwhile, made a dash and broke through the Royalist lines at Littledean, reaching Gloucester with few losses. Realising that Maurice's troops were committed in the Forest of Dean, the Parliamentary forces immediately moved north, destroyed Maurice's bridge of boats, took the vulnerable Tewkesbury, and seized Upton Bridge.[10] The latter would have cut off the Royalist forces but the force holding it was too weak to withstand Maurice's eventual counter-attack. Parliament's forces retreated without damaging the bridge, and then, with both forces on the east bank of the river, came the eventual showdown at the battle of Ripple Field on 16 April 1643, at which Waller's Parliamentary forces were comprehensively defeated.

It was part of a wave of Royalist successes. Waller tried to counter it by attacking Worcester on 29 May; artillery fire was exchanged but assaults on the city gates were repulsed. Heavy losses and the fear of Royalist reinforcements persuaded Waller to retreat. He commandeered all the boats his men could find, and ordered that the wounded, and his artillery, should be ferried back to Gloucester by river, while he reached the city himself two days later.[11] Worse was to follow: the defeat of Parliament in the battle of Roundway Down in Wiltshire on 13 July 1643 and the subsequent loss of Bristol, with its large cache of armaments, to the Royalist cause.

Control of the Severn was within the king's grasp if he could capture Gloucester. This would have placed all of the valley's resources, and those of south Wales, in his hands, to supply and reinforce his field army. If he could have taken Gloucester the outcome of the war might have been different. But the siege was a failure. Before it began on 3 August Charles informed the town's leaders that their situation was hopeless and that a relief force could not come to their aid. Several sources give an account of the siege of Gloucester, one of the most important of them written by John Corbet, chaplain to the governor Edward Massey, a key eyewitness. He well understood the importance of Gloucester and its position on the Severn: 'the center, garden and granary of the kingdome, the block-house to the river of Severne, and a barre to all passages betweene Worcester, Bristol and the sea, to stop of entercourse between Oxford and Wales'.[12]

The city was surrounded, and three days into the siege the Welsh contingent began a bridge of '20 flatt boats' to unite forces on either bank of the Severn.[13] Edward Massey, Gloucester's governor, was initially pessimistic and wrote to Parliament about the low levels of ammunition, morale, and loyalty of the townspeople. The defenders were not idle, however. Initially 'out-guards' were posted 'at each corner of the Isle of Alney for securing thereof and the river of Seaverne', although the positions were subsequently abandoned.[14] The earl of Stamford sent out a raiding party by boat to wreak as much havoc as was possible before retreating.[15] Ten days later, on 31 August, Sergeant-Major Ferrer crept along the riverbank to surprise the enemy at Llanthony; they took cover behind a wall, upon which the artillery of the city was then directed.[16] All of these tactics bought time for an army of 10,000 infantry and over 3,000 cavalry, led by the earl of Essex, to march from Kingston-upon-Thames.

The imminent arrival of Parliament's army was enough to lift the siege. By chance, a rise in the Severn flooded the approaches to the city and gave Gloucester an extra line of defence.[17] On 5 September the army besieging Gloucester retreated to Birdlip Hill and henceforth concentrated its efforts on barring Parliament's route back to London. Once at Gloucester, Essex sent a detachment north to Tewkesbury. Here the Parliamentary forces constructed a bridge of boats across the river, which the Gloucester garrison used to bring in resources from the west bank of the Severn. They then pressed further to Upton to secure the bridge, giving the impression that they intended to attack Worcester from the west side.[18] Throughout, the Royalist army kept its distance, only realising later that its best chance of success would have been to meet Parliament in an open battle. Worcester was beyond the reach of an army short on provisions, and the earl of Essex probably never intended to attack it. Instead he marched east and took Cirencester by surprise, plundered its military stores and marched his replenished army back to London.

The capture of Bristol by the Royalists profoundly shifted the balance of power in the Lower Severn valley. Royalists commanded the Severn Sea and the passage at Aust, which

Westgate Bridge, Gloucester, in 1793, by C. Catton. The timber span was removed during the siege of Gloucester in 1643, closing off any easy access to the city.
(© Gloucester City Council)

remained an important route between Bristol and south Wales. Parliament had troops stationed at Frampton to stop maritime incursions from Royalist-held Berkeley Castle. On the west bank Sir John Winter controlled the passage at Newnham, which he used to launch raids across the river. Parliamentary forces took up positions at Arlingham to defend the crossing from the opposite bank.[19]

Edward Massey had a frigate built at Gloucester to defend the river close to the city. It was also sent on raids up and down river, with a crew of experienced mariners and a party of marauding soldiers carrying off whatever spoils they could. A surprise attack was made on Chepstow, where the Royalist garrison was largely stood down, a Captain Carvine was killed while he supped in the George Inn, and a Bristol vessel bound for Worcester was seized. It was laden 'with oyle, wine, sugar and other commodities', perhaps including ordnance.[20] Royalists increased their naval presence to prevent such losses happening again.

Parliament needed to prevent the Royalists from establishing a permanent garrison at Beachley, which would have allowed them to control all the coastal traffic from the Severn and Wye. Prince Rupert, with a party of 500 soldiers and cavalry, began to fortify Beachley. A bank is said to have been dug, which extended half-way across the narrow neck of land between the Wye and Severn, beginning at Sedbury Cliff on the bank of the Severn. It was probably the bank which can still be seen at Sedbury Cliff. This was at one time thought to have been part of Offa's Dyke, but recent archaeological investigations have shown that it was a separate feature, although it existed as early as AD 956,[21] which suggests that the Royalists merely improved the existing fortifications. According to John Corbet, half of the enclave was protected by the bank, the other half by a hedge. Today, the bank still protects the eastern side but on the western side it is mostly eroded. Parliament knew that it would have to time its attack exactly right. At high water Royalist ships guarded the rivers and came close to the shore. But the Severn has a phenomenal tidal reach so at low water the ships retreated far from the shore into deeper waters, and were of little assistance to land-based forces. The first Parliamentary attack drove out the Royalist forces but, having no command of the surrounding waters, they withdrew, allowing the Royalists to re-take Beachley and improve the defences, by re-cutting the ditches and erecting a palisade on the bank. A second Parliamentary assault in October 1644, also made at low tide, was equally successful. Royalist forces were forced back to the river, among them Sir John Winter, who escaped in a waiting boat, while others are said to have drowned. Again Parliament could not hold the position and so simply destroyed the palisades and hedges.[22] For the loss of only ten men Massey killed 70 of the enemy, and took 170 prisoners, two pieces of cannon and 200 muskets.[23]

By 1644 the struggle to control the Severn was turning in Parliament's favour. Lydney was captured, although Sir John Winter managed to burn his house 'White Cross' to prevent its sequestration.[24] Upstream there was a series of raids on enemy positions. Thomas Fox led a daring nocturnal raid on Bewdley. The bridge was difficult to cross on account of its bridge house, which was closed at night, so Fox probably made a surprise attack by fording the river at low water. The main achievement was the capture of Thomas Lyttleton, governor of Bewdley and the most prominent native Royalist in

Worcestershire. Meanwhile Thomas Mytton, for Parliament, launched a surprise attack on Atcham Bridge, but it was repulsed by a stronger Royalist force. Montford Bridge was the focus of a skirmish on 3 May 1644, when Parliamentary cavalry captured '100 new pressed soldiers from Denbighshire ... as they were going to Shrewsbury'.[25]

The failure of the Royalists' Thames Valley campaign of 1644 saw Charles retreat and, once again, seek to put the Severn between his own and the Parliamentary forces. His destination was Shrewsbury. Worcester was too weakly defended for the Royalist cause and in any case, the experience of a year earlier persuaded Charles that the Parliamentary army could cross the Severn at Tewkesbury and attack Worcester from the west as well as the east. Charles crossed the river at Worcester in early June and then moved northwards to Bewdley, while the opposing forces shadowed him on the opposite bank of the river. Despite having twice the armed force of Charles, Sir William Waller could

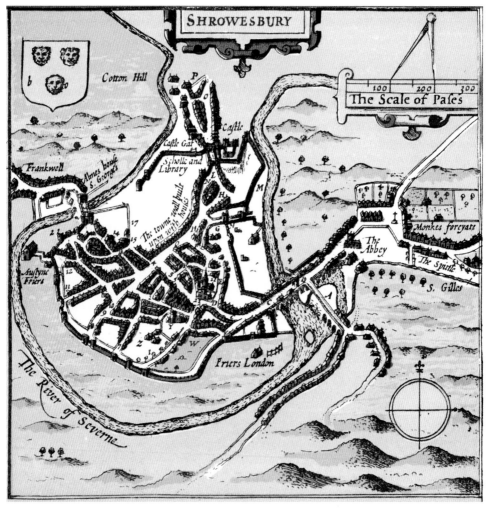

John Speed's map of Shrewsbury shows the town's naturally defensible position. The river acts as a moat around the town, except on the north side where the castle was built.

not engage him in battle because the bridges at Worcester, Bewdley and Bridgnorth were too heavily defended. From Bewdley, however, things took an unexpected turn. Parliamentary forces had travelled away from the Severn towards Stourbridge, hoping to reach Shrewsbury before the king's forces could march there on slower riverside roads. Waller then hesitated, calculating that a Royalist army in Shrewsbury was in no position to cause mischief, given that the Midlands was now firmly under Parliamentary control. Charles, meanwhile, convened a meeting of his council of war at Bewdley on 14 June in which he introduced a new tactic to give Parliamentary forces the slip. The cavalry was deployed to give the impression that the army was still active in the area, while the musketeers boarded boats and sailed down to Worcester, where the king attended the cathedral church on Sunday 16 June. With poor intelligence, Waller did not realise what was happening until Charles and his army had made their escape.

The strategic importance of Shrewsbury was demonstrated after its capture by Parliament in February 1645. The Royalists had already lost control of mid Wales and with it the Upper Severn. Parliament took Welshpool in August 1644, on 17 September won the battle of Montgomery, which was fought close to the river Camlad, and took Powis Castle in October. Shrawardine Castle, upstream of Montford Bridge, was garrisoned for the Royalists by Anglo-Irish men recruited by Sir William Vaughan. In order to reduce cover for attacking forces, the church and much of the village was taken down. Parliament had nearly taken the castle in October 1644 when they captured Vaughan and twelve of his officers while they were celebrating Holy Communion. Somehow Vaughan managed to escape into the castle, leaving Colonel Mytton with only the lesser officers as his trophy.[26]

Royalists had held Shrewsbury since the beginning of the Civil War, although the inhabitants were not wholly Royalist in sympathy, and it was an important military base where munitions were stored, and had been commanded by Prince Rupert and his brother Prince Maurice. Under the command of Sir Francis Ottley the town's defences, which were already among the best of the Severnside towns, Shrewsbury still having its medieval town walls, had been strengthened by the digging of trenches on the south and west sides of the town. But none of this could provide a defence if the town was betrayed from within.

In February 1645 Prince Maurice moved north to attack Chester, leaving Shrewsbury all the more vulnerable when Parliamentary intelligence sources learned that it was guarded only by a small contingent of troops – mainly men recruited from Ireland who had recently lost out to the enemy near Montgomery. Shrewsbury was attacked and taken on the night of 22 February. An advance party, sent in by boat, sawed down the wooden palisade forming the outer defences. Apparently these men were not challenged, almost certainly because there were sympathisers within the town. One or more of them probably opened the town's castle gate, and perhaps also the gate in St Mary Water Lane, allowing Parliamentary forces to enter freely. Colonel Thomas Mytton, who led the attack, perpetrated one of the most gratuitous acts of cruelty of the whole war when he selected 13 of the defending troops, branded as Irish (i.e. Roman Catholic) mercenaries, and ordered that they should be hanged. (Prince Rupert retaliated by hanging 13 men at Whitchurch a

Berkeley Castle was taken in 1645, helping Parliament gain control of the Severn estuary. Roundheads scaled the walls with siege ladders, a throwback to medieval warfare.

Shrawardine Castle was razed to the ground following its capture in 1645, leaving little more than a mound in a field by the lane to the old ferry.

The ruined tower of Bridgnorth Castle leans at an angle greater than that of the tower of Pisa. It is virtually all that remains from the destruction of the castle after its capture by Parliament in 1646.

month later.)[27] In military terms, the Royalists' loss of some 200 soldiers was insignificant compared to the military supplies and foodstuffs that simultaneously fell into enemy hands. Shrewsbury was also on the route between Oxford and north Wales, the latter being a major recruiting ground for the Royalist army, and it controlled the Upper Severn valley. With the loss of Shrewsbury, Montford Bridge, the bridge at Atcham and a nearby Severnside garrison at Longner Hall also fell into Parliament's hands.

Following his defeat by Cromwell's New Model Army at Naseby on 14 June 1645, Charles retreated westwards again, having sent Prince Maurice ahead to secure the bridge at Worcester. Charles went to Bewdley, where he apparently stayed at the Angel Inn on Load Street for two nights before heading into south Wales, leaving a few men to guard Bewdley Bridge.[28] Behind the barricade of the Severn Charles intended to recruit a new army and take the fight back to Parliament. The superior numbers and tactics of the king's opponents were beginning to tell, however, and within a year the war was effectively over, although it continued in isolated incidents into 1647. The Royalists surrendered Berkeley Castle in 1645, although the Governor, Sir Charles Lucas, had sworn that 'he would eat horse flesh before he would yield, and man's flesh when that was done'.[29] Roundheads scaled the walls with siege ladders and killed 40 cavaliers as they tried to surrender, which frightened the remainder of the garrison into giving in. The isolated Shrawardine Castle fell to Parliament at the end of June after a siege lasting only five days. The garrison was allowed to march away to Ludlow but to prevent the castle's re-fortification it was destroyed.

Hostilities ceased on the Severn, for the time being, in 1646. In March Bridgnorth fell. The Royalist rearguard retreated into the castle, setting fire to part of the town behind them, apparently as revenge because the town refused to provision the garrison for a month's siege, and held out until April. A second fire was started after the defending artillery struck St Leonard's church, which had been requisitioned as a powder magazine (the Royalists stored their ammunition in the town's other church, St Mary Magdalene).[30] After the Royalist surrender the castle was largely destroyed.

Worcester was besieged from early June, as this isolated pocket of Royalist resistance stubbornly refused to yield. Parliamentary forces took their time surrounding the city and taking control of its bridge. Bargemen from Holt brought boards downstream and these were used to construct a bridge of boats at the upper end of Pitchcroft, on the north side of the city, wide enough for Parliamentary foot soldiers to cross eight abreast. Now all branches of the Parliamentary forces could communicate with ease. It is true that a temporary bridge is vulnerable if left for a period; heavy rains at the end of June caused the river level to rise, and Henry Townshend thought that 'if the river on the late rain had risen but a foot higher their Bridge of Boats had been broken and come down the river, their army parted, and we might have destroyed them'. It was a forlorn hope and would have been, at worst, a temporary setback for Parliament. 'But we were not so happy nor lucky.'[31] Worcester Bridge was seized on 9 June but it was two weeks before Parliamentary forces had taken up positions on the south side of the city. Worcester finally surrendered on 23 July, the last Royalist garrison on the Severn to fall. As Henry Townshend, who had been in the city throughout the siege, commented: 'by having Worcester you have the key which opens all the passages on the river Severn, debars His Majesty of all succour from the Welsh, and in substance the Crown itself'.[32]

The defeat and subsequent execution of Charles I in 1649 brought civil war hostilities to a temporary close, but there was a brief reprise two years later. His son, the future Charles II of England, was crowned king of Scotland on New Year's Day in 1651 and henceforth assembled an army to win back the English crown. He entered England on 3 August 1651, won a skirmish near Warrington and on 23 August entered Worcester, where his army was well received by the city folk. Worcester was to be his headquarters. The rich and fertile valley of the Severn could provide for his army of mainly Scotsmen, who were exhausted after the long march south. Charles ordered the rebuilding of Worcester's defences and according to Nicholas Lechmere his 'numerous army, most Scots, some English' were sent out of Worcester to 'break down Upton, Bewdley, Powick

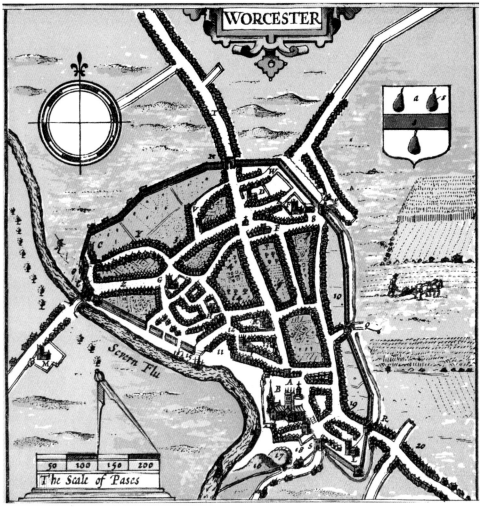

John Speed's map of Worcester shows the extent of the walled city
and the position of its bridge.

and Brandsford bridges', of which the latter two are on the river Teme.[33] Charles tried to muster local men for his army, but with such embarrassing lack of success that his plan to launch an offensive gave way to a defensive strategy. Parliament forces were by now on the march. Repairs and additions were made to Worcester's fortifications, but Charles divided his forces between those manning the city's defences and those encamped on the west side of the river, protected by the Severn and the Teme, a relatively safe haven once the bridges had been eliminated.

From this point onwards the Royalist strategy quickly unravelled. Upton was only lightly defended. On August 29 a small band of 18 Parliamentary troops made their way across the bridge on a single plank spanning the two broken bridge arches. 'They mounted it as though it was their wooden Pegasus, and so scrambled across to the opposite side', according to Lechmere.[34] The advance party was noticed by the Scots, who took refuge in the parish church by the bridge, where they prepared to resist. During a fire-fight between the advance party and the Scots, General Lambert ordered his dragoons to ford the river, which they are said to have done slightly further downstream – 'about a pistol shot from the bridge'.[35] It was late summer and the river level was probably near its lowest, but fording unknown waters was still a dangerous challenge, and involved at least wading in the water if not swimming. Encouraged by the dragoons' success, the cavalry followed, and the Scots were soon outnumbered. As soon as the defenders were driven back, more planks were laid over the demolished arches, allowing yet more troops to pass freely over the bridge. The Scots were routed. Cromwell came to Upton later in the day and ordered the bridge to be repaired, placing General Fleetwood in command.

Now that they had secured Upton Bridge, Parliament's forces had access to the west side of the Severn, from where they could cut off Charles's retreat into Wales, and prevent any Welsh reinforcements from joining him. But the main focus was on attack. The east bank, outside the confines of the city of Worcester, was in Parliament's hands. Fleetwood would attack on the south-west side by crossing the Teme at Powick Bridge. All that was needed was a force to cross over to the west bank of the Severn and attack from the south-east side, and Charles would be trapped and driven back over Worcester Bridge and into the city. The Council of State described the strategy: 'There is a bridge of boats preparing above the confluence of the Teme and Severn. When ready this will be a line of communication between the two armies, and we shall speedily force them to fight, or starve, or run if they can break through; the latter will be most likely.'[36] In the event two temporary bridges were prepared. General Lambert travelled as far south as Gloucester, commandeering all the boats he could find. One bridge was built just upstream of the confluence with the Teme, and another about 50 yards upstream on the Teme itself. Contemporary sources suggest that the bridges were assembled downstream, tied together and laid with planks, and towed upstream from Upton by Fleetwood's men on the day of the battle. According to Robert Stapleton, in a letter to Parliament, the crossing points were first cleared by a preliminary assault, or 'forlorn', but their success may have been helped by the fact that the Scots never expected such audacious structures to be thrown across the river.[37]

On 3 September Cromwell's Roundheads, 28,000 men, attacked. Fleetwood's men advanced on the west side of the Severn, crossing the Teme at Powick Bridge as planned. The principal force attacked by crossing the temporary bridges. Charles is said to have viewed developments from the best vantage point in the vicinity – the tower of Worcester Cathedral. The outnumbered Scots resisted for several hours but then were defeated, with the loss of two to three thousand men. They retreated back across Worcester Bridge into the city, but could not defend the bridge itself. Roundheads went in after them, and Cromwell sent a detachment northwards to take Bewdley Bridge and prevent their escape. Attempts to regroup and counter-attack from within the city walls failed abjectly. Among the few who escaped was Charles himself, probably by St Martin's Gate on the north side of the city. Violence against the defeated Scots was retributive: Major-General Harrison wrote: 'What with the dead bodies of men and the dead horses of the enemy filling the streets, there was such a nastiness that a man could hardly abide the town.'[38] Hugh Peters declared to his Ironsides on 23 September: 'You have been in Worcester, where England's sorrows began, where they were happily ended.' The Civil War had ended in the same meadows where the first skirmish had taken place nine years previously. This time the Severn had played a vital role in trapping the king's forces, and the audacious bridges of boats were decisive factors in Parliament's victory.

The march into England which ended with the battle at Worcester was sheer folly on Charles's part. Failure to muster any support among the people of Worcestershire and the Marches was embarrassing, although such reverses appear to have had no effect on the exiled prince's resolve and have been glossed over in history. What was an ignominious and humiliating defeat was rewritten as a noble failure in the years that followed the Restoration in 1660. This interpretation of events was cultivated in part by Charles himself, who publicised his miraculous (or miraculously lucky) escape from the battlefield and his eventual arrival in France, but history has looked favourably on it simply because Charles eventually regained the throne. In this final scene of the Civil Wars, and one of its most mythologised, the Severn again played a crucial role. Charles planned to flee to Swansea, where he would be able to take a boat over to France. With his companion Richard Penderel he worked his way upstream from Bridgnorth and intended to take the ferry across the river at Madeley by night. But near the river they were spotted behaving suspiciously, and fled. They hid for a while and eventually found overnight refuge in a barn in Madeley. By the following morning the area was swarming with Parliamentary troops, and they were particularly vigilant at the ferry points. The Severn being barred to him, Charles moved eastwards, and hid in an oak tree at Boscobel House. In later centuries the tree became a shrine, but the focus of pilgrimage could, but for unfortunate circumstances, have been a ferry across the Severn.

Incredibly, none of the Severn bridges were destroyed in the Civil Wars, even though they were crucial in the fighting and there was significant damage to many, such as Upton Bridge already described, and Westgate Bridge during the siege of Gloucester.[39] Drawbridges were constructed at Westgate Bridge and Over Bridge, both of which already incorporated timber spans. Bridgnorth Corporation initially considered making a drawbridge for one of the spans of the bridge, but decided against it and strengthened the town's gates instead.[40] In 1645 money had to be raised to construct a new drawbridge over one of the spans of Worcester Bridge. A year later, during the final siege of Worcester, fighting took place from the bridge but the parapets were found to be too low and therefore they were raised in brick, incorporating loop holes.[41] Worcester Bridge was not crucial to the fighting, but it had a symbolic importance, or at least a propaganda value. In an early skirmish Royalists captured three colours from the enemy and hung them up on the bridge as a trophy. Above the transom of the drawbridge the words *Civitas Fidelis* (faithful city) were written, and on the inside, *Deo et Rege* (God and king).[42]

Destruction of the bridge at Over was to be part of an elaborate plan to lure and entrap Royalist forces in their attempt to attack Gloucester in 1644. The plan, documented by Captain Robert Blackhouse, a Parliamentarian posing as a Royalist spy, was to construct a drawbridge over one of the spans of Over Bridge and Westgate Bridge, then to convince the Royalist attackers, led by Sir William Vavasour, that the drawbridge would be lowered to admit them. Artillery was trained on Over Bridge and a team of men waited beneath it ready to collapse the drawbridge with a rope. 'The bridge would have fallen in, whereby of necessity they must all have been killed, drowned, or taken [prisoner]' but, at the last minute, Vavasour's men hesitated and moved off in a different direction.[43]

Ferrymen could be forced to take sides when their vessels were commandeered to ferry troops across the river. The most conspicuous victim during the Civil War was the New Passage ferry, which was abolished during the Commonwealth and was not established anew until 1718. The ferryman is said to have tricked a group of Parliamentarians crossing from the Welsh side at low tide. They were put down on to the English Stones, a rocky outcrop in the Severn estuary near Redwick, and told that they could walk to the shore from there, but of course it was a trick and all of them were apparently drowned.[44]

Amid the chaos, normal life continued as well as it could. The Severn navigation was crucial to the war effort in the movement of soldiers, ordnance, food and fuel. However, long-distance trade was severely hindered. Charles forbade any trade between Royalist-held towns and places held by Parliamentarians, except where a special licence was granted. Prince Rupert specifically prohibited any trade with Gloucester.[45] Some people profited from the war – like the bargemen of Holt who were paid to bring down boards to make a deck on the bridge of boats at Worcester in 1646. Vessels on the river were vulnerable to plunder, especially if word got out as to the nature of their cargo. Just after the siege of Gloucester was lifted, Parliamentary forces gained intelligence that a boat at Newnham contained ammunition destined for Hereford. A raiding party of foot soldiers and cavalry seized its contents, which included two tons of match (the cord used in firing cannon), wine and other merchandise, but they did not have the wherewithal to carry it back to Gloucester by water, and it was brought to the city in horse-drawn carts.[46]

The river must also have been a conduit of information and misinformation, for mariners were a useful source of news about what was happening further afield. Each side tried to control the river, and hence the trade, at its principal towns and bridges. The point is amplified in a letter written in 1645 by the Parliamentary Committee for Shropshire: 'We lately erected a small garrison at Benthall near those places whence we have all our coal and lime for this garrison, the same, being within a mile from the river, is of much concernment to use because of carriage by water.'[47] The Royalist stronghold of Benthall had fallen to Parliament with the loss of Shrewsbury, and at last Parliament could gain a stranglehold on traffic on the Severn.

How did the conflict affect everyday life? Residents of the towns occupied by the opposing armies were not necessarily sympathetic to either cause. Edward Massey complained of the disloyalty of Gloucester's citizens, neglecting, perhaps, the possibility that they might have simply been fed up with the war, its taxes, privations and suffering. A list of 'delinquents' compiled in Shrewsbury in 1642 included the names of prominent drapers, butchers and dyers, and one Richard Proude was denounced as 'the basest knave in towne and a traitor or hippocrite and Roundhead'.[48]

Unfortunately for the native Severnside population, the valley was fertile country capable of provisioning armies, and the soldiers were not slow to exploit it. When Prince Rupert rode into Bewdley in February 1644 the borough met the cost of entertaining him and other leading Royalist officers, including £4 10s for a hogshead of claret for Prince Rupert.[49] The corporation of Worcester congratulated Prince Maurice on his victory at the battle of Ripple Field by sending claret, sack (i.e. Spanish white wine) and French white wine to Upton, at a cost of £16 17s 10d, and then welcomed him back to Worcester with a hogshead of claret and three sugar loaves, costing £9 12s 11d. As Governor, Prince Maurice expected a level of hospitality commensurate with his rank, and he was a hard drinker.[50] Horses, corn and boats were plundered, and these were the lifeblood of the local communities, some of which retaliated by forming the vigilante groups known as Clubmen. A petition was sent from Worcester to Parliament in September 1644, by which time the city had become tired of the whole affair. They complained that they 'have for the last two years been under the power of the enemy, who have exacted large sums of money from the County, besides seizing cattle and horses without payment. Your petitioners have, besides, suffered at the hands of the Parliament forces, who in their inroads and requisitions make no distinction between the ill-affected and well-affected.'[51] The citizens of Worcester paid a second time in 1651 when their property was looted by victorious Roundheads, perhaps in retribution for having welcomed Charles in the first place.

This says nothing of the threats and intimidation against the civilian population, who were warned to give no succour to the other side, as if they were powerful enough to resist them. Looting, ransom demands and sequestrations increased as the war progressed. The entry of a besieging army must have been one of the most terrifying experiences for civilians during the war. At the siege of Bridgnorth the town was burned by Royalists – who had made so many demands on the inhabitants of the town in different circumstances – and the consequences were long remembered. 'Rich and poor alike ... were left houseless, and sought shelter where they could, in the field around the town, in thickets, and under rocks: all their property destroyed, and their life itself in jeopardy.'[52] Bridgnorth was not a place of heavy fighting, except briefly in 1646, but the town's population did not recover to its pre-war level until about 1670.[53]

Part Four

The Working River

❧ 9 ❧
Industry

'From Coalport to Ironbridge, two miles, the river passes through the most extraordinary district in the world: the banks on each side are elevated to a height of from 3 to 400 feet, studded with ironworks, brickworks, Boat Building Establishments, Retail Stores, Inns and Houses, perhaps 150 vessels on the river, actively employed or waiting for cargoes; while hundreds and hundreds of busy mortals are assiduously engaged, melting with the heat of the roaring furnace; and though enveloped in the thickest smoke and incessant dust, are cheerful and happy.'[1]

Charles Hulbert's vision of Ironbridge at the height of its activity (if not its prosperity) reminds us that the downriver traffic on the Severn was in large part a consequence of the industries on or near its banks. Industry was drawn to the river for several reasons. The raw materials it needed were found there; it needed water for the production process; it served the riverside towns; the Severn was the means by which goods were despatched to customers.

When we think of industry on the Severn, we are bound to think of the river's part in the Industrial Revolution, but it has been a focus of industry since Roman times, the pattern of work on the riverbanks changing over time as the river changed. In time, industry came to be concentrated in the upper half of the river rather than the lower, but it was not always so. In Roman times iron was smelted at Worcester using iron ore shipped upstream from the Forest of Dean, and probably using local forests to supply the charcoal. Monasteries, as ever, had an important role in industrial development. Shrewsbury, Tewkesbury and Gloucester abbeys all had mills near the Severn but in each case the water was supplied from tributaries – the Rea brook, Avon and Fullbrook respectively. In the Middle Ages fulling, dyeing and tanning were industries of the major towns, but as woollen manufacture increased in scale and mills were upgraded with the adoption of waterwheels, these old established industries gravitated upstream to the purer waters of mid Wales. Economics prompted a similar shift in the clothing industry from its medieval centres like Gloucester to mill towns like Newtown and Llanidloes. Brewing was a traditional riverside industry that grew to an industrial scale in the 19th century; Holbrook's Vinegar Brewery, the shell of which stands at the confluence of the Severn and Stour at Stourport, was the town's oldest native industry until it ceased production in 2005.

An obvious use of the river might be thought to be as a supplier of water for water-wheels, use of which developed in the Middle Ages, and remained the main motive power for industry until the end of the 18th century. According to Celia Fiennes, who visited Worcester in the late 17th century, 'the water just by the town encompasses a little piece of ground full of willows and so makes it an island, part of which turns mills'.[2] Perhaps she was referring to the wheel pumping domestic water to the city which, like the waterwheels beneath arches of the Shrewsbury's Stone Bridge and Bridgnorth Bridge, was driven by the current (known as an undershot wheel) – a design not deemed to be an unqualified success. Other mills with undershot waterwheels must once have existed – one is shown in a print of Calcutts ironworks in the Ironbridge Gorge, published in 1788 – but they can only have represented a minority of mills on the river. With most mills the water was channelled to the top of the waterwheel and the gravity of water in the wheel's buckets made it turn. Overshot waterwheels could be powered with far less water than an undershot waterwheel, but there needed to be sufficient 'head', i.e. the fall of the river had to be sufficient to feed a waterwheel of at least three metres diameter. In practice there were only a limited number of places where this was possible without drawing off water so far upstream that maintaining an artificial watercourse, or leat, was impractical.

Where the river was narrow enough, a reservoir could be created within the river by constructing a weir across it. This has the drawback that once a weir has been built the river is no longer navigable. The lowest weir on the Severn is at Pool Quay near Welshpool; upstream are several more, used to supply a succession of agricultural

The Severn at Stourport, showing the former Holbrook's Vinegar Brewery

and textile mills. Further downstream the most effective way to exploit proximity to the river was to site the mill beside a tributary stream. The result is that in the Welsh section of the river there are Severn mills, but in the English stretch of the river there are tributary mills.

The earliest water mills in Wales were used to grind corn. Caerhowel Mill was mentioned as 'juxta Aquam Sabrine' in 1252, when Henry II allowed water to be diverted from the main channel to the mill. It continued to be used as a corn mill until the 1870s.[3] Many of the 19th-century woollen mills were on the site of much older corn mills, including Llanidloes Mill, first mentioned in 1293, and Beander Mill in Newtown, first documented in 1330.[4] One of the most effective ways to draw water off the river was to cut a straight watercourse across the neck of a meander, allowing water to supply a wheel directly and be discharged back into the river, all in a straight line. This was done at Goron Ddu, downstream of Abermule, and at Pool Quay.[5] Little is known about some mills, because they were short-lived. There was a Penarth Mill by 1635, close to the splendid timber-framed house of that name near Newtown, and there was a house called Graig Mill by the river at Mochdre near Newtown, but there is no other evidence of there having been a mill there.[6]

The prosperity of Llanidloes and Newtown relied on the industrialisation of the woollen industry. The area had some obvious advantages, not least the abundant sheep on its hills. The purity of its water also made it attractive for the cleaning process known as 'fulling', in which woven fabric is thickened and strengthened by pressing and kneading it with soap, then rinsing it in clean water. Fulling mills are sometimes known as walk mills from the use of a leat in which millers pounded the cloth with their feet

The Bridgend Mill at Llanidloes, now converted to flats, was built in 1834 and stood next to an older corn mill; both mills drew their water from the same weir on the Severn.

during the rinsing stage. There were water-powered fulling mills on the Upper Severn in the Middle Ages. One of the earliest documented examples was at Beander, next to the corn mill, which was in existence in 1330, swept away by a flood in 1382 and rebuilt; it eventually ceased working in the 17th century. An advertisement for the sale of the Milford factory in Newtown in 1831 summed up the importance of the river Severn (and in Llanidloes also the Clywedog) as a source of power and purity: 'The factory and fulling mills are constantly supplied with a powerful stream of water from the Severn, driving 4 wheels, with ample power to work the said carding engine and stocks. The water of the Severn is much prized for its superior properties in the dressing of flannels.'[7]

Unfortunately the textile mills could not rely on the Severn as a means of navigation. For that, factories had to await construction of the Montgomeryshire Canal, which remained uncompleted until 1821, but then allowed goods to be shipped from Newtown to the Ellesmere Canal and thus the nationwide canal network. To feed the canal, water was pumped from the Severn just below Newtown. There are also two curved weirs below the town at Penarth from where water was diverted into a leat that fed the canal.

Once a good location had been established for a corn mill, and the water supply had been made reliable by building a weir, that place tended to remain attractive for as long as water was a motive power for industry. Bridgend Flannel Mill, originally known as the Town Mill and now converted into flats, is the best survival of the Severnside woollen industry in Llanidloes. It was built in 1834 beside the earlier corn mill and continued working into the 1930s. The corn mill was supplied by building a weir across

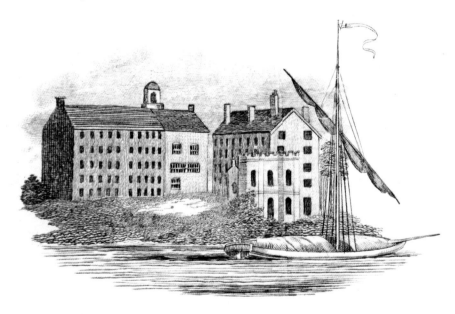

Charles Hulbert's cotton mill on the bank of the Severn in Shrewsbury was a commanding riverside presence but not a commercial success, and stayed in operation for less than thirty years.

the Severn, creating a reservoir that was later used by the flannel mill (the weir collapsed in 1932). Other Severn woollen mills also exploited the site of earlier corn mills. There was a corn mill at Caen y Coed in Llanidloes before a fulling mill and carding factory was erected there in 1809.[8] Craigfryn mill at Newtown was also said to have once been a corn mill.[9] Milford was the site of a corn mill but in 1810 William Tilsley built a new weir to supply the new carding mill, which was equipped with ten carding engines.[10] At Beander, fulling and carding mills were added alongside the corn mill in about 1806 and became the Oversevern woollen and corn mill, at least until the woollen mill burned down in 1848.[11] The flannel mill was rebuilt and was working again by 1858, although it had ceased trading by the 1890s. The weir that supplied it has now vanished and the site of the mill was destroyed when a flood embankment was built in the 20th century.

Textile manufacture extended as far as Shropshire in the 19th century. A woollen mill was built at Shrewsbury in 1789 but after a decade of struggle it was partly converted to dwellings before its purchase in 1803 by Charles Hulbert, an optimistic Lancastrian who vainly hoped that he could compete with the northern mill towns. Hulbert's mill lasted little over a decade but the building survived, largely converted into tenements that became an Irish enclave later in the century.[12] The site of Bridgnorth's Greyfriars later became Southwells Carpet Factory, essentially overspill from the centre of carpet manufacture in Kidderminster. Above Bridgnorth the old Severnside mill at Pendlestone Rock, briefly a forge in the late 18th century, was converted in 1845 to a mill spinning yarn for the carpet industry. It continued to draw water from the river Worfe, first to power a waterwheel, later a turbine.[13]

The weirs at Cilcewydd and Leighton Bridge, almost opposite Welshpool, were built by the Leighton Estate in the mid 19th century and belong to the last phase of the Severn as a source of motive power. Leighton was the rural estate of the Liverpool banker John Naylor and is one of the most remarkable examples of high-Victorian estate development in Britain. It is especially notable for the impressive range of pioneering technology that

The mill at Cilcewydd is one of the few surviving corn mills on the upper river that drew water directly from the Severn. The mill was built in 1862 for the Leighton estate. Power was provided by water turbines, the arched intake for which has now dried up.

was introduced into farming and related industries, which included the use of water turbines. One of most important of the turbine installations was housed at Cilcewydd corn mill, built in 1862, which is otherwise a conventional mill by the river, although separated from it by the railway line. The level of the river is now lower than it once was, leaving the arched intake from the river high and dry. From the other weir hydraulic rams pumped water to reservoirs for use in the turbines elsewhere on the estate.

At Mill Farm, Pool Quay, is the site of the former abbey corn mill of Strata Marcella Abbey, where water was drawn a fair distance from the river, by means of a weir. The weir was constructed by the abbey, which was founded in 1170, perhaps as early as the late 12th century. By the 19th century it was said to be 17 feet (5.2 metres) high and so was a substantial undertaking. There are various records of its repair, such as an agreement for repair works in 1657-58, but it was fatally breached in a flood in 1881, after which no attempt to repair it was made and the nature of the river bed here changed appreciably in a short time.[14] Water was diverted at various times to power a succession of industrial enterprises. For most of its working life it was a corn mill, first mentioned in 1291 as the property of the abbey, and known as Crowther's Mill in the 17th century. It continued working into the 19th century and had only been shut down for a couple of years before the weir was breached. The corn mill used comparatively little water, and the spare capacity allowed a succession of other industrial enterprises to be built alongside it. From the 1690s there was a lead smelting works; lead ore was brought from Llangynog in the Tanat valley and smelted lead pigs were exported down river from Pool Quay. After

The corn mill at Benthall was typical of Severn valley watermills. Its waterwheel was fed by a tributary stream rather than the river. In the late 18th century it became a tourist attraction for visitors to the Iron Bridge. (Ironbridge Gorge Museum Trust)

the 1770s the lead works was replaced by an iron forge, then by a fulling mill and from 1802 also a mill for carding and spinning wool. From 1835 this was redeveloped into a flannel mill and a dye house, which worked until 1858, after which there was a barytes crushing mill which lasted until 1879 when a saw mill was established.[15] The latter ceased working when the weir collapsed. The weir was the lowest weir on the Severn until the 19th century, and hence the limit of the navigable river. It also marks a shift in the character of industry on the Severn, not unconnected with the navigation. Upstream the mills are either agricultural or belong to the textile industry. The Pool Quay mills mark a significant shift. Although their history shares the characteristics of the upstream mills, they also reflect the greater diversity of industries found further downstream.

The navigability of the river and its volatility were among the reasons why traditional water-powered industries were not found on the riverbank. When travellers visited Shropshire to take in the wonders of the newly-built Iron Bridge in the late 18th century many of them were sidetracked by the sight of an enormous waterwheel on the south side of the river that powered Benthall corn mill. Reckoned to be 60 feet (18.3 metres) in diameter, the wheel was still occasionally in use in the 1920s.[16] Further downstream, Swinney Mill below Coalport was also depicted by some of the Picturesque artists of the early 19th century. It started as a corn mill but was eventually employed in grinding raw materials for the chinaworks. The best of the Severn tributary mills is now the restored Daniels Mill at Bridgnorth. In its present form it dates from only 1855, but there was a mill here in the 15th century and it continued working until 1957.[17] Another fine

The Abbey Mill at Tewkesbury receives its water from the Avon, despite being at the edge of the Ham, the water meadows by the Severn. There was a mill here in the late 12th century but the present mill was built in 1793.

example of a tributary mill is the abbey mill at Tewkesbury. The mill was founded in the late 12th century, but the building that can be seen today was built in the late 18th century. It is fed by the Mill Avon, an artificial cut from the river Avon that was widened in the 15th century and now looks like a river in its own right. Here the machinery was powered by undershot waterwheels that relied on the strength of the flow. One of the waterwheels is still visible.

Industry on the Severn has relied in large part on the proximity of accessible raw materials. Building stone was shipped up and down river from the Middle Ages, including from the sandstone quarries at Highley, source of building stone for many large projects, including Worcester Bridge. Coal mining began near Highley in the early 19th century, but it ceased in the 1820s. Then in 1877 the Highley Mining Company was formed, and coal was mined here until 1969, with a further colliery opened on the opposite bank at Alveley in 1935, but by this time the coal was transported by rail, not river. There are two places where minerals can be found actually in the river. The inhabitants of Tirley found coal on the river bed which they dragged up in summer using nets, often having raked the river bed first.[18] At Preston near Shrewsbury there was a seam of coal in the river bed, which could be won by fishermen dragging the bed and putting the material through a sieve.[19]

The story of Severn's extractive and manufacturing industries is dominated by the Ironbridge Gorge. Coal was the basis of the industrialisation of the Gorge and it was already mined commercially as early as 1575, when the landowner James Clifford was in trouble for dumping spoil in the river. A pamphlet written in 1660 urged that the river Stour should be made navigable, because the shortage of wood had created a market for coal as domestic fuel. It was reckoned that about by this time 100,000 tons of coal was mined in the East Shropshire coalfield and shipped to the major Severnside towns of Bridgnorth, Bewdley, Worcester and Shrewsbury.

The demand for coal spawned some technological innovations too. By 1605 there were wooden railways on which coal was taken from Broseley mines to Severnside

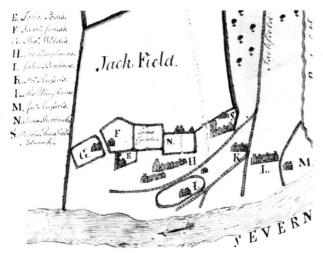

A plan of the riverside at Jackfield in the mid 18th century shows the wooden railways that had already been in existence for nearly a century and a half. Among the riverside buildings is a 'mug house', a cottage with a kiln on the end. (© Shropshire Archives)

wharves. The idea spread to the Madeley bank and in 1741 a wooden railway nearly a mile in length was built from the pits to Loadcroft Wharf below Coalbrookdale.[20] Steam engines were also pioneered by coalmasters dependent upon the river trade. The first mine pumping engine was erected in the Lloyds, between Ironbridge and Coalport, in 1719, only seven years after the first recorded installation of a steam pumping engine anywhere.[21] Samuel Simpson noted another innovation adapted to the unusual terrain of the steep-sided gorge. In 1746 he noticed that 'the coals are conveyed down in the following manner: a large barrel or wind is fixt at the top, on which runs a large chain; at each end of this is a wooden wagon that will hold about 2 tons each. This chain reaches to the river; and when one wagon is loaded at the top, it sets going gradually, which brings the empty one up and so continues until the vessel is laden.'[22] The inclined plane so described was to become a familiar sight in Shropshire as elsewhere. An alternative way of getting coal to the river barges was tried in 1786 when William Reynolds drove a tunnel into the hillside, with the aim of drawing out the coal horizontally to the river-bank instead of vertically to the pit head. By chance his tunnel hit upon a trapped well of tar, the original scheme was abandoned and the tar was extracted instead.

Coal appears to have been so plentiful that experiments were made to find new uses for it. Several by-products of coal were pioneered in the Ironbridge Gorge. Martin Eele set up kilns for the distillation of coal to produce, tar, pitch and oil, beside the Severn at Jackfield in the 1690s. In the 1770s there were similar ovens adjacent to the riverside Madeley Wood Ironworks and a few years later Archibald Cochrane, the ninth earl of Dundonald, set up ovens for distilling tar and pitch by the river at Calcutts. Coal attracted other industries to the Ironbridge Gorge. Lead ore mined in mid Wales and in Shropshire was smelted in the Ironbridge Gorge, just as it was at Pool Quay. Ore was shipped from Llandrinio to Ironbridge, where there were lead smelters on the south side of the river at Benthall, and on the north side at Coalbrookdale, which Samuel Simpson described as 'vastly poisonous, and destructive to everything near it'.[23] Lead pigs were then exported by river. Likewise, limestone from the area's quarries was brought to the riverside where it was burned in kilns, and then exported by river as lime.

Apart from coal, the East Shropshire coalfield contains profitable deposits of clay and iron ore. It was iron that defined the historic character of the Ironbridge Gorge and was the most prominent Severnside industry for a hundred years from the mid 18th century. Unlike other industries, ironworking needed a source of power even for small-scale production. Whether for smelting, where power was needed to blow the bellows, without which the required temperature would never have been reached, or for forging, which needed large hammers to 'shingle' and shape the iron into bars, waterwheels were the sole source of power until the end of the 18th century. With a few exceptions, iron-works were established close to the Severn but on its tributary streams. The best known of these is the Dale brook at Coalbrookdale, where waterwheels were erected, at various times, in five different places, for two blast furnaces, two iron forges, a mill for boring cannon and engine cylinders, and a mill for making frying pans. Other ironworks were close to the river. A blast furnace was built at Leighton, just above the head of the gorge, and was working by 1632. Iron pots were cast there that were transported on the Severn, but it also supplied pig iron to a forge at Sheinton on the opposite bank of the river, which was working by 1637.[24] It was one of the first ironworking enterprises to be positioned close to the river to exploit the proximity of transportation.

The trend continued in the 18th century. Whereas in the 17th century there were iron forges scattered across rural Shropshire, in the 18th century new ones were sited on tributary streams close to their confluences with the Severn. Tern Forge was built in the early 18th century at Atcham, on land that would later be evacuated to make way for Capability Brown's Attingham Park. It was part of an ambitious enterprise that included brass manufacture as well as iron. Wrens Nest Forge, built about 1770, is sited on the Dean brook close to the site of an older corn mill, the water supply for which it appropriated. In 1760 the Coalbrookdale Company also built a forge at Pendlestone near Bridgnorth, known as Rock Forge, which drew its water from the river Worfe. There had been a mill on this site since at least 1227 (and it was later converted to the mill for spinning yarn mentioned above).[25] By 1778 an old mill at Eardington on the Mor brook had been adapted as a forge, and by 1790 there was a forge at Hampton Loade. None of these new works was in the Ironbridge Gorge or the coalfield, and yet Hampton Loade and Eardington remained working well into the 19th century, as long as the navigation was a viable form of transport. There was a similar concentration of ironworks in the Stour valley, in which the river ports of Bewdley and, later, Stourport, were crucial.

There were also developments along the riverside in the Ironbridge Gorge, where almost every industrial enterprise had its own wharf. In 1756 a partnership of coalmasters and businessmen set up a riverside ironworks at Madeley Wood, better known as Bedlam, which had the advantage of being close to high-quality iron ores and next to the Severn. The only disadvantage it possessed was a lack of obvious water supply for the waterwheels. By the mid 18th century steam engines were employed regularly to pump coal mines, and were also used at ironworks to recycle water for waterwheels when the natural supply of a stream or river was insufficient. At Bedlam, water was channelled from the Severn into a sump, from which it was pumped up to a header tank for two waterwheels. It is the only known example where the source of water for a waterwheel came from below rather than above.

Another ironworks was built downstream at Calcutts in 1766, close to the Jackfield wharves where the early railways had been built. Surprisingly little is known about the works in its early days, but in 1786 it was acquired by Alexander Brodie. Brodie erected a steam engine and concentrated on casting cannon and ships' stoves, his chief client being the Board of Ordnance. Calcutts probably supplied the cannon that were fired in anger at Trafalgar. Later the ironworks was owned for a decade by William Hazledine, who used it to supply his riverside foundry and engineering works at Longden Coleham in Shrewsbury, source of ironwork for bridges and many other large-scale projects. Even less is known about a Severnside ironworks at Barnetts Leasow, which operated for just over 30 years from 1797 and was powered by steam engines instead of waterwheels. The success of the iron industry stimulated the growth of manufacturing that used iron as its raw materials. Brodie's cannon foundry and William Hazledine's engineering works are good examples. Another was the engineering works of John Hazledine erected on the riverbank at Bridgnorth, where pig iron was bought in and engines were shipped out. Among the latter was the pioneering steam locomotive *Catch-me-who-can*, designed by Richard Trevithick, which worked on a circular track in London in 1808 to publicise the feasibility of steam locomotion.

Not every colliery or ironworks in the East Shropshire coalfield could be sited along the river, a disadvantage that was solved by the construction of the Shropshire Canal, which was completed in 1793. It was only eight miles long, but passed across the East Shropshire Coalfield on the north side of the Severn, descending to the river level by means of an inclined plane, below which was a canal-river interchange at a place that soon acquired the name of Coalport. Coalport differed from the older and larger canal-river interchange downriver at Stourport because it was conceived from the outset primarily as a centre of manufacturing. William Reynolds, ironmaster and entrepreneur, had lavish plans to create a new industrial town at Coalport and some of his vision was realised. The north bank of the Severn was ripe for development. The river had been bridged a little downstream at Preens Eddy as early as 1780 (this later became Coalport Bridge). By 1800 Thomas Telford could describe Coalport as 'striking proof of the good effects of an improved inland navigation'. Already 'houses to the number of 30 have been built here, and more are still wanted, to accommodate the people employed at a large china manufactory, a considerable earthenware manufactory, another making ropes, one for bag making and one for chains'.[26] There was also a timber and boat yard where the canal's tub boats were constructed. William Reynolds became the joint owner of a ferry that operated for over a century and was used by employees of the various Coalport enterprises who lived on the more populous south side of the river in Jackfield.

The Calcutt Ironworks, as viewed in 1788. Calcutts was famous for casting ordnance during the wars with France between 1793 and 1815. On the right is a small corn mill.

The clay industries of the Ironbridge Gorge were established earlier and although less well known than the iron industry, thrived long after the area's ironworks had closed. Pottery manufacture began in Broseley parish in the 17th century. At this time it was made in 'mug houses', which were basically cottages with a kiln on one end (and should not be confused with public houses of that name), but by the 18th century the industry had expanded and plates, dishes, jars, coffee pots and tea pots were made and exported by river. There was even a distinctive 'Jackfield ware', a vitrified black earthenware used for teapots and decanters, as well as the drinking vessels used in the Severnside inns. White clay was suitable for making clay tobacco pipes, production of which boomed in Broseley at the end of the 17th century with the rising popularity of tobacco, itself one of the chief imports carried to the district by river.

The story of porcelain manufacture on the Severn begins not in Shropshire but in Worcester. The Worcester Porcelain works was established in 1751 by Dr John Wall, who had purchased Warmstry House, a grand house with gardens extending to the Severn, where he set up his factory. The riverside was the ideal location for such an enterprise because it allowed coal, and later soapstone and china clay, to be imported and stacked in an open yard by the river. The works started by producing blue and white porcelain but soon branched out into a range of Rococo designs. From the 1780s it was owned by Thomas Flight, and after a visit by George III and the granting of a royal warrant in 1788 it became the Royal Porcelain Works. By this time Thomas Turner,

Coalport Chinaworks was established in 1796 beside both the Severn and the Shropshire Canal, and was one of the largest manufactories of its kind.
(© Ironbridge Gorge Museum Trust)

who had been apprenticed at Worcester, had left and moved to Shropshire, where he set up a rival porcelain works at Caughley in 1772. The Royal Porcelain Works eventually moved away from the river. Robert Chamberlain left the original Worcester works in the 1780s to start his own porcelain decorating business on a fresh site, and bought out the original company in 1840. His new works on Severn Street was beside the Worcester and Birmingham Canal.

The porcelain works built at Caughley in 1772 proved to be too far from the Severn, although it had its own wharf at the Rovings, where there was also a boat yard. John Rose, who had been apprenticed at Caughley, established a new porcelain works at Coalport in 1796, on a site between the river and the canal. It was a logical move. China clay was imported by river, although the works also used local clay. Carriage of fragile goods by river was not a problem; the Severn had regularly carried wares from the Staffordshire Potteries. By 1799 Rose and his partners were in control of Caughley, and they ran it until 1814, when John Rose purchased a neighbouring pottery at Coalport and created one of the largest ceramics factories of its time. There was also a small enterprise by Walter Bradley manufacturing Coalport Delftwork in the last decade of the 18th century, the precise location of which has never been identified.

The brick and tile industry began in the 17th century too, but it made its greatest impact on the riverscape of the Severn much later. The manufacture of bricks and tiles thrived on the south bank of the river after the iron industry declined in the early 19th century. Clay was effectively a by-product of mining operations. Because it was the least valuable of minerals, veins of it were often exploited after the coal and iron reserves of a pit had been exhausted. The Bower Yard Brick and Tile Works stood close by the Iron Bridge on the south side of the river and was built not long after the bridge. The last barge to leave Ironbridge was laden with firebricks from Bower Yard when it left on its ill-fated journey to Worcester in 1895 – it struck Bridgnorth Bridge and sank. The works continued into the 20th century and in its latter days as the Benthall Stoneware Company produced sanitary pipework.[27] Nothing survives of the works now but you can still see pipes embedded into the bank to act as a retaining wall beneath the road.

Brick-making is a dirty business and its huge waste tips along the riverside changed the character of the Ironbridge Gorge. No longer sought out by the Picturesque traveller, unsightly tips along the bank helped to render the Ironbridge Gorge an eyesore to contemporary eyes. The coalfield that had been one of the first to prosper was one of the first to enter terminal decline, which is why Ramsay Macdonald described the Ironbridge Gorge in 1930 as a 'summary of the nation's problems'.[28] In time, and beginning with original thinkers like John Betjeman and John Piper who had an eye for the beauty of dilapidation, the fortunes of Ironbridge were turned around, and it became Britain's first post-industrial heritage landscape, an experiment in living with history that has been pursued just as vigorously at Gloucester Docks.

But we are not quite done with industry. The decline of the old industrial economy saw the rise of the new Severnside industry of electricity generation, which took advantage of the Severn's supply of abundant cooling water. A power station was built at Stourport in 1926, followed six years later by the Ironbridge A power station (both

The cooling towers of Ironbridge B power station are a prominent East Shropshire landmark and stand by the river at the entrance to Ironbridge Gorge.

of these were of the same generation as Battersea). Stourport's power station was taken down in the 1980s. Ironbridge A was eventually superseded by Ironbridge B, which began generating in 1969. The latter's four reddish-brown cooling towers command the skyline in the approach to Ironbridge from the east. Despite its unashamedly modern design the power station has attracted little opprobrium, testament to the care exercised in placing the structures in the landscape. Much more controversial are the nuclear power stations in the Severn estuary at Berkeley and Oldbury (and the two nuclear power stations at Hinkley Point in the Bristol Channel). The sites were chosen because the Severn could supply unlimited quantities of cooling water. On the estuary they are not in built-up areas, although Gloucester and Bristol are less than 20 miles distant. Berkeley was the first to enter operation, in 1962, with two Magnox reactors and a designated output of 300MW. It was decommissioned as long ago as 1989. Oldbury is a Magnox nuclear power station, with two nuclear reactors, that started generating electricity in 1967 and closed in 2012. It will be another 80-90 years before the reactor will be safe to dismantle and the site can be cleared. On a good day the power station supplied 435MW, enough for the needs of Bristol and Bath. At Oldbury 75 million litres of sea water were pumped into the condensers in the turbine hall every hour. In a nuclear power station the energy generated by the reactors produces steam to drive turbines. The sea water was not converted to steam, but used to condense the steam so that the condensate could be pumped back to the boilers.

The end of the road has not necessarily been reached for power generation in the Severn estuary. Schemes for a Severn barrage are as old as the 19th century and if ever implemented would have a significant impact on the character of the river, not least because the Severn bore would be history. Oldbury remains on the government's list of preferred locations for new nuclear power stations, and 150 hectares of land next to the current site have been designated for one. Whatever the future of Severnside industry, it seems likely to be in the generation of electricity by nuclear or tidal power at the mouth of the river, and perhaps wind power at the source.

✎ 10 ✎
The Working River

Coracles, floats (or flottes, flotes, drags or cobbles), picards, brigs, frigates, sloops, wherries, punts, barges, trows, boats (including cock or cockle boats, tow boats and long boats), tugs and lighters are some of the craft that have plied the waters of the Severn. As long as people have lived by the Severn there has been cross-river traffic, and perhaps some of the earliest settlers found their new homes by sailing up or down river. It is difficult to find an artist who portrayed the Severn in the 18th and 19th century who did not include some form of craft on the river. Artistic convention may account for this in part, but it reminds us that until recently the Severn was the hardest working river in Britain, both serving and facilitating the establishment of industries in the Severn valley, and benefiting areas that had access to it, such as the Midlands manufacturing district.

As George Perry wrote in 1758: 'The river is of great importance on account of its trade, being navigated by vessels of large burden more than 160 miles from the sea, without the assistance of any lock: and from thence into the adjacent countries: also great quantities of grain, pig and bar iron, iron manufactures and earthenwares; as well as wool, hops, cider and provisions, are constantly exported to Bristol and other places, from whence merchants' goods are brought in return.'[1]

The Severn trade grew in importance throughout the Middle Ages as it was navigable as far inland as Pool Quay near Welshpool, beyond which a weir constructed by Strata Marcella Abbey made the river impassable. The estuary and coastal trade was the first to develop. The Severn's tributary streams, or pills, provide many natural harbours on the lower river, and there ports such as Lydney and Newnham grew up. Lydney was a Roman port from which iron ore and charcoal were exported, but most ports are known only from the Middle Ages. A quay at Berkeley Pill, for example, would have been protected by the castle. Boats put in to a basin at Frampton Pill that was still used for landing coal in the 18th century, and there was a bridge across the pill by 1584.[2] On the opposite bank, a quay on Grange Pill was part of Woolaston Grange, owned by Tintern Abbey, and was built in the 12th century, initially of timber. River and sea craft docked there, and fish, timber, stone and livestock were probably traded from the quay. A mile upstream, the Cone Pill quay was established by the late 13th century and used by naval frigates as late as 1646; esparto grass was imported to Cone Pill in the late 19th century for a paper mill. The quay at Grange Pill did not last so long, becoming a victim of riverbank erosion; it had been abandoned before its probable destruction in the storm and flood of 1607 that inundated the south Wales and Somerset coasts.[3] Lydney Pill had shipyards and wharfage near the parish church by the 13th century.[4] Newnham was also an important medieval port serving the Forest of Dean, trading in timber, oak bark for tanning, and iron.

For long-distance trade the chief river ports were Gloucester, Tewkesbury, Upton, Worcester, Bewdley, Bridgnorth, Shrewsbury and Pool Quay. The place name 'lode' refers to an embarkation point, or a road leading to it, and describes either a ferry crossing or a wharf. In medieval Shrewsbury there were quays at Yrkeslode, Bulger Lode, Chadlode, Cord Lode, Frerelode (or St Mary's Water Lode) and Cripple Lode.[5] The term was also current into the 19th century; at Bridgnorth, Foster's Load, Skinner's Load and Friar's Load were all flights of steps from which vessels were unloaded. Other examples include Loadcroft wharf at Coalbrookdale and Load Street in Bewdley. St Mary de Lode church was close to the earlier medieval quayside at Gloucester. Gloucester has unfortunately lost this early quay, which was on the branch of the Severn that dried up during the Middle Ages. The new Common Quay, below the confluence of the two (medieval) Severn streams, was in existence by 1364 and continued to serve commercial vessels until the 1960s.[6] The one medieval town that owes its existence specifically to the river trade, as opposed to beginning as a defensive burh or growing up by a church or bridge, is Bewdley, which had emerged as a river port by the early 14th century, perhaps because it was a natural transhipment point. Upstream from here smaller vessels were needed to sail the shallower waters.[7]

A view of the busy riverside at Stourport in the early 19th century

The rise of Bewdley was evidently resented in Worcester, where in the 14th century a dispute arose that provides the earliest documentary evidence that the new port had become established. In 1308 two Bewdley men, Ralph de Bewdley and Adam de la Halle, complained that their cargoes had been seized and they themselves had been imprisoned at Worcester. Disputes like this frequently arose between the river ports on account of the fierce competition for trade. Illegal tolls remained a problem for much of the later Middle Ages, as shown by an ineffective Act of 1430 designed to prevent toll gathering at Worcester. Bristol men also complained in 1464 of dues, including payment in wine, exacted on vessels being hauled upstream. Worcester gained a partial victory when it established the right to exact dues from vessels that tied up on its quays, which in practice meant that under Worcester Bridge watermen ran the gauntlet of blandishments to stop and tie up. In extreme cases rocks and other missiles were thrown at them. Bewdley men were not always innocent, however. The Bewdley watermen were well organised at an early date and tried to prevent non-local vessels passing through the town. In 1411 'on the eve of St Michael last past, lying in wait near Bewdley with great force and arms they had seized upon a great drag or flote going to Gloucester, and made the masters of it cut in pieces the said flote in the said river, or otherwise they would cut off their heads'.[8]

An orderly river trade was vital to its prosperity, and despite the evidence of disputes it would be wrong to conclude that the trade was entirely dysfunctional. Even as late as the 16th century it appears that downstream trade consisted mainly of raw materials like wool, leather, skins, coal and timber, while upstream traffic was in manufactured goods, notably wine, soap, iron, pepper and exotic fruits like oranges and raisins. This may reflect a trend that went back further into the early medieval period.[9]

The 19th-century quay at Bridgnorth retains the steps, or 'lodes', down to the waterline.

From the 17th century there were changes as upstream traffic reflected the greater reach of Bristol as a trading port. The Severn drew in trade from a wide hinterland. The Warwickshire Avon was navigable to Stratford, the Wye to Hereford, the Teme to Ludlow (although Powick Bridge prevented any through-navigation into the Severn), while short stretches of the Tern and Vyrnwy stimulated riverside industries on those rivers. Attempts made in the 17th century by Andrew Yarranton to improve the Salwarpe and Stour river navigations were unsuccessful, however. Severn river ports had access to the coast of south Wales and south-west England, but the most significant trading destination was Bristol. Trade with London was also lucrative for the Severn region, whether or not goods were transhipped at Bristol. By the 1740s a 'land bridge' allowed goods to be carried on a reliable road between John Jones' wharf at Gloucester and Richard Ainge's warehouses at Lechlade on the Thames.[10]

Manufactured goods like iron pots, nails and earthenware were sent downstream, and raw materials like iron ore and semi-finished iron for the Midlands manufacturing trade were sent upstream from the many ports such as Cone Pill and Lydney Pill serving the Forest of Dean. With increasing efficiency, by the end of the 17th century, goods from Manchester and Staffordshire were brought by road to Shrewsbury, then Bridgnorth and Bewdley, for transportation down the river. Sir Richard Whitworth, writing in 1766, reported that 'large quantities of pot-ware from Burslem are conveyed

Trows unloading at Gloucester Quay in 1858, an oil painting by Edmund John Niemann.
(© Gloucester City Council)

on horses' backs to Bridgnorth and Bewdley and thence sent to Bristol for exportation. I should not forget the number of packhorses, about one hundred and fifty, go weekly with woollen cloth and various other kinds of merchandise from Manchester through Stafford to Bewdley and Bridgnorth for exportation, computed yearly at three hundred and twelve tons'.[11]

Bulk goods included coal and charcoal, pig iron or semi-finished iron, timber for shipbuilders, planks for coopers, oak bark for the tanning industries, and wool for export. The Shrewsbury Draper's Guild marketed wool from mid Wales, which was sold under the misleading name 'cottons'. Most of these bulk goods were traded downriver.

Among the exotic imports that found their way to the Severnside towns via Bristol was tobacco. In 1689, for example, Samuel Gough's trow the *Samuel* left Bristol with a cargo including three baskets of Spanish wine, one barrel and eight bags of tobacco that weighed 12,637 lbs.[12] Tobacco had become popular by the late 17th century – in 1699 over 350 tons of tobacco left Bristol on Severn trows. Imported fruit was also sought after. Worcester consumed 9,000 boxes of oranges and lemons in 1691, imported by barges and trows and distributed via street vendors. Mineral water from the spa at Bath and Hotwells in Bristol were sent upstream in the early 18th century.[13] Preserved foodstuffs were popular. A list of foodstuffs brought upriver from Bristol sounds like the ingredients of a Christmas pudding: currants, raisins, figs, prunes, walnuts, ginger, sugar, molasses, treacle, sherry, rum and brandy. Although the river was a significant food supply in its own right, there was a large market for preserved fish, mainly herrings caught in coastal waters and salt cod from Newfoundland.

Records of journeys made in the 17th century recorded in the Gloucester Port Books suggest that most carriers sailed with mixed cargoes. John Farley of Shrewsbury sent his trow the *John* downriver in 1691, and the vessel left Gloucester carrying 200 crates of earthenware, 13 packs of Manchester wares, 4 hogsheads and 2 barrels of salt [from Cheshire], 3 packs of linen cloth, 2 trusses of serge, 7 tons of cheese and 36 bundles of calfskins.[14] In 1699 the *John and Mary*, owned by John Beale of Bewdley, embarked for Bristol with '20 tuns of iron and iron wares, 4 tun pott clay, 12 packs and fodges of Kitterminster stuffs, 3 trusses serge, 60 reame paper, 2 packs thread, 1 tun timber stuffs'. On its return journey three days later it left Bristol with '200 shott, 4 bundle rags, 2 pipes olive oil, 2 tuns rape oil, 4 tuns grocery, 4 barrells pitch, 1 runlett oyle, 3 baskets Spanish wine, 22 hogsheads tobacco weighing 9703 lbs'.[15]

Before the industrial revolution, agricultural produce was the major export from Shropshire. There were rich dairy farms in north Shropshire and Cheshire, and cheese, the least perishable of dairy produce, was shipped in large quantities. In 1713 the *Prosperity* shipped 230 tons of cheese in 17 voyages from Shrewsbury.[16] Bacon, the least perishable form of meat, and grain and fodder crops like peas and beans were also traded downriver, while hops and cider often came upriver. Timber and building stones from Shropshire and Montgomeryshire were among the earliest bulk goods to be transported by river and remained so into the 19th century. Bark for the tanning industry and charcoal for the iron industry were also important cargoes. Coal was shipped from the Ironbridge Gorge to the Worcestershire and Gloucestershire towns from before 1600,

A Severn trow with top sail makes its way upstream from Gloucester,
without the aid of bow haulers.

A barge makes its way upstream in the tidal stretch of the river.

allowing it gradually to replace wood as the principal domestic fuel. For obvious reasons, it was not shipped in mixed cargoes but in coal boats. By 1758 'upwards of 100,000 tons of coal are annually shipped from the collieries about Broseley and Madeley to the towns situate on its banks'.[17] Coal, iron and, later on, bricks continued to be staple goods on the river until the decline of navigation in the mid 19th century. Iron in semi-finished forms continued to be traded up and down river from the Forest of Dean, where it was smelted into pig iron, to Shropshire forges, where it was converted into malleable bar iron, and thence to Bewdley or Stourport for distribution to small Black Country forges that manufactured finished products. By the mid 18th century there was also a large trade in imported pig iron for the Midland forges. In 1752 Reinhold Angerstein estimated that 2,000 tons of imported iron were carried upstream every year, and while in Shrewsbury he saw several vessels carrying charcoal downriver, all headed for the Midland forges and the port of Bewdley.[18] Exports from the Lower Severn ports were different, concentrating on grain and other foodstuffs, and timber and iron from the Forest of Dean.

Trows were spoken of as early as the 15th century but as late as the 16th century they had a capacity of only 12-18 tons burden. Size of trows steadily increased from the 17th to the 19th century, up to 90 tons. Trow is a word often used loosely to describe vessels on the Severn, but it referred to a specific type of vessel in a set. 'Sets' of vessels were operated by the main carriers on the Severn, and comprised trows, barges and boats, or 'cock boats', in descending order of size. Operating a set allowed the flexibility necessary to keep trade moving at times of low water, the smaller boats being able to navigate shallower waters. Even as early as the 16th century Samuel Blacknedge of Worcester had four vessels worth £32, while Arnold Beane had six – the *Ragged Staff*, the *Old Speedwell*, the *Spy*, the *Luke*, the *Butterbox* or *Swallow*, and the *Black Pear* – worth a total of £17.[19]

George Perry, writing in 1758, described a trow as being about 80 feet (24.4 metres) long and up to 20 feet (6 metres) wide. It had main and top masts up to 80 feet (24.4 metres) high, set slightly forward of mid-ships, and some trows also had mizzen masts, all with large square white sails. Masts could be lowered to allow them to pass under bridges. The crew had covered cabins but the merchandise was in open holds, protected from the rain by oiled skins or tarpaulins. Trows had a shallow draught, which enabled them to avoid running aground on the river's fords and sandbanks. They did not have keels; a keel was not needed in the river and would have been an impediment in shallow waters. Below Gloucester draught boards were let down to act as temporary keels, otherwise it would have been impossible to sail in estuarine and coastal waters. In any case, trows were unstable away from the river, where the shallow draught became a liability. They were vulnerable to capsizing in stormy weather and if they ran into a hidden sandbank were liable to turn broadside and roll. Owner Harris of Droitwich lost a trow coming out of the Avon from Bristol in 1829. Three years later his trow *Hope* struck a sandbank seven miles below Gloucester and turned over. Its cargo of timber was recovered, but the remainder of its cargo of groceries and leather, worth £100, was lost. It was his third loss in three years. Owner Barnett lost his trow on the journey to Bristol in 1836.[20] William Harrison of Newnham drowned when his trow was overset by the tide in 1753, and in 1767 and 1768 Bewdley and Worcester trows were lost in gales off Gatcombe.[21]

Barges were smaller, from 20-50 tons burden, and most of them were probably built for river navigation only. George Perry described them as being 40-60 feet (12.2-18.3 metres) long, single-masted with a square sail. Boats were smaller still, but the classification is only a general one. George Perry also mentioned frigates (the general meaning of which is a diminutive vessel), which may have been an alternative name for a boat. The vessels that sailed on the Severn were not strictly classified, and nor were they built to standard designs.

For the journey downstream the trows and barges relied on the current, and could hoist their sails if the winds were favourable. When the level of the river rose after heavy rainfall, known as a 'fresh', 'freshet' or 'flash', passage downriver was greatly speeded up, although more hazardous as it was more difficult to navigate the shallows and avoid vessels travelling upstream. On a fresh it was reckoned in 1786 that 60-80 vessels could leave Shrewsbury one morning and be in Gloucester the following morning.[22] Sails were also used on the upstream journey, but if the wind was not strong enough, the vessels were pulled by teams of bow haulers. After 1810, horses pulled most of the vessels upstream but bow haulers survived in reduced numbers for as long as the Severn above Bewdley was a river of commercial navigation.

The nearer the source the smaller the river, and the more chance that there would not be enough water for the boats to navigate it. In November 1725 James Baker complained that he could not send a consignment from the Pool Quay lead smelting works because of a lack of 'bargewaters'. Worse, from November 1740 to the autumn

A barge lowers its mast to pass beneath Westgate Bridge in Gloucester, drawn by Joseph Farington.
(© Gloucester City Council)

of the following year the water was so low that no vessels could sail from Pool Quay. Below Shrewsbury periods of idleness were fewer, but traffic was stopped in winter by ice, for example in the well-documented flood years of 1795, 1830 and 1854, and also in 1684 and 1695, when frost fairs were recorded in London. At times of low water a barge could sail with a reduced cargo, but in the 1850s, when the navigation was in serious decline, John Randall claimed that 'there are often three, four or five months in the year when barges cannot navigate the river with a freight equal to defray the expenses of working them'.[23] Watermen carried oars and shafts to help with steering, and also to help lift the barges from the fords they grounded upon. Above Stourport the fords are still evident, although the level of the river is kept artificially high by managing the outflow at Llyn Clywedog. Below Stourport, before the dredging of the river in the 1840s, there were 24 fords in the 20 miles to Upton, and a further seven in the 19 miles to Gloucester.

There were many losses of trows and barges on the inland river. Thomas Beard recorded the loss of four vessels at Eaves' Mount in Shropshire in 18 months of 1831-2. Benjamin Doughty's barge was 'broke through the middle', Adam Oakes' barge ran aground, 'drifted to the burst above Bowneys and filled full of water', and Widow Edwards' barge, loaded with pig iron, also ran aground, took on water and 'broke thro the middle and the men were obliged to swim ashore out of her or lose their lives'.[24]

The men who possessed and managed the carriers on the Severn were styled 'owners', such as Owner Harris mentioned above. Occasionally women were responsible for managing a business, usually after they had been widowed. Although widows regularly managed all kinds of businesses they more frequently took to the river trade than, say, the iron trade. That there were so many widows simply reflected the dangerous nature of working on the river. Between 1690 and 1770 three heads of the Asbury family of Bridgnorth carriers were predeceased by their children.[25] In cases where an owner lost his life the widow stepped in until the son was old enough to take on the business in his own right.

By the 18th century owners transported goods between customers, but at an earlier date they were also wholesalers, and wealthy with it. Roger Brooke of Worcester left in his will over £300 worth of property in the 16th century. Another contemporary Worcester boat owner was Arnold Beane, who on his death still owed money to his suppliers, who were coal miners from Madeley and Bridgnorth. It seems that he purchased the coal in south Shropshire and sold it in Worcester and perhaps Bewdley. Likewise the groceries brought back to the Middle and Upper Severn from Bristol had been purchased wholesale by the boat owners, who sold them to the local grocers. Thomas Jackson was described in 1701 as a trowman and cheese factor, showing his ownership of one of the staple Severn cargoes, but by the 18th century it was more usual for carriers to combine work on the river with the ownership of riverside inns and public houses.[26]

The role of carriers in the Severn trade extended beyond simple haulage; they were the arbiters of the goods that were shipped. When the Botfield family established an ironworks at Old Park in the East Shropshire coalfield in 1790 it was obliged to use established carriers to deliver iron to customers. It was already a 'long established rule' that contracts to supply iron specified a place of delivery – not its ultimate destination, but one of the wharves on the river at Coalport, Stourport, Gloucester or Bristol. Iron was weighed at its delivery point on the river and an invoice drawn up on that basis. If iron had been lost in transit, as it frequently was, it was the supplier, not the carrier, who was out of pocket. The carriers were therefore in a pivotal position between supplier and customer, and arguments between ironmasters and carriers were inevitable. The Botfields hired an agent, George Pugh, to ensure that the iron was weighed correctly. By the 1820s the main carriers in the iron trade were William and George Devey of Bewdley, Danks & Co, J.G. Amies, Matthew Heath, Belsham & Co and York and Worthington of Stourport, and Thomas Nevett of Bridgnorth. In 1827 William Botfield abruptly terminated his contract with Thomas Nevett, who was blamed for mixing up his cargoes on the wharf at Coalport, but for a replacement he could only turn to another carrier from the same hereditary fraternity of river men, George and William Devey.[27]

The river was navigated by expert watermen who knew the currents and shallows of the river. The crew were usually described as watermen or occasionally mariners. They wore distinctive flannel frocks; a putrid corpse pulled from the river at Tewkesbury in 1822 was identifiable as a waterman by his dress,[28] and the waterman who robbed a woman at Worcester in 1764 might have achieved greater anonymity if he had remembered to remove his frock.[29] As a tribe, watermen had a generally low reputation, and sometimes earned it. The 1830s diary of Thomas Beard, a Benthall waterman, gives a pungent impression of watermen's unruly ways with its sad chronicles of hard drinking

Edward Burney's view of the Iron Bridge, published in 1789, shows a team of bow haulers
pulling a trow.
(© Ironbridge Gorge Museum Trust)

and domestic violence. There are picaresque tales of watermen dining off the rabbits, wildfowl and game that could be poached en route. 'The true waterman is primitive in his habits', wrote John Randall in 1858, 'a waiter upon Providence, who will stand for months looking into the stream, patiently waiting for a fresh to carry him down. You may tell him by his appearance. He has a broad back, legs which a flunky may be jealous of, swelled like skittle pins at the calves, he is a hard drinker, a heavy swearer, given to gasconade and good living'.[30] The latter aspect of his character found ample opportunity to fulfil itself in a trade that took men away from their home towns. At night, ship keepers kept watch on vessels and their cargoes while the rest of the crew patronised the riverside inns and brothels. It was a small community. If Thomas Beard in Jackfield knew that 'Teddy Lloyd had his pockett picked by the whores at Gloster' it was probably common knowledge. Likewise that 'John Transom was catch'd in bed with another man's wife at Worcester by the whoman's husband and the man stuck a pickel in his backside which caused him to run away without his clothes'.[31] Heavy drinking was also a prelude to another form of misadventure. Thomas Beard chronicled the drowning of Job Speath, Joseph Madelin, John Lister, Edward Harriss, John Beard, John Malpas and Thomas Davy in his diary. The crews of four Severn trows, belonging to Devey, Belsham, Harris and Barnett, took advantage of the riots in Bristol in 1831 to rob the Custom House, but could think of nowhere to hide their booty but aboard their own

This 19th-century copy of Lord Burleigh's map of Elizabethan Shrewsbury shows four bow haulers pulling a barge upriver. In the background are the ruins of the Dominican friary on the river bank and St Mary's Water Lane, leading up from the river through an arch, which remains standing. (© Shropshire Archives)

vessels, where it was quickly discovered. The crews were taken into custody, leaving their trows unusually stricken.[32]

Neither were bow haulers much esteemed beyond the riverside communities, although they at least could excuse their drinking habits as necessary refreshment. In Bewdley they were hired by trowmen in the Mug-House Inn on Coles Quay. Bow haulers were the principal motive power for upstream journeys, the sails being of only supplementary use. Lord Burghley's map of Shrewsbury of 1575 shows four bow haulers. According to Celia Fiennes, who visited Worcester in 1698, a trow was pulled by six to eight bow haulers.[33] Both might be accurate, reflecting the increasing size of vessels on the river over time. A team of bow haulers probably only worked on a specific section of the river, allowing them to take a boat back home at the end of the day. Although the Quaker ironmaster Richard Reynolds decried bow hauling as 'the means of harbouring and collecting persons of bad character', bow haulers efficiently combined to protest at the proposed bill for a Severn towpath in 1786. Bow haulers resisted the introduction of horse-drawn trows using the towpaths and responded by obstructing them, often in person and en masse. In 1832 a troop of Scots Greys were called in to restore order in Worcestershire after bow haulers, believing that the Acts establishing the towpaths had expired, set about blocking the paths and preventing watermen from shackling their horses. Nine watermen were arrested.[34]

Improvements in the navigation were a sign that its viability was under threat so that it needed to be improved to compete with rival forms of transport. Watermen

A view of the Severn at Bridgnorth in the late 18th century. The small boat on the right is probably one of the wherries that offered a regular service to the river ports between Shrewsbury and Gloucester.

successfully lobbied against a bill presented to Parliament in 1786, according to which improvement of the Severn would have seen the construction of 16 locks between Diglis and Coalbrookdale. Bargemen were against it, rightly fearing that locks signalled tolls and the bureaucratic control of the river. They preferred a free river in a state of nature, even though it spelled the long-term decline of the navigation because of its unreliability compared with canals and, later, railways. One improvement scheme that did come to fruition was the construction of the towpath from Bewdley to Shrewsbury, which allowed vessels to be hauled more cheaply and preserved the independent spirit of the watermen. Charges were levied on the horses, not the vessels they towed.

The other form of traffic that flourished in the 18th century was the transport of passengers. 'In the morning, I went on board the wherry [at Shrewsbury], breakfasted at Atcham, dined at Bridgenorth, drunk tea at Bewdley, and at 9 at night arrived at Worcester.' So began the journey of William Owen in 1750, as he left his native Montgomeryshire for a career at sea.[35] According to the *Gentleman's Magazine* the river offered good value for money: 'safe and commodious stage wherries constantly ply … from Shrewsbury and Worcester to Gloucester, and back again, wherein a whole family may be carried, with bag and baggage, sixty or seventy miles for a trifling fee'.[36] In 1734 Thomas Pococke boarded a wherry in Shrewsbury to travel by river to Worcester and then continue to London by stage-coach.[37]. He found it an agreeable way to travel – 'fine meadows on each side the river, and low hills covered with wood'. Wherries invariably set off from public houses – the Marquis of Granby in Gloucester, the Green Dragon in

Coles Quay in Bewdley, now known as Severnside North, retains the character of the 18th-century river port, with its quay, brick houses mostly of the 18th century and two older timber-framed houses.

Bewdley and Bridgnorth, and the Britannia or Wherry in Shrewsbury. A rowing boat of shallow draft, a wherry could carry passengers and small packages.

The heyday of the wherry was the latter half of the 18th century, before the significant improvement of the road network and of course before the railways. In 1773 John Price of the Wherry Inn in Shrewsbury offered a service to Gloucester that involved an overnight stay at the Green Dragon inn in Worcester, arriving at the Mermaid in Gloucester the following day. The upstream journey was even longer, leaving on Wednesday afternoons, requiring overnight stays in Worcester and Bridgnorth, and arriving in Shrewsbury on Friday afternoon.[38] By 1803 the service from Shrewsbury had ceased – Shrewsbury's Wherry Inn had become the Old Wherry Inn by 1828 – but it continued to operate lower down the river until the middle of the 19th century. A wherry service began from the Sea Horse Inn at Bewdley in 1783, travelling to Stourport and Worcester on Mondays, Wednesdays and Fridays, and making the return journey on Tuesdays, Thursdays and Saturdays. Richard Wintle of Newnham travelled up from Worcester in 1783 with a consignment of tobacco: 'I got all the tobacco put on board a Wherry for Bewdley wch I accompanied leaving Worcester between 11 and 12 o'clock in the forenoon and arrived at Bewdley about seven in the evening, landed the goods and got it into Mr Kenrick's Warehouse where we weighed the whole of it the same night. After we had done I returned to the Black Boy Inn [on the hill above the town] where I slept.'[39] John Crump sailed twice weekly from Bewdley to Worcester in 1840. The last wherries were the market boats that carried passengers and goods to the regional markets, like the Friday night wherry that left Bewdley for Worcester's Saturday market as late as 1850.[40]

The Severn navigation was at its peak in roughly the same period – the 18th and early 19th century – spurred on by the growth of industry and commerce, and by the canals

The canal-river interchange at Stourport

Coalport Warehouse was erected across the terminus of the Shropshire Canal,
just upstream of Coalport Bridge. A barge is moored upstream, and next to it is a canal
narrowboat, a regular sight in the latter days of the navigation.
(© Ironbridge Gorge Museum Trust)

that interlinked with the river. The Staffordshire and Worcestershire Canal opened in 1770 and linked the Severn with the Midlands manufacturing district. Interchange basins were constructed beside the river at a new site near the mouth of the Stour river, around which the canal town of Stourport developed. With the rise of Stourport began the decline of Bewdley as a river port. It was long a local myth that the townspeople refused to have the canal interchange at Bewdley, to their lasting regret, but in fact topography prevented the canal from running this far upstream. Bewdley's decline has had the happy consequence that the town retains the atmosphere of an 18th-century river port, with Georgian buildings characterising the long river front of Severnside and Coles Quay. 1771 saw the opening of the Droitwich Canal, by which means salt was transported to the river at Hawford. Another canal settlement was created at Coalport, near the downstream end of the Ironbridge Gorge, site of the interchange between the Shropshire Canal and the river. Completed in 1793, the canal gave the coal and iron industries of the East Shropshire coalfield access to the Severn. Other canals were less significant. The Worcester and Birmingham Canal opened in 1815 and joined the river at Diglis below the city. The Herefordshire and Gloucestershire Canal did not reach Hereford until 1845, by which time the opening of the Gloucester and Sharpness Canal had taken away the trade from the hazardous Severn estuary, although locks and weirs as far upstream as Stourport had made the lower navigation more reliable. The upper navigation beyond Stourport was, however, in terminal decline, faced with competition from the railways.

The decline of the Upper Severn navigation was accelerated by the improvements to the Lower Severn made in the mid 19th century. Another factor was the comparatively small size of Severn trows and barges and the difficulty for seagoing vessels of piloting the tidal stretch of the river to Gloucester. However, Gloucester survived while other river ports declined in the 19th century by admitting sea-going vessels. There had always been long-distance sailing from the Lower Severn ports; Tewkesbury traded with Irish ports in the 17th century. The number of seagoing vessels at Gloucester and the Lower Severn was to increase, however. As early as 1764 Hawkins Pyrke & Co, operating out of Newnham, ran the *Severn*, a brig (i.e. brigantine, a two-masted coastal vessel) that traded directly with London.[41] Trade from Gloucester shifted away from the river when the new Gloucester and Sharpness Canal was completed in 1827 from Gloucester to the estuary at Sharpness. Traffic became focused upon the new Gloucester Docks rather than the old riverside quay. Sloops, schooners, barques and brigs became common sights in the estuary, but in time they too were gradually superseded, by steamers and motor vessels. Seagoing vessels could now import grain and timber to Gloucester at all times of the year, irrespective of the tides. Goods could be transhipped at Gloucester and continue their journey upstream on the river, although by the 1850s rail transport was another option, and the opening in 1862 of the Severn Valley Railway, which followed the river from Bewdley to Shrewsbury, borrowed the topography of the river to create a more convenient and reliable mode of transport. By the 1870s the seagoing vessels had become too large even for the canal and a new dock was built at Sharpness.

Gloucester Docks stands at the head of the Gloucester and Sharpness Canal, where there was an interchange with the river. This view is from the Barge Arm and shows warehouses of the 1830s.

Cargo was transported upriver long after it ceased to be traded downriver. Inward cargoes included the traditional metals and foodstuffs, but now timber was imported upriver, whereas it was once an important downriver cargo. Steam tugs towed long boats upriver to the canal interchanges at Worcester and Stourport. Powered and unpowered barges up to 90 feet (27.4 metres) long, and capable of carrying 130-150 tons, were hauled by tugs from Avonmouth and came upriver as far as Diglis Wharf at Worcester and Nelson Wharf near Stourport. Grain barges served flour mills in Gloucester and Healings Mill in Tewkesbury. In 1938 the steamer SS *Argentina* ran aground off Sharpness laden with maize from South America. Barges operated until the late 1960s, when they could no longer compete with road transport, and one of them, *Sabrina 5*, is moored in the Barge Arm at Gloucester Docks, next to the National Waterways Museum. Tanker barges carrying petroleum products continued to Stourport until the 1960s, until pipelines had superseded the need to transport goods on the river. These were unwieldy vessels. One struck and fatally damaged the Haw Bridge in 1958 and another struck the Severn Railway Bridge in 1960.

River transport of course required boat-building. Coracles are probably the most ancient of all the known craft of the river. Small enough to be carried on a man's back, they were simple bowl-shaped craft constructed of wooden laths and a hide of animal skin or, latterly, calico. Giraldus Cambrensis mentioned them in 1190; at that time they were used for angling and river crossing, much as they were down to the mid 20th century. On the Severn the coracle was used on the middle and upper reaches of the river. Ironbridge coracles differed slightly from Shrewsbury coracles, which in turn were different from Welshpool coracles.[42] Even in Ironbridge Eustace Rogers claimed that he could distinguish a coracle made by himself from one made by Jackie Williams of Coalport.[43] Coracles were as individual as the men who made them, and were made with materials to hand. An Italian visitor noted on visiting Ironbridge in 1787 that coracles were constructed of flexible willow boughs covered with horse hide. By the 20th century Eustace Rogers was using unbleached calico sealed with tar and pitch.[44] The coracle man, unlike the watermen, developed an intimate relationship with only a small stretch of river, and had little or no knowledge of the rest of it.

The use of coracles declined rapidly in the 20th century. David Ruscoe, aged 73 in

Tommy Rogers at Ironbridge, with coracle strapped to his back. A coracle was always a portable vessel.
(© Ironbridge Gorge Museum Trust)

1936, described making them in Montgomeryshire with ash laths, but said that this was a modern method. In his youth 'the frameworks of coracles I saw were made out of strong briars pulled from hedgerows'.[45] The Rogers family of Ironbridge were the last traditional coracle makers (as opposed to the thriving revival of coracle making and use at Ironbridge and elsewhere). In their minor celebrity status the essence of the coracle men was distilled into this one family. Eustace Rogers came to represent the universal coracle man, although his real significance in history is that he was fundamentally a local man, and distinctive because of it. His father Harry Rogers (1887-1967) enjoyed an intimate relationship with a two-mile stretch of river. Having been a cabin boy on Severn barges from the age of eight he was adept at all the river crafts. It was said that he could lasso a floating tree trunk like a cowboy reining in a buffalo. During the floods of 1947 he was out in his coracle, skilfully manoeuvring around animal carcasses on the fast-flowing river, rescuing homeowners stranded in their bedrooms. His son Eustace Rogers (1914-2002) became a tourist attraction, aided by the rapidly growing heritage industry of the Ironbridge Gorge, sought out by royalty and an international coterie of journalists. Rogers obliged them by building coracles using animal skins, trying to replicate the construction of the craft as they had been made in prehistoric times, and his coracles were shipped as far afield as Bremen, Haifa in Israel, Australia and New Zealand.[46]

The next oldest vessels were probably the floats or flottes. These were rafts used to transport bulk items like timber and were undoubtedly the most dangerous way to navigate a river. Water was the ideal way of transporting large timbers and the trade was characteristic of many rivers in the Middle Ages. Timber from Montgomeryshire

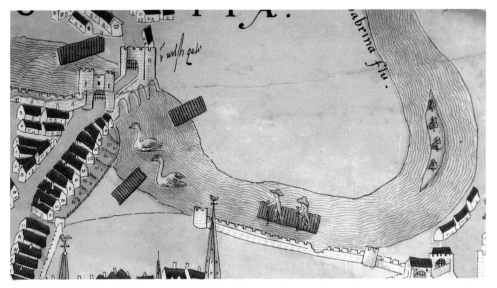

A raft, or float, of timber travelling downstream is shown on a 19th-century copy of Lord Burleigh's map of Shrewsbury. The raft is approaching the most dangerous part of its journey, where it had to shoot the bridge. Such rafts had a poor safety record even by medieval standards. (© Shropshire Archives)

and the Wyre Forest was floated downriver to build ships for merchant vessels and the Royal Navy, and was of course used in the building trade. The most hazardous aspect of a river journey was shooting the bridges, and there were many accidents. By way of compensation, in 1285 the residents of Montford were given leave to charge a toll for floats passing under the bridge, and to levy a fine if they hit and damaged the bridge.[47]

Most of the vessels that plied the Severn were built on the Severn. Boatyards once lined the river, but the general trend over time was for boat building to become concentrated in fewer areas. Specific references to boat and ship building on the Severn appear in the 16th century and later. For example, the repair of Tewkesbury town quay in the 16th century incorporated two slipways, and trows were under construction there and at Lydney Pill in the 17th century.[48] Naval vessels were built in the lower river and estuary ports in the 17th century. Daniel Furzer, master-shipwright at Lydney Pill, built the 306-ton, 22-gun frigate *Forester*, launched in 1657, and the 620-ton, 54-gun frigate *Princess*, launched in 1660. Accumulation of sandbanks soon became a problem for navigation by sea-going vessels, and after building another 620-ton frigate, *St David*, this time with 64 guns, at Cone Pill Furzer moved to Portsmouth and construction of naval vessels on the Severn appears to have ceased. Merchant vessels continued to be built and there was a mini-boom in coastal-vessel construction in the late 18th century at Newnham, Gatcombe and Awre, while Lydney's shipyard remained in business until the late 19th century.[49]

Other Severn boatyards were large enough only for the construction of river craft. John Bowen's panorama of Shrewsbury in the 1730s shows a boat yard near the Welsh Bridge, while the Harwood family were boat builders and operated the ferry from the

The Coalbrookdale Company built a castellated warehouse at Loadcroft Wharf in 1834, which expressed confidence in the future of the Severn Navigation at a period when it was already in decline.

Bishop Percy's house at the foot of the Cartway, leading to the quayside at Bridgnorth, was built in 1580 for Richard Forster, a bargemaster, and shows how the watermen made handsome profits when they were also the owners and distributors of their cargo.

Boathouse Inn. Gother's Yard at Benthall in the Ironbridge Gorge survived until the 1880s, while the Beard family of Jackfield were still building craft in the 1890s, probably only pleasure craft. In the late 18th century innovative local ironmasters sought new uses for iron, and this included in 1787 the launching of an iron barge, the *Trial*, constructed at John Wilkinson's Willey ironworks near Broseley. This was, as far as is known, the first iron-hulled vessel. The prototype was not deemed an unreserved success, but the idea was. By 1820 the Onions family of Broseley operated four such barges.[50]

The trows and barges have long since gone, with the odd exception. A trow built in Benthall in 1807 survived until 1938 when it sank in the Bristol Channel while under tow, a smaller trow built at Chepstow in 1894 was restored in the 1980s. But if the vessels have gone, along the river the quays, warehouses and inns have often survived. The Powis Arms, now a house, defines the limit of the navigation at Pool Quay, although it is set back from the river. In Shrewsbury, St Mary's Water Lane, and the medieval arch that opens on the quayside, is the medieval Frerelode, beside which is the Union Warehouse of the 1820s, now converted to flats. In Ironbridge, the Coalbrookdale Company's castellated warehouse of 1834 dominates the riverbank, and set further back are the 18th-century inns and warehouses from the heyday of the navigation. Bridgnorth, the relative importance of which declined just as that of Ironbridge was reaching its peak, still retains some of the character of a river port, especially in its steep Cartway from the high town to the river, on which many watermen lived, and where the fine timber-framed Bishop Percy's House, built by the bargemaster Richard Forster, can still be seen. The waterfront retains its Town Quay below the bridge, with steps, or lodes, descending to the waterline. Bewdley is the best preserved of the river ports, on both the town and Wribbenhall banks, where quays, houses, inns and the Mug House still line the river. In Worcester, where the river is dominated by the cathedral, there are still warehouses, now converted to flats and restaurants. But for a thorough makeover it is Gloucester Docks that reminds us that regeneration is more than gentrification and economic opportunity, but that on the Severn we are always living with the past.

❧ 11 ❧
Fish

The Severn is a great natural resource, 'known to teem with life and to furnish a supply of agreeable and nourishing food'. But whereas there has always been a powerful lobby on behalf of agriculture, 'how seldom do we hear of our fisheries,' noted the *Shrewsbury Chronicle* in 1828, 'in reference to the capital occupied, the population employed, or the supply to our wants and comforts which they yield'.[1] It remains true. Nothing on the Severn has been abused and squandered more than its abundant gift of fish.

The tidal river and estuary once hosted a multitude of species, a good impression of which is given in the list of fish caught in the Severn Estuary in the early 17th century, compiled by John Smyth, steward to the Berkeley family. Smyth lists 57 species, including herrings, mackerel, prawns and swordfish, as well as common species like conger eels, salmon and sea trout. The lists also includes more exotic sounding species, such as jubetas (young whales), thornpoles, sand flooke, huswife, sun-fish and sea tad – names from the language of a lost culture. In 1819 a 60-foot (18.3 metres) whale was caught at Frampton.[2] Upriver there were also numerous species of freshwater fish, many of them listed by Thomas Telford as found in the Shropshire Severn in the late 18th century: salmon, trout, flounders, pike (admittedly rare except in Montgomeryshire), grayling, perch, eels, shad, bleak, gudgeons, chub, roach, dace, carp, ruff, bullhead, loach, stickleback, as well as lampreys and lamperns.[3] Even making allowances for shifting habitats and the changing economy of fishing and culinary tastes, it is impossible to escape the fact that the river's natural history has sadly diminished, and with it an interesting culinary heritage.

Salmon, eels and lamprey are the fish most especially associated with the river. The largest fish ever claimed from the river was a sturgeon caught in the weir below Shrewsbury Castle in 1802. It was said to have been either 8 feet six inches or 9 feet (2.6-2.75 metres) long, weighed 192 lb and was full of spawn. The trophy fish was displayed in a small museum in Shrewsbury School, where it was doubtless scrutinised by the school's most illustrious scholar, Charles Darwin.[4]

The salmon may not be the largest but is undoubtedly the aristocrat of Severn fish. Salmon enter fresh water every year to spawn, usually beginning about February, and swim up to the headwaters of the Severn in Wales, to lay their eggs in the hillside streams. The fish seek out gravelly parts of the river, in which they make a channel in which to lay and fertilise their eggs. The salmon are now exhausted and thin, having lost half their body weight; the scales have turned hard while the flesh, if it were eaten, would be grey and tasteless. Salmon barely feed in the river, and they return to the sea at a sluggish pace until they can begin to rebuild their strength in the ocean. The young fish, known as pinks, also have no need to fear human predators, although they are easy prey for eel and pike.

The salmon is a creature of mythology. In Celtic Christian culture salmon were popularly supposed to have swum in holy wells. The fish was a sign of an otherworldly presence, since deities could transform themselves into animals, of which the salmon was one. The point is illustrated in 'How Culhwch won Olwen', one of the stories in the *Mabinogion*. Culhwch seeks the hand of Olwen, but first he must complete a series of tasks that will take him on crazy adventures across Wales from Plynlimon to the Severn Sea. Among them he must find the huntsman Mabon, son of Modron, with whom he must hunt the fearsome boar Twrch Trwyth. Culhwch seeks out his cousin Arthur, who deploys some of his finest warriors to help, but Mabon is difficult to track down. They enlist the help of various creatures that are able to communicate with humans – the Ouzel of Cilgwri, the Stag of Rhedynfre, the Owl of Cwm Cawlwyd, and the Eagle of Gwernabwy, who directs them finally to the Salmon of Llyn Lliw. The Eagle of Gwernabwy had once sought food as far from home as Llyn Lliw: 'When I got there I sank my claws into a salmon, thinking he would be food for me for a long time, and he pulled me down into the depths, so that I barely got away from him. What I did, I and all my kinsmen, was to set upon him and try to destroy him. He sent messengers to me to make peace with me, and he himself came to me, to have fifty tridents taken out of his back.'[5] The salmon knows where to find the divine hunter Mabon: 'With every flood tide I travel up the river until I come to the bend in the wall of Caerloyw [Gloucester]; never before in my life have I found such wickedness as I found there.' Two of Arthur's warriors, Cai and Gwrhyr Gwalstawd Ieithoedd (Gwrhyr Interpreter of Tongues), rode on the salmon's shoulders to Gloucester, where they were able to talk to Mabon son of Modron in his prison. The salmon in this story is not just an imaginary whim. It is as wise as the salmon in Irish literature, in which the salmon come and go between worlds, a characteristic that was surely drawn from observing the mysterious migratory habits of the fish.[6]

The life cycle of the eel is no less incredible than that of the Salmon of Llyn Lliw. The migratory and spawning habits of eels are one of nature's more intractable mysteries. Having reached maturity in the freshwaters of Europe, they return to the Sargasso Sea to spawn in depths of 500 fathoms, and then die. The larvae then float across the Atlantic and congregate in large shoals in the Severn Sea as transparent elvers up to 3 inches (7.5 centimetres) long. The Bore helpfully washes them into the river, where they swim up into the freshwater and make themselves at home in the muddy banks. While they grow they are yellow-bellied, sometimes known as gelps, and when they reach maturity after about seven years they change colour to silver. Eels were caught in the Severn during all stages of their life cycle.

The fish more closely associated with the Severn, and especially Gloucester, than any other river was the lamprey. Lampreys of the Severn grew to about 26 inches (66 centimetres) long and weighed 3-4 pounds. Lamprey swam into the river in early spring, especially the Worcestershire and Gloucestershire stretches, being much less common in Shropshire. They spawned in the fresh water of the Severn and then swam out to sea where they thrived as parasites on other fish such as salmon, cod and haddock. Lamprey are eel-like vertebrates and have neither jaws nor scales (for the latter reason they have never been kosher). Instead they have mouths with long protruding tongues on which there are horny teeth, and instead of gills they have seven breathing holes along the sides. They clamp their large mouths to their victims, rasp off the flesh and then suck the host's blood and bodily fluids, effectively turning their prey inside out.

The lamprey is among several species of fish that spawned in Severn waters until weirs were built on the Lower Severn in the 19th century. All of them were particular about the exact spawning ground. It was once common knowledge that 'although the river Avon, at its mouth near Tewkesbury, exactly resembles the Severn, and there joins it, yet no Salmon, Shad, Lamprey or Lampern, ever mistake their course, or go up the Avon'.[7]

Some of the earliest written records of the Severn concern the taking of fish. The best known aspects of Severn fishing are the catching of migratory fish, the commercial or large-scale fishing of which is at least as old as the earliest written records. Most large-scale Severn fisheries caught their fish in weirs or basket traps, although there were also riverside fishponds, the banks of which can still be seen by the overgrown riverbank at Buildwas Abbey. An alternative, tidal pools, were created by Tintern Abbey at Woolaston in the 13th century.[8] Fisheries on the Severn appear in Anglo-Saxon charters from the 7th century at Aust, and there is reference to a fish weir in a charter of AD 706 for Ombersley. They are mentioned in the 10th century in the laws of Hywel Dda, and probably existed at Tidenham, where Bath Abbey had a large estate with 104 fish weirs by the 11th century. The prior of Bath Abbey laid claim to every other fish caught in the parish, and all of the sturgeon, porpoise, herring and sea-fish, forbidding the selling of fish without his knowledge and consent. Domesday lists 53 fisheries on the Tidenham estate at places like Beachley and Sedbury.[9] In the freshwater section of the river Domesday records at least eight Severn fisheries in Shropshire and six in Worcestershire, which were valued according to their render of eels. Over 40 fish weirs are known to have existed in medieval Shropshire.[10]

The momentum behind the proliferation of fish weirs was provided by the monastic estates, which were in large part responsible for economic growth at the start of the second millennium. Edward the Confessor granted the Deerhurst estate to Westminster Abbey in the 1060s, including its fish weirs. Of 23½ fish weirs in Worcestershire at Domesday (one of the weirs was on the county boundary, presumably), 16 were owned by monasteries.[11] Brewood Priory had a weir at Withlakeswere near Bridgnorth; Great Malvern Priory had a weir at Dowles; Bordesley Abbey was partly endowed with a fishery at Areley Kings near Bewdley; Evesham Abbey's two fisheries at Ombersley were said in Domesday to yield 2,000 eels per annum. The Severn at Worcester was dominated by Worcester Priory, which had fisheries at Grimley, Hallow (granted in 1117), Bevere, Henwick and Timberdene.[12] In 1376-77 76,000 kidells, a form of basket fish trap, were made and laid down on the same weirs. Tewkesbury Abbey had its own weir at 'Stenwere'. Gloucester Abbey dominated the fishing industry near the city; it had weirs at Gloucester, Churcham, Minsterworth and Framilode. The priory of Llanthony Secunda had its own weirs at Gloucester, Hempsted, Elmore, Awre, Ham and Tidenham. St Augustine's Abbey in Bristol owned weirs at Ashleworth and Arlingham.[13]

For obvious reasons, shallow waters or riffles were the preferred location of fish weirs. Freshwater weirs consisted of a wattle fence in one or more V-shaped configurations and supported by piles and braces. Fish were funnelled to the apex, where there was a gate, accessible by catwalk, across which the net was placed.[14] However, large structures in the river were an impediment to those who wanted to navigate its waters freely. As early as the 13th century quarrels broke out over the navigation of the river, in which weirs could impede passage. For this reason, contemporary references to fish weirs are usually connected with the navigation, which may also explain why there are few references to the upper section of the river beyond Pool Quay, where the river was not navigable. The characteristic way around the problem was to incorporate a side channel, known as the gutter (or 'barge gutter' or, at the Coton Hill fish weir in Shrewsbury, 'flash'), which vessels could navigate. The weir was constructed between the bank and an artificial or natural island, or bylet (or eyte, ayot, neyte or naight). River craft could also be a

A fish weir on the upper Severn at Montford, painted by F.W. Seville in 1897
(Courtesy of Shrewsbury Museum and Art Gallery)

danger to fish weirs, as happened in 1839 at Preston near Shrewsbury, when a barge broke through the fence, claiming that the gutter was too shallow to sail through.[15] The barge gutter was also effectively a fish pass, allowing migrating salmon and eels to swim freely upstream. Fish weirs were sometimes part of a larger enterprise, of which meadows with withy beds were particularly important, as dried withies were used for basketwork. Castle fish weir in Gloucester also incorporated a mill and several weir houses, all of which were burned down during the Barons' War in 1264.[16]

Fish weirs declined from the 16th century beyond the tidal limit of the river. Flood damage was not repaired and eventually bylets were washed away, as happened at Bewdley where the weir was disued by the mid 17th century. The last weir, at Preston near Shrewsbury, went out of use after a flood in 1910.

On the tidal river, methods of catching fish that were current in the 20th century were probably adapted from much earlier methods that were in use on the monastic estates. The most common method of catching fish in abundance on their migratory travels was by various forms of basket traps, arranged in rows known as hedges or weirs. Sea-hedges or foreshore weirs were an effective means of catching fish with minimum effort. Basketwork traps made from willow or osier, which will stand immersion in water, are known variously as putts, putchers, grigs, hives and kidells (hence 'kettle of fish').

Use of basket traps was still common into the 20th century, and it is from then that most of our knowledge is derived. Putchers are baskets woven from withy and hazel (and latterly metal frames constructed of galvanised wire and then aluminium) attached in lines to racks across the tidal stretches of the river, in which salmon inadvertently became trapped when the tide was ebbing and they were seeking deeper water. The baskets can be stacked several rows high and, because of the height to which the tide rises, remain submerged at high water. If one basket out of every hundred contained a salmon when the tide ebbed away, that was regarded as a reasonable catch. Larger baskets were known as putts. They were made up of three cone shapes – kipe, butt and foreweel – superimposed on one another, and were designed to catch everything from shrimps to salmon. In the Severn estuary putts would be laid out as many as 120 in a line

Salmon putts at Berkeley at low tide, photographed in 1964 (© Gloucester City Council)

Top left: Herbert Woodward with his putcher weirs at Berkeley, photographed in 1964
Top right: Frank Cadogan with his lave net, photographed at Awre in 1912
Left: Bill Turland with a salmon caught in his lave net at Lydney in the 1930s
(© Gloucester City Council)

which, in combination with the hedge, stretched for three quarters of a mile across the river. However, their use declined rapidly in the 20th century. They were unsuitable in a modern age when the river carried so much rubbish downstream, fishermen lacked the skill and time to make them, and perhaps the economics of fishing made fishing for small fry unprofitable.[17]

Regulation of salmon fishing in the 19th century acknowledges that salmon were over-fished, but also highlights the scale of organised fisheries that existed at that date. Landlords leased their sections of the bank to fishermen, whose weirs occupied the optimum points for construction and access to the putchers. Lord Fitzharding, for example, leased four fish weirs at Sharpness in the 1860s – Venus Rock, Hayward's Rock, Botwell Rock, Bull Rock – with an estimated 1,600 putchers. At Aust and Redwick R.C. Lippincott had seven fisheries – Gravel Weir, Folly Weir, Salmon Weir, Lower Salmon Weir, Upper Salmon Weir and English Lakes – with an estimated 2,140 putchers. 20th-century decline was rapid. By 1970 the Severn River Authority administered only six weirs with just over 4,000 putchers.[18]

Other ways of catching salmon were tailored to the prevailing conditions on different stretches of the river, and were among the traditional methods of catching salmon mentioned by John Smyth in 1605. One of the traditional methods was to catch salmon in lave nets, which are nets attached to a Y-shaped frame made from ash or hazel, although their use has rapidly declined and is now confined to the estuary near the Second Severn Crossing. Fishermen catch salmon in low water on the ebbing tide and, although they developed agile salmon boats that could float in only a few inches of water, a fisherman could only lave salmon while standing on the river bed. Salmon are fast swimmers, so the fisherman has to have sharp wits and agile limbs. Because they swim close to the surface an experienced eye can spot the loom of the fish and, if he knows the river bed well enough, will be able to plot its course as the fish tries to swim out to deeper water. The net is placed and lifted as the fish enters it. The frame is then inverted and stuck in the ground, leaving the salmon suspended in the net; it is killed by a blow from a 'knocker', much like a policeman's truncheon.

An alternative is to use a net from a stopping boat, crewed by a single man in the fast-flowing channel of the river. This mode of fishing was probably invented in the early 19th century. Over the side of the boat is a net on a V-shaped frame, constructed of poles up to 25 feet long, forming an entrance 30 feet wide. In 1866 there were stop-net fisheries at Lydney Pill, Coneybury Elm, Etloe, Bull Rock and Wellhouse Bay, and the season lasted from 2 February to 8 August. This is the most dangerous form of salmon fishing as the strength of the current or the tide is liable to overturn the boat. Two stopping boat men were drowned in the mid 20th century when their boats overturned and they became trapped in their nets. (In desperate circumstances the men usually try to throw their gear overboard, knowing that they will be able to recover it upriver later.)[19]

Long nets were used further upstream in the Gloucestershire and Worcestershire stretches of the river, where it is feasible to span the entire channel. First the river bed was dragged with a heavy chain to remove any large objects like tree trunks washed down in winter high water, which would tear the net. The net was let out across the river on a punt and then one end is taken slightly downstream so that the line is diagonal

Stopping-boat fishing at Wellhouse Bay, Gatcombe in 1964. The net is suspended below the boat and is raised by a counter balance when the fish strikes. (© Gloucester City Council)

across the current. Any fish swimming upstream have little chance of escape. The downstream end of the net is then taken by the punt which crosses the river, with the net closing in a horseshoe around any fish unfortunate enough to have been in that stretch of the river. Long nets were used for salmon fishing up to the 1930s from Framilode. It was an effective mode of fishing in the deep-water stretches between Tewkesbury and Minsterworth, especially the pool known as Madam Pool. But the haul was meagre by commercial standards – three or four salmon in the net was considered a good catch, and sometimes there were no salmon at all.[20]

Long nets were not universally popular on the river, because by effectively trawling the whole channel, they undermined the efforts of fishermen upstream. In 1613 long-net fishing at Upton, Holdfast and Ripple angered hundreds of fishermen further upstream in Worcestershire and Shropshire, and they petitioned the Quarter Sessions to put a stop to it. It was claimed that the long-net fishermen took all the fish (sometimes 60 salmon at a draught), and what they did not take they drove back, so that the river upstream was devoid of fish.[21] In the 20th century the practice was made illegal, and was only undertaken at first light, when the water was low; this was known as a 'dawner'.[22]

In the 1930s Samuel Phillips, who lived at the boat house by Leighton Bridge, near Welshpool, remembered as a boy salmon fishing in the Severn in February. As they migrated, salmon were caught in a net between two coracles, a practice that was only possible for a few nights a year. Samuel Phillips remembered that the entire catch was sold to Shrewsbury fishmongers, and this practice was continued until it was prohibited under a bye-law of 1890. Ever ingenious, men like Phillips took to setting night lines

Long-net fishermen at Callow Pill in 1973, with their catch of salmon
(© Gloucester City Council)

across the river, on which there were several baited hooks, but that was also in time prohibited. Nets, meanwhile, were put to other uses. 'Will nets' were fixed across brooks and ditches when floodwaters were receding – an energy-efficient way of catching pike as they were returning to the main channel.[23]

Elvers arrive in the spring, and were usually fished at night in March and April, preferably just after high tide or, at spring tide, about an hour after the bore had passed. Home-made nets with long handles were used to scoop the elvers out of the water. The special skill was not in knowing how to fish, but when. It was evidently popular in the early 19th century and presented an unusual sight, with lines of men along the banks at high tide, taking out the elvers, 'caught in a kind of sieve made from hair cloth, fixed to a long pole', probably their dinner and tomorrow's breakfast.[24] Over roughly half an hour the yield would slowly increase, gradually filling the buckets into which the translucent worms were decanted. Still alive, the elvers would squirm in the bucket in their attempts to escape, under a 'froth like newly drawn beer'.[25] In 1943 four men took three hundredweight of elvers in one night near Tewkesbury. Given that there are reckoned to be 90-100 elvers to one ounce, the haul would have been upwards of 170,000 elvers. Elvers were once a delicacy in the Severnside towns and villages of Gloucestershire, although they were little esteemed further away from the river.

Should the elvers survive and grow to full maturity in the freshwater of the Severn, as eels they will have to run the gauntlet of fishermen a second time when they migrate in the autumn. Eels migrate en masse, usually between the last and first quarter of the moon, usually between sunset and midnight, and they like stormy weather with muddy

Shrewsbury viewed from Coton Hill. In the foreground is the bylet known as The Flash and fishermen with a net spread between two coracles in what was once a fish weir. Beyond them a masted vessel can be seen passing through the barge gutter.
(Courtesy of Shrewsbury Museum and Art Gallery)

water in the river. Basket traps for catching eels on their migration have a long history – for example, in the 14th-century *Luttrell Psalter* traps are illustrated placed within a mill race, as was common practice until the 19th century. The baskets were known as putcheons and weels (or wills), depending on their size. They were also an effective way of catching lamprey. In the middle of the 20th century, when Brian Waters was documenting the fishermen of Worcester, he knew that it was a dying craft. Changing culinary tastes had made eels and lampreys old-fashioned, and there was a feeling that putcheons would not be seen along Severn Street for much longer, nor punts in the river. His record of the local fishing culture was a valuable gift to posterity. Who would have known, for example, that fishermen in the early 20th century wore bowler hats, and that their fathers and grandfathers had fished in top hats, the cast-off gifts of the men who bought the fish? The Severn Street fishermen were usually part of a family tradition. For example, in the early years of the 20th century the Jenkins family made their living by eel and salmon fishing, putcheon-making and occasionally labouring on the quayside unloading coal or china clay. April to August was the time for making putcheons, which were woven from withies that grew on the riverbank around Tewkesbury; then eel fishing occupied them till the end of the year, followed by salmon fishing in the early months of the new year. Nets were also occasionally used to catch eels, the most popular spot being the narrow channel at Llanthony, just below Gloucester. The nets, with a finer mesh than salmon long-nets, were fixed across the current, and in the centre was a funnel, or 'cod', into which the eels invariably swam.[26] Eels were also caught in the Upper Severn, although by different methods. Long lines were laid across the river at night with hooks attached to them, but the practice appears to have died out by the early 20th century.[27]

Fishing rights were based on tradition. John Smyth was steward to the Berkeley family in the early 17th century and his description of the fishing there may reflect fishing rights as they existed in the Middle Ages. The fisheries of Berkeley belonged to the lord of the manor. In one week all of the fish caught from one tide were given to the lord of the manor, and those caught in the next tide were given to the parson. Anybody could fish with a lave net and take any fish, except for salmon, lampreys, shad and Fishes Royal (sturgeonseal, thornpole and porpoise) – fish that were claimed by the crown, on behalf of which the lord paid a special bounty. The system was known as the 'gale' and was administered by the lord's agent, or galor. The manor claimed half the value of all the fish sold. By a custom designed to reinforce these manorial rights, fish caught in Berkeley manor were brought to the market cross, where they had to remain for an hour before the fishermen were allowed to carry their catch and sell it elsewhere. Based on ancient traditional rights and privileges, the system eventually proved unworkable and a system of licences was introduced, whereby the right to fish was a simple financial transaction.[28]

The enduring image of a Severn fisherman is one earning only a modest living, but proud of his independence and able to turn his hand to other jobs when necessary. Many eel fishermen must have combined their angling with other occupations. Severnsiders kept eel boxes in the water, in which live eels could be kept until they were needed for sale or for the fisherman's own table. Before the Second World War Worcester fishermen took their putcheons downstream to Severn Stoke and Upton, returning to hawk their baskets of live eels from door to door. Elvers were once sold in pint mugs around the streets of Gloucester and were fried alive. Frampton-upon-Severn had an elver-eating competition and there was a local tradition that elvers were an effective aphrodisiac. Now it has become prosaic and businesslike; elvers are sold to elver stations who sell them on to foreign buyers.

Fishing has been a declining business ever since the demise of the monasteries in the 1530s. In Worcester, one fisherman in 1552 owned five boats and £5 worth of nets, but by the end of the century most fishermen had only one boat and nets worth shillings.[29] By the end of the 18th century salmon could be had for between 1s 6d and 2s 6d per pound in the high season between Michaelmas and May. This was apparently cheaper than in the early part of the century, when the lion's share of the catch was sold to London fishmongers.[30] In reality the London market was needed to sustain the lives of the fishermen, but market forces made excessive demands on the river's resources, and the natural abundance of the river was diminished. Decline of the river's fish stocks is also ascribed partly to the building of weirs below Stourport after 1835, which had inadequate fish passes that prevented spawning fish from travelling upstream. The long-term trend has been one of decline of species and of numbers. In 1811 an association was formed 'for the preservation of young fish in the Severn', and by 1849 there were 'fence months' when salmon could not be caught.[31] Demands on the riverbank caused the closure of some of the in-shore salmon fisheries, such as the building of the Severn road and rail bridges, and facilities for the intake of Severn water for Berkeley and Oldbury power stations. Pollution has also had its effect on the quality of the water. In this respect the motor barges of the 20th century have done far more damage than traditional barges and trows. Meanwhile industrial waste from tributary rivers and effluent from Gloucester sewers have adversely affected the quality of Severn water for migratory fish. In 1883 an estimated 30,000 fish were caught in nets and traps, a figure that fell steadily to just over 5,000 in 1959, while only 3,900 salmon were caught in 1970.[32]

Nothing has so far been said of fishing for subsistence and pleasure, the combination of which must have been the experience of the majority of Severn fishermen over the centuries. River men like Harry Rogers of the coracle-making dynasty at Ironbridge had such an intimate knowledge of the river that they could tickle trout, catch salmon, lay eel lines and knit nets.[33] Fishing for pleasure is one of our oldest leisure pursuits and surely began on the Severn long before the time of Chaucer, who wrote: 'like a fisherman, as men may see any day, he baits his hook with pleasure so that many a fish is crazed until he is seized therewith'.[34]

Angling with baited hooks has a long history, evidence for which is the bone hooks that have been recovered from many of Britain's rivers. Fly fishing was popular by the 18th century when, at Bridgnorth, bare-legged anglers fished from the shallows for gudgeons, blays and samlet, the latter 'only four or five inches in length, and … of a most delicious taste'.[35]

An older, and perhaps the oldest, method of fishing was the skill of spearing fish, a practice that did not die out on the Severn until the early years of the 20th century, when the 1911 Fisheries Act made it no longer possible to obtain a licence. In 1923 spearing of all species of freshwater fish was prohibited, but at one time many fish were caught in this way, including salmon, eel, flounder and pike, although salmon spearing was outlawed as long ago as 1534. Salmon spears were essentially forks with between three and nine prongs. Eel spears were similar, usually with up to five prongs. Eel-spearing was carried out from boats, from banks, or from muddy foreshores or mud flats at low tide. The objective was to identify and trap eels that were lying in mud, but not to run them through. The spears were designed to hold an eel between the prongs. The handles were at least eight feet long, and perhaps up to 30 feet long if the eels were speared from the deck of a trow.[36] In winter the murky depths of a deep pool at Wainlode were a favourite haunt of eels, and the banks of the pool were consequently just as attractive to fishermen.[37]

Another traditional method of catching eels was known as sniggling or patting. Izaak Walton mentions that it was practised on the river Lea in the 17th century. The idea is very simple. Bait, usually a worm, is attached to a needle and twine and pushed into a muddy bank or undercut, the kind of places where eels like to search for food. When the eel takes the twine it is easily pulled in. Salmon, especially those that had swum themselves into shallow water on the ebb tide, were taken with gaffing-irons, essentially a stick with a C-shaped hook, which the fishermen used to swipe the fish sideways out of the water as it attempted to swim between his legs.[38] Other methods in the upper river depended upon an intimate observation of the river and its ripples. If a fishermen spotted the 'loom' or ripple made by the female as she made her nest in the small gravel the spot would be marked, and at night the fishermen would return with a spear or dart.[39]

Fishermen with nets at Quatford in the late 18th century

It was in the 19th century that a conflict developed between fishing for subsistence and for pleasure. In 1839 the Shrewsbury Severn was described as good for fishing salmon, pike, grayling, trout and perch, but it was stated that it would be better if it was not being spoilt by 'excess of poaching with illegal nets'.[40] A long-established method of fishing for salmon had suddenly been demonised, and the traditional fishermen had become the enemies, not the keepers, of the river's heritage.

Hunting and fishing rights became a symbol of privilege and eventually a source of tension. The right to fish from the riverbank belongs to the owner of the bank, who usually leases the rights to commercial fisheries, although many riverside farmers were also part-time fishermen. Anybody, however, may fish wherever the tide flows, but the distinction between the river and the tideway has been the source of many disputes among lawyers as well as fishermen. Access to the fish of the river was therefore restricted in a way that navigating the river was not. Occasionally the resulting tensions have boiled over, even as early as 1376 when 60 people took part in a mass assault of Ombersley's fisheries, which belonged to Evesham Abbey, and fish to the value of 100 shillings were taken.[41]

Henry Green, writing at the onset of the Second World War, remembered fly-fishing on the Severn as an idyllic pastime. Brought up at Forthampton Court near Tewkesbury, he fished the river from a bank and from a small boat. The thrill required intimacy with a short stretch of river, where the chub and roach lay among the withies, and the bream under the shade of an alder tree; the skill was in knowing when a trout was taking the line down deep under water. Here came men on the bicycles after work, each to their own chosen spot, 'and to a boy there was something conspiratorial in all of us hunched over our floats as shadows began to stretch out long over the surface of the water'.[42]

All classes may have participated in angling but like every other sport it could be socially segregated. By the early 19th century Lord Coventry kept a fishing box above Upton for the use of fishing parties and river excursions.[43] In the 19th century Plynlimon was within reach of mining communities and their mine captains; in 1832 Captain Medwyn claimed to have caught 81 fish from Lake Bugeilyn on a moonlit Plynlimon night. The coming of the railways made the hills more accessible. Regular newcomers included John Bright, the MP for Birmingham and owner of lead mines near the source of the Clywedog, who was said to go fishing every Sunday with his miners.[44]

Lave-net fishing was not always a professional pursuit – during the 1926 General Strike Forest of Dean miners are said to have taken it up,[45] and boys and amateurs used lave-nets to catch plaice and mullet in the tidal waters. The most infamous of these fish-ermen was the luckless Stephen Aldridge, who in the early 19th century was suffocated by a flat fish which he put between his teeth to keep it safe as he hauled in his net (once a widespread practice and still practised by the Wagenia tribe on the Congo). The fish suddenly sprang forward and lodged itself in the man's throat, causing him to choke to death within two minutes.[46]

The most common fish in the upper river has always been trout, a species that thrives in fast-flowing streams. In 1860 John Randall learned of seven men in Llanidloes who

Lampreys caught by Philip Gaskins, a retired water-bailiff, in 1977 to make a lamprey pie for the Queen's Silver Jubilee.
(© Gloucester City Council)

were able to make a living of sorts by fishing in the upper river. They could take 8-10 lb of trout daily from the river, selling it at sixpence a pound. One of the men, Hugh Jones, claimed that his son had caught a trout 22 inches (56 centimetres) long.[47] But a clash was brewing between the locals and tourists. In 1920 A.G. Bradley complained that a Welshman 'really believes in his heart that he has a traditional and unalienable right to his share of the fish' and, carefully distinguishing his target from visiting fly fishermen, raged that 'men who destroy fish by nefarious means are public enemies, not merely the enemies of this or that landowner, to be treated with the utmost leniency when caught red-handed'.[48] At the heart of this was a clash between English and Welsh traditions and an attempt to anglicise the culture of the upper river. In Wales, fish were traditionally free to all, and these Llanidloes men branded as 'too lazy to make an honest living' can also be seen as 'the rural poor'.

Fish was once a far more important component of diet than it is now. River fish were fit for kings. In 1241, for example, Henry III ordered the bailiffs of Gloucester to send to London on Christmas Eve 30 lampreys, 60 of the finest salmon, some of which were to be made into 150 fishcakes, and 200 shad.[49] In the Middle Ages meat was not normally consumed on Fridays and Saturdays, or during Lent. Manorial lords were therefore prepared to meet the expense of building and maintaining fish weirs and ponds so that fish could be served in aristocratic households and monastic refectories.

Surplus fish were sold to fishmongers, who supplied freshwater fish to all classes of society. In Worcester fish was sold at the 'king's boards', presumably in Fish Street, where roach, dace, eels, lamperns and salmon were all for sale. There was a tradition that salmon were such an abundant resource that when parents bound their children as apprentices, they stipulated a clause that forbade them from eating salmon more than twice a week.[50] Such references with their golden-age overtones add another dimension to the mythology of salmon, but it seems unlikely that the fish was ever that plentiful. The principal fish eaten in aristocratic households was not salmon but the humble eel, mainly because of their abundance in rivers. Other fish, like the twait shad, are bony, and a deft hand is needed to cut it so that the bones come away from the flesh.[51] Sturgeon was only occasionally caught in the river. Three to five times as large as a mature salmon, they became one of the Fishes Royal on account of their sheer size, and were esteemed the perfect fish for a large banquet. But there has never been a tradition of caviar being made from Severn sturgeon. John Smyth noted in 1605 that 'the belly of a sturgeon is preferred before the back, and the lesser the sturgeon the more wholesome and tender is its flesh'.[52]

Lampreys were best eaten in spring, since 'in summer the interior nerve which serves them for a backbone grows hard' and made them less palatable.[53] This may account for their reputation for indigestibility, as referred to in John Gay's 1720 poem 'To a Young Lady with some Lampreys':

> Lamprey's a most immodest diet:
> You'll neither wake nor sleep in quiet.

Strange then that the lamprey was also regarded as an aphrodisiac:

> Why then send lampreys? Fie for shame!
> 'Twill set a virgin's blood on flame.

Good money was once paid for lamprey. In 1662 Mr Townsend of Elmley-Lovett paid 13s 4d for fresh sea lamprey caught in the Severn and sent to London, and by the end of the 18th century a 3lb fish could be expected to sell for 10 shillings from Worcester fishmongers.[54] Their smaller freshwater cousin, the eel-like lampern, grow to only 10 or 12 inches (30 centimetres) long, and are roughly the girth of a man's finger. Less sought-after than the sea lamprey (although Severn lamperns were esteemed the best), by the early 19th century lamperns were stocked in Worcester shops potted and preserved, or were sold as bait to cod fishermen.[55]

The lamprey may not have been among the Fishes Royal, but it was in other ways a royal fish. Henry I died in Normandy in 1135 when, against medical advice, he ate too many lampreys at a sitting. The lamprey is said to have been King John's favourite fish, and he is said to have fined the men of Gloucester 40 marks (£26 13s 4d) for not paying him sufficient respect in the matter of his lampreys, which presumably meant that they did not supply enough of them. Henry III is said to have considered other fish insipid by comparison. Surviving recipes for lamprey indicate that tastes in the style of cooking fish were quite different from today's, as they all describe methods of preserving the fish and eating it cold. This, at least, appears to be how it was eaten beyond the Severn hinterland, but it may reflect local tastes as well, since in the 16th century most of the stock of Worcester fishmongers was of preserved fish.[56] Fresh fish may only have become fashionable after it was more difficult to obtain.

Until the time of Elizabeth I the city of Gloucester presented the monarch with a lamprey pie at Christmas.[57] Thus did the lamprey become a symbol of the river Severn and its people. In the 16th century it was eaten in the form of a coffin-shaped pie, not from a predilection for stodgy food but as a means of preserving it. The fish was first well seasoned with salt, pepper and wine, and baked in butter, then sealed under three fingers thickness of butter, in which form it would keep for up to a year.[58] The fish was eaten cold, but the sauce it was in was boiled up, spiced with wine and ginger, and eaten hot as 'gode lordys mete'. An alternative was to eat lamprey 'galantine', in which the lamprey was cooked in bread (soaked in wine and vinegar) and onions, which had been fried with any leftovers, and served as pottage.[59]

Lamprey pies fit for kings were also sold by London fishmongers, a tradition that was still strong in the 17th century when potted fish had become fashionable and had begun to supplant the fish pie. At Gloucester in 1698, Celia Fiennes noted: 'here are the fine Lamprys taken in great quantetys in their season of which they make pyes and potts and convey them to London or else where, such a present being fitt for a king; this and the Charr fish [i.e. trout] are equally rare and valuable'.[60] By the 17th century lamprey pie (and eel pie, which was baked in a similar way) was cooked with puff pastry, always with butter and seasoned in a typically British spicy-fruity way with nutmeg, salt, pepper, cinnamon, ginger, sweet herbs, currants, dates and sliced lemon, and perhaps some claret wine.[61] Recipe books give recipes for lamprey pie and potted lampreys from the 16th to the 19th centuries. In the 18th century lamprey was served at fashionable London dinner tables. Hannah Glasse, writing to 'improve the servants, and save the Ladies a great deal of trouble', advised that the best lampreys 'are taken in the river Severn; and when they are in season, the fishmongers and others in London have them from Gloucester'. Lampreys were fried in blood and herbs, garnished with lemon, or potted by baking with clarified butter and seasoning.[62] Eels were potted in a similar way, the most time-consuming aspects of the process being the skinning and splitting open of the fish.

It was the city of Gloucester that broke the royal tradition – it complained in 1832 that it had cost £12 17s to supply the king, the lord high steward and assize court judges with their annual pies. The custom of the royal lamprey pie was revived later in the century by the same city council when, looking for a gift that would distinguish the people of Gloucester from other towns and cities of the kingdom, they sent a lamprey pie to Queen Victoria in 1893 and again on the occasion of her diamond jubilee in 1897. Thereafter it became a birthday gift. In 1900 the Mayor of Gloucester wrote that 'in accordance with ancient custom … I have the honour to forward a Royal Lamprey Pie as a birthday offering … in token of the continued loyalty and affection of the Citizens of Gloucester'.[63] The annual gift was discontinued in the 20th century but lamprey pies were baked as gifts at the coronation in 1953 and silver jubilee in 1977 of Elizabeth II.

In the riverside cottages the lamprey was probably usually stuffed and baked, with fewer ingredients than the recipe books recommended. By the late 19th century, however, while the authorities of Gloucester were assiduously reviving the cult of the lamprey as the emblem of loyal Severnsiders, the locals had had enough of them. Lampreys were now rarely eaten locally; many people believed that part of the fish was poisonous, so fishmongers rarely handled them. Since then the tradition of preparing them has been lost and their ugly appearance on the fishmonger's slab has not inspired a revival.[64] In the late 19th century there was still a market for lampreys, of sorts. Kept alive in submerged large urn-shaped baskets known as hard wheels (or cunning kipes), large quantities of Severn lampreys were shipped to the east coast for use as cod bait, a humiliating come-down for such an esteemed fish.[65]

Part Five

Life and Death on the River

❧ 12 ❧
The Water of Life

The miscellany of historical sources compiled by Nennius in the 9th century cites three cities of the Severn – Wroxeter, Worcester and Gloucester, all of them of Roman origin. Urban life by the Severn is usually therefore thought of as a Roman innovation, but that may reflect a bias in the evidence. As the Roman road known as Ermine Street approaches Gloucester it is not directed at the town itself but some way northwards to Kingsholm by the Old Severn, where a fortress was built in the first century of Roman occupation. Here there was a native town or village close to the river, the earliest significant settlement known by the Severn, older than the Roman invasion and occupying roughly the position on the river that the Romans would later exploit. In subsequent centuries war, religion, communications, trade, industry and government planning have all influenced the formation of towns along the Severn. In their different ways they all show why it has been important to settle beside the river.

The site of the present city of Gloucester was first of all a legionary fortress, built in the mid 60s AD to take advantage of the favourable river crossing as a way to advance into Wales. At the end of the first century the old fortress was transformed and Gloucester became one of the *coloniae* of Roman Britain, a town built to provide homes for the colonists, specifically retired legionaries. Tacitus explained the purpose of the earlier *colonia* at Camolodunum (Colchester): 'Its mission was to protect the country against revolt and to familiarise the provincials with law-abiding government.'[1] Thus Glevum, the first town on the Severn, was built for immigrants, with the native population living outside the walls in relative poverty. Such is the way of empire. Gloucester outlived the Roman Empire, albeit in diminished form, and remained a regional power base, probably controlled by a succession of warlords, the last of whom was known as Conmail. According to the *Anglo-Saxon Chronicle* Gloucester was captured by the West Saxons after Conmail was defeated at the battle of Dyrham in 577, but the city maintained its importance in the kingdom of the Hwicce and by the 9th century had come to be regarded as the capital of the Mercian kingdom.

Virconium (Wroxeter) was a regional capital of the Cornovii tribe and grew to be the fourth largest city in Roman Britain. Like Glevum it was built in the late 1st century on the site of a former legionary fortress, and was created as a result of government initiative. *Viroconium Cornoviorum* (the town of Virico of the Cornovii) replaced the earlier tribal capital, probably on the Wrekin, and expressed the confidence of a society moving from the uplands to the lowlands. Emperor Hadrian may have visited the Severn-side city during his brief visit to Britain in 121-22. Unlike Gloucester, Wroxeter eventually declined and was abandoned as a city. The Roman way of life appears to have declined slowly after the withdrawal of Roman forces in 410. Civil authority weakened in the 6th century, probably facilitating the rise of a warlord who controlled the city. Although parts of the city were left in ruins and the economy shrank, Wroxeter seems still to have been a vibrant and viable urban community in the 6th and 7th centuries, albeit without the civic institutions that underpinned it in its heyday. It ceased to function as a city in the 7th century, largely as a result of Anglo-Saxon expansion and the subsuming of Wroxeter and its hinterland within the kingdom of Mercia. Its king, Penda, had no need of this former capital city on the Severn.

Worcester, by contrast, was only a small Roman town, owing its existence to industry and its position on the river, although there was a small settlement there before the Romans came. Imported iron ore was smelted on the banks of the Severn, its waste material (slag) being used as core for the town's bridge. A road was constructed to the salt-producing area of Droitwich, and this was the means by which salt was sold and distributed. Like Wroxeter, Worcester appears to have remained relatively prosperous after the Roman departure, and this, together with the presence of a well-established Christian community, influenced the creation of the see of Worcester in the kingdom

Paul Sandby's view of Bridgnorth at the beginning of the 19th century shows the old bridge under repair, and the town on the hill behind. Note the bylet on the left of the picture.
(Courtesy of Shrewsbury Museum and Art Gallery)

of the Hwicce, at the expense of Gloucester (which was larger) and Winchcombe, the royal seat.

Shrewsbury emerged in the 8th century, and was described as *civitas*, a town, in 901. Perhaps it filled a gap left by the demise of Wroxeter in a place that is easily defensible by the loop of the river. By 1086 the town consisted of 151 houses, according to the Domesday survey. Other towns owed their origins to their defensive positions. Saxon burhs were created at Gloucester, Worcester and Quatbridge, although the latter was relatively short-lived, superseded when Robert de Belleme began the town of Bridgnorth in 1100, in conjunction with the castle. Welshpool similarly grew up in the shadow of Powis Castle.

Llanidloes and Newtown have quite different origins, but both are at places where the river could be crossed and where regional centres grew up. Llanidloes was already a town when Edward I granted its first charter in 1280. Upton-upon-Severn is of Anglo-Saxon rather than Celtic origin, but probably had a similar reason for existing. Newtown was a new town in the commote of Cedewain, founded in 1279 by Roger Mortimer when Edward I granted a charter to hold a market at Llanfair-yng-Cedewain. Its riverside location, replacing Dolforwyn Castle on the hill, signified more peaceful times ahead, and was one of several English-inspired new towns that were built in Wales – including Beaumaris, Caernarfon and Conwy – in the wake of Edward I's conquest.

Trade and industry had a direct influence on the foundation of some Severn towns. Bewdley emerged as a town in the 14th century on account of its port, although it remained within the parish of nearby Ribbesford. Stourport was a planned development

The town of Ironbridge grew up around the bridge, acquiring its own market place and, in 1836, its own church. (© Ironbridge Gorge Museum Trust)

The riverfront at Bewdley, as viewed from the position of the old bridge that was taken down after 1795. In the centre is the five-bay Saracen House of the early 18th century, and to its left the taller six-bay Alveston House of the late 17th century.

The riverside at Wribbenhall is lined with warehouses and the houses of merchants and watermen. On Beales Corner are two 17th-century timber-framed houses, the left-hand one dated 1623, flanking three 18th-century brick houses.

of the 1770s after the completion in 1771 of the interchange between the Severn and the Staffordshire and Worcestershire Canal. Ironbridge grew up after the bridge was built and eventually overtook the older village of Madeley as the focus of local life, testament to the strong gravitational pull of the river and its bridge. Downstream, William Reynolds established a new town, known as Coalport by 1794, at the transhipment point between the Shropshire Canal and the river.

Few people have lived close to the riverbank unless they could be sure that their homes were not in danger of becoming flooded. Shrewsbury is surrounded by a loop in the river but the riverside itself was common land for grazing cattle in the Middle Ages, and is now a park. Likewise the area of Worcester upstream from the bridge (and therefore vulnerable to inundation) had a stretch of riverside common land known as Pitchcroft Meadow. Usually the poorest people lived in the vulnerable positions by the river and on the bridges, as was noted during the flood of 1795 when the poor were far worse affected in Shrewsbury than other classes, and when relief of the poor riverside folk was down to 'several humane Gentlemen'.[2] Likewise, it was the inhabitants of Bridgnorth's Low Town who suffered in the same flood. In Upton-upon-Severn the cottages on the quay and at the lower end of New Street were always the first to take in water.[3] The poorest districts in 19th-century Shrewsbury included riverside communities at Roushill and at Longden Coleham. The latter was a virtual Irish enclave inhabited by refugees of the famine of the late 1840s. More than 30 houses disappeared from Severn Street in Gloucester in the century that followed the Black Death of 1348, as the population shrank and the areas of high flood risk were avoided.[4]

The best riverside houses have traditionally been the homes of the mercantile classes. The river front at Wribbenhall includes 17th- and 18th-century properties, including an 18th-century modernisation of an early 14th-century manor house. On the opposite bank in Bewdley are similarly fine 17th- and 18th-century houses downstream

Severnside in Stourport was built in the late 18th century. Its fine Georgian house by the river expresses the prosperity of the canal-river interchange in what was the heyday of the Severn navigation.

Glansevern Hall, near Berriew, was built in 1805 near the bank of the Severn
and is shown here in its original form in a print published in 1830.

of the old bridge on Severnside South, with more modest houses on the upstream
Severnside North, formerly Coles Quay. Shrewsbury's industrial and mercantile centre
was at Frankwell, on the outer side of the Welsh Bridge, where there survives a mixture
of timber-framed houses and commercial premises of the 16th and 17th centuries.
Bridgnorth's riverside must once have been similar but few of its timber-framed buildings have survived, although one that did is the opulent and misleadingly named Bishop
Percy's House, built for a barge master in 1580.

The Severn was too prone to flooding to attract the finest country houses, but there
are many houses whose parkland borders the river. Some had laundry cottages by the
river, or extensive woodland that the watermen exploited for fuel and perhaps also for
game.[5] Glansevern House near Berriew, Berwick House near Shrewsbury, and Bevere
House near Worcester all face the river but at a respectful distance, and include the riverbank in their parkland. Other houses have been content to view the river from further
off, like Winterdyne near Bewdley, The Mount at Shrewsbury (birthplace of Charles
Darwin) and, one of the earliest, the house built in 1607 at Eyton-on-Severn, of which
only the summerhouse remains.

The most fundamental requirement of any urban community is water, both for
drinking and for washing. Nobody has ever drunk untreated Severn water unless they
really had to, but in the course of history many people have had to. If they were available, wells, springs and even tributary streams provided much cleaner water, but they
could never supply a whole town. The standard of supply to Roman Wroxeter, whose
public baths were a marker of civilised living, was not equalled in Shrewsbury until the

The public baths at Wroxeter, an important symbol of Roman civilisation, enjoyed a water supply not surpassed until the 20th century.

20th century. In Wroxeter the water table was high enough for inhabitants to dig wells, many of which have been identified by excavation, but the principal source of water was the Bell Brook, a tributary of the Severn which was dammed to create a reservoir from which water was channelled into the city. It supplied the public baths, filling the plunge pools and basins and supplying steam. Discharged water flushed the city latrines into a main drain that emptied into the Severn. Some houses even had private baths and latrines. Public drinking fountains have also been found during excavation.[6]

Of the Severn's medieval towns and cities, Gloucester was perhaps the most fortunate in its access to water. By the mid 15th century it was supplied by means of pipes laid from a spring at Matson Hill and delivered by water spouts next to the High Cross in the city. The water would have been undrinkable by modern standards as it was not filtered, but better than the silty river. Gloucester Abbey had its own source of water from the Fullbrook, where it was drawn off on Robinswood Hill, south of the city.[7] The impressive lavatorium that survives in the abbey cloister is the best surviving testament to the well-organised supply and drainage of water at the abbey. When the city was besieged in 1643 the Royalists immediately cut the water pipes from Robinswood Hill, leaving the inhabitants to rely on river water.[8] These long-established sources were later supplemented by river water, which supplied a cistern in Westgate Street for a period after 1695, when pumps were installed near Westgate Bridge in a joint enterprise between a Gloucester plumber named Thomas Nicholls and his business partners Daniel Denell and Richard Lowbridge. The scheme appears not to have been a great

The water tower at Barbourne, shown here in a painting by Henry Jarman, was built in 1770 as a service reservoir for water pumped from the Severn. It was demolished in 1957, long after it ceased to be used.
(Image from Worcester City Museum collection)

success, and it had ceased by the mid 18th century. The Gloucester Water Company was formed in 1836 and assumed responsibility for the older infrastructure supplying spring water to the city. However, in common with other rapidly expanding towns and cities of the era, established sources could not hope to meet demand, and by the early 1850s the water company could not supply the city for more than two days a week. Its reservoirs now received water pumped from the Severn, although the main additional supply came from springs near Witcombe, to the east of the city. Filtered Severn water was used again temporarily in 1893 from a waterworks at Walham, but it was not until the 20th century that Gloucester joined with Tewkesbury and Cheltenham in drawing its supply from the Mythe Waterworks,[9] which had been built in 1870 to supply water for Tewkesbury.

Until the early 17th century Worcester's drinking water came from wells within the city walls. As the population expanded, however, new sources were needed. Water was piped to cisterns in the Corn Market, via a waterwheel at the bridge, probably adapting a system that had previously supplied the cathedral. It was finished by 1623. Water was also taken upstream of the bridge for use by brewers.[10] The waterwheel beneath the old bridge was removed in 1778 as the bridge was taken down. Extensive new waterworks had already been erected at Worcester in about 1770 at a cost of £11,000. The works was at Barbourne, upstream of the city, which supplied the city with cleanish river water. Water was pumped to a service reservoir, in the form of a 100-feet high water tower that was said to be ornamented at the top with cannon.[11] It was demolished only in 1957. A new steam engine was erected in 1810 to supply the reservoir. It was paid for

The waterworks at Barbourne began supplying river water to Worcester in around 1770, but the surviving buildings belong to the steam-powered phase of the later 19th century. It is now the Pump House Environment Centre.

by a rate levied on the inhabitants, which also funded street lamps and paving of the carriageways.[12] Population growth put pressure on the city's water supplies in the mid 19th century. Further improvements were carried out at Barbourne by the erection of a large pumping works, the earliest phase of which was designed by the water engineer Thomas Hawksley and begun in 1857.

Of the major Severn towns, Shrewsbury and Bridgnorth are the least well situated in terms of water supply; both are perched on hilltops comparatively high above the water table. At Bridgnorth, the Greyfriars took over responsibility for the town's water supply in the 14th century, ensuring that there were conduits supplying water to four places in the town, including the High Cross in the high town.[13] Spring water could not meet demand, however, and was unreliable. For the first few centuries of Shrewsbury's existence the river was probably the town's main water supply. The business of carrying water to houses was onerous for householders, and provided an opportunity for water carriers to offer their services. Shrewsbury was supplied with piped spring water from 1573; stone conduits were laid from Broadwell, a mile to the south-west of the town, to cisterns on Mardol and Wyle Cop, two of Shrewsbury's main streets. They were taken down in 1703 and 1704.[14] Remarkably, however, the conduit head that was built above the well in 1578 remains standing.

In 1744 no water was supplied to Shrewsbury for several months. By this time wells existed in the town – there were apparently 16 of them in the 18th century – but they could not deliver an adequate supply. The only other bulk source of water was still the river; the challenge was working out a way of pumping it uphill to the centre of town. George Hosier was responsible for the first (briefly) successful scheme, when in 1666 he pumped water from the river bed below the Welsh Bridge up to a water tower beside the river. Celia Fiennes noticed it when she visited Shrewsbury in 1698. 'There is a water house which supplys the town through pipes with water, but its drawn up with horses and it seems not to be a good and easye way, so they intend to make it with a water engine in the town.'[15] Whether or not Hosier managed to supply houses in the town with piped water is not known, and the project was apparently defunct by the early 18th century.[16] Hosier's sole right to supply river water to the town was taken over by Robert Aldersey of London in 1705. Aldersey constructed a waterwheel under the Stone Bridge, from which water was pumped via a lead pipe uphill to the market square, a distance of 574 yards (524 metres). Here, on the site of the old Market Cross, a

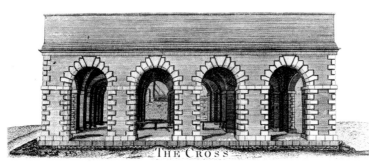

THE CROSS

'The Cross' in the centre of Shrewsbury was a water cistern that in the 18th century stored water pumped up from the waterwheel below the Stone Bridge.

succession of ever larger cisterns was built on raised pillars. The last of them was erected in 1755, a reservoir supported on groined arches, which had a capacity between 700 and 1,000 barrels of water (authors disagreed).[17] After some resistance, the waterwheel was retained when the old Stone Bridge was replaced by John Gwynn's English Bridge in the 1770s. The pumping arrangement was similar to the scheme designed by John Hadley at London Bridge. The quality of the water at the downstream end of a town that dumped all manner of refuse into the river could not have been high, and nor was the supply adequate in times of low or high water. A later water engineer, Thomas Tisdale, remembered from his youth that the wheel was once ice-bound for 12 weeks, and it was blamed for exacerbating the floods of 1795.[18] Another scheme of the same type appeared in Bridgnorth in 1717; a waterwheel close to the bridge pumped water uphill to Castle Walk in high town, where there was a cistern said to have a capacity of 6,500 gallons.[19]

In the 19th century Bridgnorth and Shrewsbury sought more efficient ways of pumping river water taken upstream of the respective towns. Bridgnorth's water pumping station was built relatively late, in 1861.[20] The Shrewsbury Waterworks Company was founded in 1827 but started inauspiciously when it was inundated in the flood of 1831.[21] From 1830 a 15 horse-power steam engine raised 172,800 gallons from the Severn every day and supplied most of the town, although not the suburbs beyond the bridges. There was also a short-lived Royal Baths, established by a surgeon named Thomas Onions, which offered showers, sauna, Turkish baths, and 'warm, salt, medicated and fresh water baths'.[22] The growing town evidently needed it, as a report on the sanitary condition of the town in 1853 repeatedly advocated the need for public baths in a town where there was insufficient water to provide for all of its inhabitants.[23] Water could not be supplied to the whole town simultaneously. Instead, it was divided into two principal areas that were supplied on alternate days, and then two sub-areas each that were supplied either from 7am to noon, or noon to 7pm. Some streets and small courts had to share a single standpipe. The better class of householders installed pumps and cisterns so that they could stock up while the supply was switched on. Even so, many complained that at times of low water the supply dried up for up to two or three weeks. The water was not filtered. A Mr Blower, who owned a warehouse in the town, complained that whenever his cistern was emptied for cleaning out in warm weather the 'water left a considerable deposit of mud, which had a very offensive smell'. Mr Hughes Clarke, a local surgeon, pointed out that the 'water was hardly fit for cooking purposes, and certainly not fit to drink'.[24] The cleanest drinking water was still the water piped from Broadwell and delivered to seven standpipes in the town's streets. The downside was that it had to be carted into the home manually.

For many people in Severnside towns and villages the only source of domestic water was at dipping places on the river. George Fowler of Jackfield drowned in 1828, having slipped into the river while fetching a kettle of water.[25] The Severn provided drinking water at Jackfield until 1913.[26] River water in the digestive system was almost as hazardous as water in the lungs. Longden Coleham, one of Shrewsbury's suburbs beyond the river, had a population of about 2,500 in the 1850s, but was supplied not from the town's waterworks, but from the river. William Ranger, reporting to the Board of Health in 1854, noted that 'in more than one instance I found that the dipping place, from which the people got the water, was close to the outfall of a sewer, and that the shore of the river round about it was covered with filth of the worst description'.[27] Despite the 1848 Public Health Act, improvements in Shrewsbury and elsewhere were slow, and some Shrewsbury folk still used the river for domestic water in the later 19th century. A sanitary inspector in 1871 found that a community of mostly Irish families living in tenements at Longden Coleham obtained their drinking water from the river, and in 1869, when a new ferry was established nearby, an old man threw water over the ferryman, who had prevented him from obtaining drinking water from the ferry steps.[28]

Improvement in the water supply to Shrewsbury was painfully slow, despite the good intentions of the town's grandees and the purchase of the town's waterworks in 1877 by the local authority. As late as 1876 a medical officer of health warned that river water should be used only for cleaning and not for drinking.[29] Shrewsbury's waterworks was rebuilt in 1896 and the building remains standing, albeit adapted as offices. It closed in 1935, when it was replaced by a new waterworks at Shelton, on the south-west side of the town.[30]

The luxury of sterilised water was only introduced in the 20th century. The story of clean Severn water begins at the Mythe, just upstream of Tewkesbury, where the first water treatment works was built in 1870 to supply Tewkesbury. From 1894 it was piped to Cheltenham as well. Sterilisation of the water began in 1912. Water is now abstracted from the Severn in a number of places, but there are none of the dramatic reservoirs with dams like those on its tributaries at Lake Vyrnwy, completed in 1888 to supply Liverpool, and Llyn Clywedog, completed in 1967. Severn water is stored and treated for use by the whole borough of Shrewsbury at Shelton. Since 1967 Staffordshire has received much of its water from the Severn; it is abstracted at Hampton Loade, stored in a reservoir at Chelmarsh, and then pumped back across the river to the Hampton Loade Water Treatment Works. Trimpley reservoir was completed in 1970 and was constructed by the Birmingham Corporation. Ironically, it is close to the point where the city's great 19th-century scheme, bringing water from mid Wales along an aqueduct, crosses the Severn.

Apart from cooking and drinking, water from the towns' waterworks was also used for laundry. So, probably, was the river. Romantic landscape artists regularly placed washerwomen in the foreground of river scenery, but while these figures were something of a cliché they were not a fiction. Towns and cities had their acknowledged washing places. The *Shrewsbury Chronicle* lamented in 1829 that the Quarry Park in Shrewsbury 'was the rendezvous of washerwomen, and the daily exhibition of garments, from the modest chemise to the inexpressible breeches' was a blot on the landscape. Women hung their linen to dry on the park's lime trees. In Elizabethan Worcester women washed their clothes in the shallower waters upstream of the bridge. In Gloucester, by Westgate Bridge, there was a water-filled clay pit that was described as a 'washing place' by 1659.[31]

Quite naturally, the Severn was for many centuries also a public sewer. That the river was a dumping ground for all manner of waste is apparent from 15th-century sources. Henry VII is said to have forbidden anyone to throw entrails, animal dung or household

Mythe Waterworks, built in 1870 to supply Tewkesbury, has grown steadily
and now supplies much of the Severn Vale.

The Hampton Loade water treatment works takes on water from Chelmarsh reservoir,
a storage facility for water extracted from the Severn, to supply south Staffordshire.

refuse over the bridge at Worcester. The city's quays and slipways were also depositories of unsavoury rubbish. Common ground beyond the bridge was set aside as a waste tip, although it was not to be used when the river was in flood.[32] All of the dumping grounds were on the south side of the city, downstream of the bridge, well below where water was extracted for domestic use. By the early 19th century the Worcester sewers were said to have been cleared and enlarged at great expense.[33] In Gloucester in 1454 the butchers were granted a place below the common quay for the disposal of offal, land on which the New Quay was extended in 1622.[34]

Shrewsbury's first public latrines appear to have been those erected on the Stone Bridge in 1564 and the Welsh Bridge in 1581.[35] Until the end of the 19th century Shrewsbury's ancient sewers continued to discharge into the Severn at 'mudholes' near the English and Welsh Bridges. There were 13 of them in 1853, but not every dwelling had drains connected to them. Instead the residents could dispose of their waste by dumping it in the river, as long as it was carried away by the current. In practice the banks were strewn with excrement, which was washed into houses in times of flood. Quite a few of the 671 houses affected by the 1852 flood must have become health hazards.[36] The Severn in Shrewsbury remained a public sewer until Coleham Pumping Station opened in 1900 to pump the town's sewage to filter beds away from the river. At Jackfield, sewage was discharged into the Severn until the 1960s.[37]

It is hardly surprising that the most popular form of liquid refreshment was beer (although coffee houses had reached Shrewsbury by the 1680s). In 1556, John Davies, who lived close to the river in Shrewsbury, sold his brewing business, which included a lead brewing furnace and a pipe bringing water to it directly from the Severn.[38] The Severn was once lined with breweries; in the great flood of 1795 barrels of beer from Berriew were washed down beyond Welshpool and proved a small consolation for the harassed inhabitants of the Shropshire riverside. Inns and ale houses brewed their own

The Tontine Inn at Stourport,
built by the Staffordshire and Worcestershire Canal Company in 1772

beer. The factory phase of brewing belongs to the 19th century; for example, Trouncers Brewery in Shrewsbury was founded in 1807, and its later buildings remain prominent by the Severn in Longden Coleham, having been converted to flats in the 1990s.

The Severn has for centuries been a river of inns and ale houses, which have always been the lifeblood of the riverside communities. They hosted manor courts (for example at the Bear in Newnham), inquests (London Apprentice in Shrewsbury, the Coffee Rooms Inn at Beachley, the Severn Trow at Kempsey, Tontine at Stourport among them), auctions and plays, and were often posting houses in the 19th century. Friendly Societies, where workmen paid into a fund to provide for them in sickness and old age, met in pubs. According to the local workman turned author John Randall, giving mugs of beer 'was an ancient mode of hiring' and as legally binding as a handshake.[39] Ale houses along the river, especially on the industrialised stretch in Shropshire, were sometimes known as mug houses, in which men were hired and paid. Bewdley's Mug House has preserved the name, and thereby something of the old culture of beer drinking. Ale houses served drink and sometimes food; inns provided food and accommodation to travellers; taverns also served wine, an important and well-documented commodity of the Severn trade.

Public houses were usually close to the waterfront of riverside towns. Bewdley's principal inns were in Load Street and served the centre of the town rather than the river community, but the town also possessed an impressive number of riverside inns and ale houses in the 18th and 19th centuries – Black Boy, Brickmakers Arms, Cock & Magpie, Duke William, George & Dragon, Heart & Dove, King of Prussia, Labour in Vain, Mersour Tavern, Mug House, Pig & Whistle, Robin Hood, Saracen's Head, Sea Horse, Severn Trow, Sun, Thurston.[40] Wherever there was any significant activity along the riverside there was a public house of some sort to serve it. They are found at ferry crossings, road-river intersections, and of course at wharves, but also in isolated stretches of the river where they could only really serve the itinerant riverside community. Examples

The Harbour Inn at Arley is an 18th-century inn that stands on the west bank of the Severn, opposite the estate village of Upper Arley.

include the Britannia in Linley and the Harbour in Arley. The Ship Inn, below Highley Station (which is itself set apart from the village) has a range of outbuildings that included stables, malthouse and brewhouse. Most bridges have a corresponding public house, like the Ironbridge Tontine Inn. Thomas Telford's London-Holyhead road had the Powis Arms in Montford Bridge and the ambitious Talbot Hotel (now the Mytton and Mermaid) built in 1775 at Atcham. The latter's fortunes declined during the railway age, but revived again in the 1930s, the age of the motor car. A new road bridge was constructed and the Welsh architect Clough Williams-Ellis re-established the hotel and rebuilt the old stables in his own style. Now its riverside garden is one of its main attractions.

Wharves attracted public houses not merely for refreshment but for the stabling of horses and occasionally to act as warehouses. The upper limit of the navigable river is marked by the Powis Arms at Pool Quay. When the canal/river interchange at Stourport was built there were warehouses and yards, but taking pride of place was the Tontine Inn. 'Tontine' refers to an insurance scheme attributed to the 17th-century Italian Lorenzo Tonti, whereby investors benefit from increasing shares of revenue as their fellow members die off. (The other Tontine Inn, at Ironbridge, was not built on that principle but appears to have copied the name from Stourport.) In Ironbridge the former Loadcroft wharf can be identified by the surviving riverside inns – the Swan and the Malthouse (formerly the Talbot), which retain their warehouse and malthouse respectively. It was common for ale house owners also to own vessels and wharves. For example, when the lease of the Llandrinio Boat, the former public house by the bridge, was advertised in 1787 it included warehouses and a wharf, and stipulated that applicants were to possess two barges and two boats.[41]

The drinking habits of the Severn watermen were legendary, incurring the displeasure of their puritanical contemporaries like the Coalbrookdale ironmaster and devout Quaker Richard Reynolds. Reynolds built 'Sabbath Walks' in the woods above the Severn in the 1790s to induce workmen away from the public houses on their day of rest. Riverside inns catered for travellers needing refreshment, and for the watermen who were engaged in thirsty work, especially the gangs of bow haulers. In his 1830s diary of riverside life, the waterman Thomas Beard records drunkenness, often ending in tragedy.[42] The presence of gangs of young men working away from home also ensured that the Severnside sex trade flourished. In 1859, when the river trade was in decline, Bridgnorth could still support eight brothels. Watermen mooring at Shrewsbury quays could avail themselves of the brothels in Roushill. Riverside districts tended to be the poorer parts of town, the natural location of red light districts and also handy for the likely clientele. A study of the 1861 census claimed to be able to identify 57 prostitutes in Roushill, many of whom made regular appearances before the magistrates: women like Priscilla Lloyd, whose son tried in 1843 after an argument 'to accomplish the filial task of throwing his mother … over Roushill walls into Severn'.[43] Not all sex was paid for, of course, as there was a liberal attitude to relations between men and women in a world where ships passed in the night, almost literally.[44] Many river people found their marriage partners at some distance, which demonstrates that, socially, the people of the riverside had more in common with river-dwellers in other towns than they did with their inland near neighbours.

Inns and ale houses reflected all social strata, although most of the riverside inns thought of themselves as respectable hostelries. Tobacco was smoked by men and women in ale houses from the 17th century – clay pipes were a staple product of Broseley, one of the first industrialised Severnside communities. In 1781 John Byng (Lord Torrington) 'entered the Bear Inn at Newnham, with a good appetite, and found a round of beef just taken from the pot, which I strove to devour, and likewise a goosebury pie'. Never slow to grumble about the hospitality or the cost of the inns he frequented in his travels, he explained that 'it is always my rule to stop about noon, at second-rate inns, and take the family fare; as one commonly dines much better in that way, and at half the expense'.[45] It was said in 1849 that 'according to the custom of the county [Worcestershire], the landladies sup with the strangers and passengers, and if they have daughters they are also of the company, to entertain the guests at table with pleasant conceits, where they drink as much as the men'.[46] Respectability had a high premium, as if the respectability of the hosts was reflected in the social rank of their guests. Thus in Henry Fielding's novel *The History of Tom Jones* (1749) a gentlewoman remarks to an inn keeper at Upton: "You people that keep inns imagine your betters are like yourselves. Indeed I expected to get nothing at this wretched place. … I suppose none but tradesmen and grasiers ever call here". The landlady fired at this indignity offered to her house.[47]

In fact the establishment prided itself on the respectability of its guests, not all of whom were commercial travellers or watermen. Henry Fielding again:

> Our travellers had happened to take up their residence at a house of exceedingly good repute [at Upton-upon-Severn], whither Irish ladies of strict virtue, and many northern lasses of the same predicament, were accustomed to resort on their way to Bath. The landlady therefore would by no means have admitted any conversation of a disreputable kind to pass under her roof. Indeed so foul and contagious are all such proceedings, that they contaminate the very innocent scenes where they are committed, and give the name of a bad house, or of a house of ill repute, to all those where they are suffered to be carried on.
>
> Not that I would intimate, that such strict chastity as was preserved in the temple of Vesta can possibly be maintained at a public inn. [However] to exclude all vulgar concubinage, and to drive all whores in rags from within the walls, is within the power of everyone.[48]

Not all riverside recreation took place in pubs. The flat ground of river valleys ensured that sport was played on the riverside. To this day Worcestershire play cricket at New Road by the river, and from 1910 until 2007, Shrewsbury Town Football Club played at the Gay Meadow, where Charles I rallied his forces in 1642. Balls were retrieved from the river by coracle. Worcester and Eyton in Shropshire both have riverside racecourses; so once did Shrewsbury at Kingsland.

Rivers are a natural magnet for relaxation and recreation. They encourage sedentary activities; Izaak Walton remarked in *The Compleat Angler* (1653) that 'the very sitting by the rivers side, is not only the fittest place for, but will invite the Anglers to contemplation'.[49] This is just as true of leaning on the parapet of a bridge as of sitting on the riverbank. But the river has never been just the province of solitude, nor have its visitors always been as passive as they appear in the works of landscape artists. Rowing and coracle racing have a long pedigree. Boat racing was well established at Tewkesbury by the mid 19th century; coracle racing, once beginning at the Regatta Field, remains a popular annual event in Ironbridge. Captain Matthew Webb learned to swim in the Severn near Ironbridge, and put his skills to good use when he became the first man to swim the English Channel in 1875. In 1879 the Ironbridge Floating Swimming Bath Co constructed in the river a bath 50 feet long by 16 feet wide (15.2 by 4.9 metres) in the form of wooden spars secured by petroleum barrels acting as pontoons. In 1880 it was a popular resort, attracting 432 visitors in one week, but it was short-lived, unable to withstand the winter conditions. Later Ironbridge swimming pools were simpler affairs. In the 1920s the schoolmaster at Coalbrookdale taught his pupils to swim in the river at Buildwas where, at the end of a narrow channel by a bylet, he had stakes driven into the river bed and interlaced with brushes to form a small pool.[50] A swimming bath was also created in Bridgnorth in 1878 by erecting pontoons in the river and covering the pool over with a pitched roof.[51] Diving into the river on hot days has been a popular pastime in Shrewsbury since Porthill Bridge was built in the 1920s.

Shrewsbury's Quarry Park has been a place of formal recreation since the ground was planted with trees in 1719. Previously it had been common land outside the town walls. A few years later Dr Richard Pococke praised the 'pleasant walks by the river side, some of them planted with limes, which, together with the fine river, make it a most delightful scene'.[52] By the early 19th century it had gained a reputation as a 'cool and sequestered situation', with 'the graceful sweep of its noble avenue and ambient river'. Plays were apparently once held in the Dingle (i.e. the original quarry), including *Julian the Apostate* in 1565 and the *Passion of Christ* in 1567.[53] According to Joseph Nightingale, writing in 1810, the combination of its fine trees and riverside location made it superior to Kensington Gardens, and yet 'it is, however, but little frequented, except by soldiers and washer-women, being chiefly used as a convenient spot for drilling recruits and drying linen'.[54] John Byng agreed. On his first visit in 1784 he noted that the riverside provided a promenade where the quality could see and be seen, but returning in 1793 he sought 'the place of genteel promenade; but not a creature there! Where I expected to have seen the gay world!'[55] In the early 19th century a more sequestered spot could be found by taking a ferry crossing below the English Bridge that led to the Underdale Tea Gardens, advertised as a 'quiet rural retreat'.[56]

During the same period the banks of the river at Worcester became a popular place for walking. Tea Gardens, known as Porto Bello, opened on the west bank. It was the perfect place 'to appreciate the beauty of the river of the vale of Severn, of the city enlivened with its lofty spires, graced with its light and elegant bridge, and backed by the sublime towers and pinnacles of its cathedral'.[57] Further downstream was a riverside walk to plantations near the confluence of the Teme, which in 1651 was the last battle-ground of the Civil Wars.[58]

The railways made other places on the Severn available to all. There was a Severnside walk and picnic area at Arley Castle by the 1860s, accessible by boat or train. The Severn Valley Railway allowed ramblers to walk along sections of the riverbank that had previously been beyond their bounds.[59] Members of Birmingham's Sparkhill and Greet Institute enjoyed an eventful annual outing to Arley in 1891. Two of their members fell from the ferry, while a small party later hired a rowing boat with the intention of visiting Bewdley, only to collide with the outrigger of a vessel coming the other way and sink. There were no serious casualties, only sodden clothes and red faces.[60] Fishing parties came to Arley to trawl for pike or fly-fish for trout.[61] The Abbey Inn at Buildwas, also made accessible by the Severn Valley Railway, was popular with anglers, artists and cyclists by the end of the 19th century.[62]

Hitherto inaccessible stretches of the riverbank became the destination of boating trips, especially with the rise of pleasure cruising from the mid 19th century. The decline of Severn trade left a surplus of vessels on the Severn, and under-employed barges were converted to pleasure boats for day trips, which seem to have been especially popular with the inhabitants of the industrialised Ironbridge Gorge. The deck of the barge was festooned with flags, banners and perhaps flowers, awnings were put up to create a covered saloon, and space on the foredeck was provided for a brass band. Their destination was often 'Apley Terrace', the mile-long terrace, also known as Belle Vue, owned by the ironmaster W.O. Foster. Here local societies, schoolchildren and works outings disembarked for picnics.[63]

Severnside festivals have a long history. The Severn is the backdrop to the Upton Jazz Festival; fairs were held by the river in Ironbridge and Jackfield. 'Jackfield Wake

The village of Upper Arley descends to the river bank and the slipway of the former ferry, which was replaced by a footbridge only in 1972. It was the picturesque destination of many outings, especially after the Severn Valley Railway opened in 1862.

was celebrated on Monday, after the usual fashion – drinking and fighting', reported the *Shrewsbury Chronicle* in 1859. The only diversion appears to have been 'a duck hunt upon the Severn, with dogs' but even that went awry when two of the canines set upon one another.[64] Castlemeads in Gloucester hosted several agricultural shows and in 1909 was host to the Royal Show. Over 88,000 people visited the site, access to which required the construction of a temporary bridge near the old quay. But the most ambitious of all riverside festivals were, and still are, in Shrewsbury. An annual fair was held at Kingsland at Corpus Christi, which fell on the second Thursday after Pentecost, and was instituted in 1317. After the Reformation it was transferred to the second Monday after Trinity Sunday.[65] By the 16th century a procession with flags, drums, fyffes and a figure dressed as Henry VIII made its way from the town across the river to Kingsland.

Sir Henry Sidney, Lord President of Wales, enacted his own ideas for a Severnside pageant on St George's Day in 1581. A procession led from the church of St Chad, in the centre of the town, to Gay Meadow, by the Stone Bridge, for a Merry England pageant, with performances by boys and schoolmasters from the town's four free schools. Sir Henry left Shrewsbury by river, and was seen off by 'serten scollars of the free scoole' waiting on a bylet opposite the Blackfriars, 'apparelyd all in greene, and green wyllows on their heads', lamenting in verse his departure:

> The water nymphs, our sisters deare,
> Do take our Lord away …

So tickled was Sir Henry that he is said to have repeated the event the following year.[66]

The river seems often to have inspired public celebrations. By the early 19th century 'an annual gala is generally given by the young gentlemen of Shrewsbury School' every June. Boats could be hired, and picnic parties set off upstream as far as Berwick and the Isle, and downstream as far as Atcham. The Shrewsbury Show was also still ongoing in the 19th century. The procession, which now included costumed figures of Henry I (who granted the first charter to the borough), Henry VIII and his wives, Edward VI (founder of Shrewsbury School), and the various trades of the town took two and a half hours to reach Kingsland, where several thousand people are said to have enjoyed the festivities.[67] But despite this mid-century peak, the Shrewsbury Show was in long-term decline, and ended when the land on which it was held was purchased by Shrewsbury School – which moved from the centre of town to the old foundling hospital, from which it looks imperiously down on the town – and for the villas that became the Kingsland suburb.

Public criticism of the Show centred upon perceived levels of drunkenness and violence. It was a familiar accusation and symptom of a social change in which the affluent classes sought more sophisticated entertainment than traditional fairs and wakes. Since the 1870s the Shrewsbury Flower Show has been held in the Quarry Park; the West Midlands Agricultural Show was also held on the riverside. Neither of these has been aimed at a universal audience like the older wakes and fairs, but both, perhaps unconsciously, hark back to a much older heritage of riverside entertainment.

✎ 13 ✐
Flood and Freeze

On the walls of the Shalimar restaurant in Shrewsbury are photographs of past floods, in which the building, on the old Abbey Foregate close to the English Bridge, is shown bearing the brunt of several inundations since the 1960s. The photographs are displayed like certificates of survival in a part of the town that has been liable to floods ever since Shrewsbury was built. A more common way to celebrate the survival of floods is to mark the high water level on a building. Cast-iron plaques on the wall of the old churchyard at Upton-upon-Severn record the great floods of the 19th century; inside the church door at Tirley is the flood line of 2007; painted lines on the door of the Boat Inn at Coalport record floods of the 20th century; and tablets at Watergate in Worcester allow you to compare flood levels of the 18th, 19th and 20th centuries. These markers are ephemeral, depending upon the fate of the buildings to which they are attached. Once there were markers on the wall of Mrs Davies' house in Frankwell, Shrewsbury, and on the city wall and in the former North Parade in Worcester.[1] The Shalimar has survived many inundations on a street where the oldest building was built in the early 15th century. But when flooding has occurred in Shrewsbury in recent years it has usually been Frankwell, beside the Welsh Bridge, that has drawn the media attention. It has picturesque timber-framed buildings, a hint that if such buildings have endured centuries of flooding and are still standing, floods may be more survivable than sensationalist headlines suggest. Indeed, Frankwell was inundated nine times between 1576 and 1602. On Saturday 10 January 1596 the water reached 2 feet (0.6 metres) deep in the Myntons' house in Frankwell, and the family was forced upstairs until Monday morning. The same thing happened at Christmas 1601: 'it troubled them sore in washing down their walls, ovens and furnaces to their great hindrance and losses beside'.[2]

The Severn is a volatile river. In normal flow it has an olive-green, rippling surface but when the river is in flood the water turns a ruddy silt-brown, the ripples vanish and in the middle of the river is a current of water flowing swiftly, smoothly and menacingly. Its wide catchment area in the rain-drenched Welsh mountains, the many rivers that flow into it and the preponderance of towns and villages along its course explain why it has become notorious as a river of floods.

Top: A tablet marks the high point of the
1852 flood on the wall of the
old churchyard in Upton.
Middle: Flood marks on the wall of the
Water Gate indicate that 1770 was the
worst year for flooding in Worcester.
Bottom: Flood levels on the door of the
Boat Inn in Coalport.

Flooding is a subtle thing, affecting different sections of the river in different ways. I remember that while I was working at Ironbridge in the 1990s, the head of the Ironbridge Gorge would often flood, leaving the Wharfage under water, but half a mile downstream at Madeley Wood the water never covered the road along the bank. Atcham church, precariously sited on the riverbank, has never been known to flood, protected for long by the bridge just upstream and since 1929 by two bridges. Flood levels are variable, so whereas the highest flooding of many sections of the river around Worcester and Tewkesbury occurred in 1770, in Shropshire the worst event was in 1795 and in Wales in 1852. This is where plaques come in useful. Flooding in Shrewsbury in 1831 started a debate about the relative magnitude of the 1795, 1809 and 1831 floods. If it was not for the plaque on Mrs Davies' house in Frankwell, recording the level of the 1795 flood, then many folk would have argued that the 1831 flood was higher, rather than 'a few inches lower'.[3] 1947 was the year of the most severe flooding in the 20th century, followed closely by 1960. At the Mythe Water Treatment Works near Tewkesbury it was thought that the 1947 flood level was probably higher there than any previously recorded flood, even that of 1770, although Tewkesbury Abbey did not flood in 1947 but did in 1770.

Many factors contribute to the severity of floods. Bridges, especially those built with thick fortress-like masonry piers on the river bed, have the effect of impeding flood-water, especially when large objects like ice blocks, tree trunks, drifting boats and even buildings, are jammed up against the bridge, impounding the water upstream. Modern agricultural methods have resulted in increasing amounts of water running off the fields. Increasing areas of tarmac have also meant that river levels now swell faster than they once did. Attempts to manage the Severn's flow by means of dredging, the construction of locks and weirs, and especially the construction of the Clywedog reservoir, have been effective at augmenting low river levels, but less effective at reducing flood levels. Options to relieve the flood risk after the severe floods of the 1990s and 2000 included establishing upstream storage lakes, bypass channels, permanent flood barriers and underground storage chambers, but none were really practical. Instead a system of demountable defences was devised, which could be erected quickly in the event of an imminent flood. In Bewdley £11 million was spent in building 800 metres of permanent and temporary defences, designed to protect 175 houses from a 1 in 100 year flood.[4] The cost, at over £62,000 per house, reflects not so much the value of property as the awesome power of the river.

One factor that contributed to severe floods in the 18th and early 19th centuries, as also in 1947 and 1963, was a prolonged freeze. In 1947 the winter freeze and the subsequent flooding was a nationwide phenomenon, recorded in such detail that it is possible to understand how it takes an exceptional combination of circumstances to result in severe flooding. Precipitation of snow and sleet was brought on from January by unremittingly low temperatures. Conditions remained Scandinavian throughout February,

Flooding at Frankwell, by the Welsh Bridge in Shrewsbury, in 1899
(Courtesy of Shrewsbury Museum and Art Gallery)

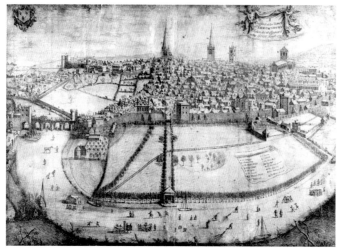

Shrewsbury in the Great Frost of 1739. In the foreground of the river is a printing press set up to sell souvenir prints. (Courtesy of Shrewsbury Museum and Art Gallery)

The frozen river at Shrewsbury, 2011

unrelieved by any warm front, which is unusual for Britain. The average maximum daytime temperature during February 1947 was just below freezing. There was snowfall as late as 10 March, but the next day a warm front set in, bringing heavy rain and a rapid thaw. The Severn basin rapidly filled. In Worcester the river level rose by three metres in 24 hours. The mid Wales stretch of the Severn flooded on 16 March, Shropshire on 18 March, Worcester and the tidal Severn on 20 March. Other major winter freezes occurred before precipitation and river flow were monitored. For example, river freezes are recorded at Tewkesbury in 1607-8, 1739-40, 1776 and 1814.[5] But the river was more prone to freeze further upriver, especially where the tide had no influence and where bridges slowed the river flow. The great freeze that began on Christmas Eve 1739 froze the river from Tewkesbury as least as far upstream as Shrewsbury, where the river was frozen for eight weeks. Crowds in Shrewsbury could walk on the ice from the Stone Bridge to the Welsh Bridge (as they did in 1963).[6] An impromptu frost fair was held; a tent was erected in the middle of the river in which a sheep was roasted, and a printing press set up on the ice issued a special souvenir print. The same thing happened in Shrewsbury in 1770 and in Worcester in 1795.[7] As far as is known, all of the printers chose the same quotation, taken from a source not usually associated with frozen northern winters – the Bible:

> His hoary frost, his fleecy snow
> Descend and clothe the ground;
> The liquid streams forbear to flow,
> In icy fetters bound.[8]

What we know about the levels of flooding earlier than the mid 18th century is minimal, but the proliferation of regional newspapers from that period on has given us vivid anecdotal accounts of flooding, while the systematic recording of river levels allowed a more scientific appreciation of flooding in the 20th century. The 18th-century antiquary Thomas Phillips chronicled Severn floods and earthquakes, when such things were evidently considered to be acts of God. Apparently in 1673 a small whale came up the flooded Severn and was taken in Shrewsbury. A dolphin measuring 3 feet and 4 inches (1.01 metres) long made the same journey in the 1748 floods, and was caught after becoming trapped in one of Shrewsbury's weirs.[9] The 19th-century antiquary Charles Hulbert compiled a far more ambitious list of major inundations, including five floods of the 17th century, several medieval floods, including an auspicious flood of 1066 after the river had been frozen for 14 weeks, and five major floods of the first millennium.[10] Such events are chronicled in the way a nation records its wars and its rulers.

The earliest documented flood on the Severn is the account of the Duke of Buckingham's Water by Raphael Holinshed. In 1483 the duke had assembled an army of Welsh mercenaries and headed for Gloucester, where he planned to cross the Severn, meet with fellow conspirators and march on Salisbury to confront Richard III. Alas, before he could reach the Severn the river flooded and remained high for ten days. 'By this floud the passages were so closed, that neither the duke could come over Severn to his adherents, nor they to him. During the which time, the Welshmen lingring idelie, and without monie, vittels, or wages, suddenlie scattered and departed.' The severity of the flood clearly took riverside communities by surprise, assuming that Holinshed's apocalyptic account is credible: '… men were drowned in their beds, and houses with the extreme violence were overturned, children were carried about the fields swimming in cradles, beastes were drowned on hilles'.[11] The description provided a blueprint for later authors, even as late as the 19th century when Emily Lawson, describing the flood of 1770, claimed that 'infants were seen floating in their cradles over the submerged fields'.[12]

The flood of 1795 can have taken nobody by surprise, for when the conditions are right for flooding the question is never 'if' but 'when'. In the slightly cooler climate of the 18th and 19th centuries it was heavy snow, a big freeze and subsequent thaw that signalled the imminent deluge. February was usually the danger month, and the great flood of February 1795 occurred after just such a freeze. In Bewdley large blocks of ice, the outriders of devastation, appeared on the river on Monday 9th, but the real drama began when the ice continued to melt and swell the river. On Tuesday night and early Wednesday morning the river rose rapidly in Shrewsbury. The town was more or less cut off, since no carriages could cross either of the bridges, and the mail arrived via a bridleway on the north side of the town. Many houses in the lower part of the town – Frankwell, Coleham, Coton Hill and Abbey Foregate – were under 10 feet (3.04 metres) of water, deep enough to flood their bedrooms. Inhabitants were rescued and relief supplies were delivered through the upstairs windows. Water also inundated Shrewsbury Abbey: 'The Abbey church presented a very singular and almost ghastly appearance; the graves in the chancel and aisles collapsed, and it appeared as though at the call of the last trump they had given up their dead.' Further downstream at Ironbridge two houses were washed away just below the Iron Bridge and disaster was averted at the riverside Madeley Wood blast furnaces only by preventing the inundation from coming into contact with the tap-holes of the furnaces, where molten iron coalesced at over 1,500°C. At Coalport the river rose so much that the Severn and the parallel Shropshire Canal

Flooding by the English Bridge at Shrewsbury in the 1880s
(Courtesy of Shrewsbury Museum and Art Gallery)

formed a single sheet of water. In the diary of Thomas Bancks of Severnside in Bewdley, on the Tuesday the ice had abated and the river began to rise. On Wednesday the water entered his house, and on the Friday 'I was on the bridge, water was running up over the two ends of it, part of the fence walls were washed away and the pavement broken and fell in the river while I was on the bridge'.[13]

The deluge was not so severe further downstream but even so, the riverside inhabitants of Worcester were forced to the upper rooms, their cellars flooded, and they too received emergency supplies by boat. The flood level in 1795 was said to have equalled the high water mark of the flood of 1672, which was 10 inches (0.25 metres) lower than the high water of the flood on 18 November 1770, as recorded on the city wall.[14] Meanwhile in Gloucester the lower part of the city was inundated, Westgate Street was navigable for small boats and the new jail was encircled by an impromptu moat.[15]

In 1795 the people of Bewdley and Tewkesbury could see the floods coming. Strange then that in 2007, with flood defence schemes and sophisticated monitoring of the river flow, the summer floods came as such a surprise. On 19 June 58mm of rainfall fell in two hours in the Bewdley area, overwhelming the pumping station on Severnside North, with a result that foul and storm water flooded about 100 homes in the town. Despite being only the 14th wettest July since records began in 1766, the flooding in 2007 was so severe because the rain fell in such a short space of time. The intensity of the rainfall on 20 July, and the inability of drains to cope with it, was the ultimate cause of the severe flooding. Many weather stations recorded rainfall in excess of 25mm per hour, and Pershore College of Agriculture recorded 120mm for the day.[16] According to the Environment Agency the normal July river level at Tewkesbury is 0.5 metres, but it rose to a peak of 5.43 metres, exceeding the level of 5.3 metres at which the 1947 flood peaked. Tewkesbury Abbey was flooded for the first time since 1770. The situation was rendered comical (except for the victims) by the failure to install temporary flood defences at Upton and Worcester, because the barriers were stored in Kidderminster and could not be transported to their destination because the roads were flooded. The barriers at Upton would have been overtopped in any case.[17]

Even when the inhabitants of riverside towns know when a flood is coming they can be caught out by the speed of its rise. The river rose by 6 feet (1.8 metres) in one hour in Worcester in the spring of 1811.[18] The 1852 flood was particularly devastating to Upton, where Dunn's Lane, High Street and New Street were unexpectedly inundated: 'In houses that had been thought to be out of flood's way, the muddy waves surged against the window sills, filled the cellars and bubbled up through the stones of the kitchen floors.' A woman living at the Goom-stool Cottages near the river in Upton said that 'the water was but got to a couple of doors off when I went to the bake-house and to do some errands; they said on the bridge that Severn was coming on unaccountable, and I ran home, and to be sure he was half-way up the kitchen, and my chayney ornaments were swum off the dresser into the back yard'.[19]

The level of water is one thing. What the river takes away is another, and the damage that those floating things do to riverside property yet another. Before dawn on 22 January 1546 a flood brought down part of the Stone Bridge in Shrewsbury, including the lock-up in which an incarcerated felon suddenly found himself exposed to the elements;

he apparently survived because he had been shackled to the floor.[20] In 1795 houses by the Welsh Bridge in Shrewsbury, the counting house at Preens Eddy Bridge at Coalport and houses just below the Iron Bridge were swept into the water. In 1809 some of the riverside houses at Ironbridge were said to have subsided by 12 inches (0.91 metres).[21] Near the rivers in Tewkesbury in 1770 the floods overwhelmed the entire lower storeys of houses, which contained nearly all of a household's possessions.[22]

In the 1795 flood, the riverside timber yards of Shrewsbury lost their stock, which all disappeared downstream as floating battering rams. Tree trunks are particularly hazardous in floods. Mrs Pettyt, who lived in the toll house at Wribbenhall in the mid 20th century, remembers: 'When the river was in flood, one could lie in bed and hear the water lapping through the bridge, an occasional thump would mean another tree trunk hitting the buttresses.'[23] The flood of 1795 also caused irreparable damage to the bridges at Buttington, Buildwas, Bewdley and Stourport. In March 1579 shops on the Stone Bridge in Shrewsbury were destroyed when a float of timber struck the props of the projecting buildings, bringing the whole lot down. Vessels breaking from their moorings were equally powerful battering rams. In the flood of 1848 a coal barge struck Worcester Bridge with such force that it broke in two, part of the vessel floating five miles downstream to Clevelode before it could be recovered.[24]

Another riverside industry was brewing, and brewery stock was also vulnerable to being swept away by floodwaters. Barrels marked 'Berriew' floated down the river in 1795 and were washed ashore in Shrewsbury, presumably with their contents intact. Three men in a boat tried to salvage one of the barrels as it passed along by the Cann Office ferry in Shrewsbury. Alas, their boat overturned. One of the men was washed far down stream and drowned; another clung to a bush and was rescued by someone who threw him a rope. The third man, Mr Johnson, who worked for the Cann Office on the riverside, swam for his life and was fished out of the water by a passerby 200 yards (183 metres) further downstream at Coleham. He was helped into a neighbouring house but died soon after.[25]

The loss of personal property was made more acute by the fact that the riverside dwellers were often poor. On the floodplains in rural areas, farmers saw their livelihoods floating away to oblivion. 'On Friday and Saturday', observed the *Shrewsbury Chronicle* in February 1852, 'pigs, bread, articles of furniture, farming implements & co were observed floating down the river' in Montgomeryshire. In February 1831 losses from Welsh farms extended even to fences, haystacks and outbuildings. Their most valuable asset, however, was livestock. A procession of cattle and pig carcasses was one of the more lamentable sights during Severn floods. Pigs were especially vulnerable, as in the 19th century they were commonly confined to sties and had no chance of escape. In 1852 many Welsh people were said to have taken their pigs upstairs with the other household valuables. Likewise stables were a death trap for horses if there was not sufficient advance warning to move them. But none of this was new. At Michaelmas 1586 a flood in Shrewsbury brought down the river a dung heap with several pigs walking up and down on it. Eventually the dung heap broke apart, depositing its cargo in the river. Pigs are poor swimmers.[26]

Shrewsbury's new Water Works was inundated in 1831. A similar fate, with far-reaching consequences, befell the Mythe Water Treatment Works in 2007. The works had flooded before in 1947, and nearly did so in 2000, but in those cases there was sufficient advance warning to make preparations and ensure the continued supply of drinking water from its service reservoirs. 2007 was different because it happened so quickly. The works was closed down on 22 July. Its Hewlett and Churchdown service reservoirs continued to supply Tewkesbury, Gloucester and Cheltenham, but by the end of the day the taps started to lose water pressure, then dispensed discoloured water with sediments before eventually running dry. For up to ten days most of its 350,000 customers relied on alternative supplies from bottles, bowsers and the tankers that re-filled Hewletts reservoir.[27] A potential catastrophe was also avoided by shutting down the Walham electricity sub-station, on the north side of Gloucester, which supplies half a million homes in Gloucestershire and south Wales. The Environment Agency erected 1,000 metres of flood barriers and was able to pump out the critical areas and avoid a catastrophic and expensive shutdown. Customers supplied from the nearby smaller Castle-mead sub-station, also in a vulnerable position on the floodplain, were not so lucky, and power to 42,000 homes was cut while flood defences were erected.[28]

Modern media have ensured that the apocalyptic horror experienced by flood victims is widely known. In Tewkesbury in 2007, Bridget Lockyer returned home to find the ground floor flooded, a bewildered dog, possessions floating in the back garden and scared children.[29] Scenes of distress were little different to what they had been in 1795 in Shrewsbury: 'The scene in many places was distressing in the extreme. The aged parent weeping, not for the safety of herself – for that of her daughter – the daughter for the infant, many of whom were taken from their room windows into boats and carried upon men's shoulders into the streets, and provided for in different houses.'[30]

Severe flooding brings with it a quota of heroism, tragedy and stupidity. Great snow and frost in 1634 brought ice down the river, breaking Coleham Wall and Shrewsbury's warehouses, and becoming blocked by the Stone Bridge. Richard Davies, a trowman, was made Honorary Burgess for his help in breaking up the ice, to his own considerable danger when his boat was sucked under one of the arches.[31] 'Navigable' is a relative term in times of flood. During the 1947 flood Harry Rogers in his coracle had the most effective means of transport on the fast-flowing river, but he had to be alert to dodge the animal carcasses floating downstream.[32] In the December 1753 floods a boat capsized in Frankwell, Shrewsbury with 11 people aboard, one of whom drowned.[33]

The flooding in Newtown in February 1852 came on quickly, even after three days of torrential rain. Once it overflowed the banks, residents and shopkeepers had little time to respond. 'Across Bridge Street from the Back Lane into Church Street, the water rushed with the impetuosity of a mountain torrent', according to the *Shrewsbury Chronicle*.[34] At the time, John Handy, a woolstapler, was walking up Church Street. Either he had no time to escape, or he underestimated the strength of the current, and was swept away into the river. His beached corpse was found the following morning two miles downstream. Usually, however, there is enough time to flee from the rushing waters, and flooding is not as fatal to human life as it is to animals and property.

We should never underestimate the recklessness of youth in extreme circumstances. At Coton Hill in Shrewsbury in 1831, 'some youths who ventured in the stream on a boat, were driven over the street and over some low walls which bound it, and were at last upset on a muck heap in a field considerably distant from the bed of the river'. During the same flood 'bargemen in a fishing coracle sailed, for a wager, over the Town walls at Roushill and under an arch of the Welsh Bridge'.[35] In 1795 three intrepid nutcases tried to rescue a cabin that had been swept away from Cooper's timber yard. One of the men jumped from a boat on to the cabin and was trying to fasten a rope to it when they suddenly realised that the English Bridge was closer than anticipated. According to the newspaper the man leapt back into the boat and all three men flung themselves in the bottom as the vessel just went through the space between the arch and the raised water level. They were rescued half a mile further downstream. The cabin went to pieces.[36]

Flooding is called a natural disaster, but really it is a human disaster. The river is simply going about its own business and is only ever itself; the fault lies ultimately with a society that refuses to acknowledge the floodplain as a natural, if occasional, part of the river. The Severn has resisted our attempts to tame it. As William Camden described the river in Gloucestershire, 'sometimes it overfloweth its banks, and wanders a great way into the neighbouring plains and then returneth back as conqueror of the land'.[37] This can be used to advantage, especially as floodwaters fertilise the ground they inundate. In Awre, Minsterworth and Slimbridge there were extensive commons beside the river, and in the latter the earl of Berkeley reclaimed part of the floodplain as meadow, protected by high banks.[38] Shrewsbury's town walls were built well above the riverside, leaving an extra-mural riverside common, now known as the Quarry Park.

On the upper section of the river between Llandrinio and Buttington the flood banks, or 'argaes', are set back from the riverbank, a practice at least two centuries old. The advantage is that the banks create a broad channel for the floodwater, but the system has its drawbacks if it is too successful. Adjoining land 'has been found to be much less fertile' than in places where the water is allowed to flood the adjacent fields, and 'in some places it has occasioned the banks to be disregarded'. The compromise solution was to fix 'troughs with a swing gate or valves' to allow controlled flooding of pasture.[39]

After the flood comes the clean up. As Emily Lawson observed in 1869, 'a great flood is a fine sight and would be an enjoyable one' were it not for its legacy. 'The walls and floors of the inundated houses are not thoroughly dry for months, and the inhabitants suffer from severe coughs and inflammatory attacks, or, it may be, lifelong invalidism, rheumatism, or sciatica.'[40] She may be wrong about the details, but she is broadly right about the reality. It is not just water that inundates homes, but the mud, the refuse, and the bacteria the river carries in it. It is surprising, then, that the victims of floods have such short memories. The 20th century was comparatively light on Severn flooding, with the notable exception of 1947. More than two decades later studies showed mixed feelings about flooding. In the floodplain around Shrewsbury a study revealed that less than half of the people thought that flooding was a problem, and only just over a quarter thought that the river would flood again. Another study, on the Lower Severn, asked people what they thought caused flooding. The majority of responses blamed rainfall and hydraulic engineering, but three out of the 42 participants found answers in Genesis: 'If the water enters the house, that is an act of Nature; if one is driven upstairs or on to the roof, that is an act of God; but if one should have so incurred His displeasure that one is swept away, then *that* is a flood.'[41]

∞ 14 ∞
'Found Drowned'

Sabrina is the most famous victim of the river. When she 'dissolv'd into that crystal streame' nobody ever drowned so beautifully, descending into limpid water as an act of purification. Mortals, on the other hand, mix with the silted river bed, where their muddy, bloated and disfigured corpses quickly lose all the individuality and dignity of a living person. Drowning must be one of the worst forms of death for those unlucky enough to be conscious of it, and recovery of the body is a grim task which was once the responsibility of men who worked on the river. One of the worst sights for the Upton watermen was 'the swollen, disfigured corpse of some long-drowned man who has been missing for weeks, in village or town far away up the river'.[1] The time taken to recover drowned bodies has been widely variable. For example, when Stephen Price fell into the water at Bewdley in March 1903, Harry Edgington, a Great Western Railway signalman, jumped in to try to save him. Price's body was pulled from the water hours later. Edgington was fished out at Stourport, but not until a further six weeks had passed.[2] James Chesterton was a 60-year-old waterman from Droitwich who fell overboard near Bevere Lock in December 1886 when the river's strong current caught the tiller, which unfortunately knocked the steersman into the river. Crew members saw his body go over the weir, but it was 11 months later that the body was recovered. The riverbed can hold down a body for a considerable length of time if the current is favourable. In the case of Chesterton the inquest heard that 'the river was at that time in flood and it is surmised that Chesterton's body was held to the bottom by the flood deposit with which it was overlaid, until the present freshet on the river washed it clear again and it floated to the top'. The body was recovered by Charles Webb, who knew Chesterton and was described at the inquest as having 'had great experience in the recovery of bodies', but even he could not be certain that the body was that of his fellow waterman. All Webb could say was that Chesterton had prominent teeth and so did the corpse.[3] The Ironbridge coracle men Harry and James Rogers reckoned that, together with their father Tommy, they recovered over 80 bodies from the Severn, and rescued a few people too, in a period spanning the late 19th to the mid 20th century.[4]

After a matter of only weeks a body that has lain in the river is difficult to identify. In 1828, when the body of George Northwood of Wentnor was taken out of the river at Ironbridge a month after his disappearance, he could be identified only by his clothing, which matched that of a missing-person description issued by his friends in the *Shrewsbury Chronicle*.[5] Modern forensic science has improved techniques of identification, and pathologists' reports, often grisly reading, have replaced the process of identification traditionally carried out by the riverside community. Formerly, local people

A contemporary view shows the sudden and devastating
inundation of the Somerset and Gwent Levels in 1607.

were closely involved in difficult tasks such as recovery and cleaning of the bodies. At the inquest into the death of Emily Harris at Worcester in 1859 two local women gave evidence: 'Mrs Clara Higgs and Mrs Murby, two women who had washed the body, described its appearance. Both eyes were blackened; there were marks on the throat, and a discoloration of the left breast, which was swollen considerably.'[6]

Death in the Severn can be categorised either as accidental or as the consequence of suicide or murder, but it has not always been easy to come to a satisfactory verdict on the cause of death. When a corpse has lain in the river for months or even years, a post-mortem cannot provide a definitive explanation, and even when the body is recovered quickly the evidence can be ambiguous. Two examples were the cases of James Sefton and Annie Jane Davies, who drowned in the Severn at Worcester in 1835 and 1869 respectively. Both died at night. Sefton had been seen carrying a silver watch earlier in the day, but when the body was recovered his watch pocket had been turned inside out and the watch had gone. Foul play was suspected but could not be proved. A post-mortem revealed that the deceased had received a blow to the head when still alive, but this could have been caused by an attack or by a fall that rendered him unconscious and so prevented him from saving himself when he fell into the river.[7] Annie Jane Davies was only 17 and it subsequently emerged that she had a complicated love life. She had agreed to marry a Stourbridge man, but kept it secret from her parents by giving a false name when the banns were read out in church. On the night of her death she had complained that she was being followed, but there was no evidence of foul play. A police constable had heard the splash of the body entering the water at 12.45am and was quickly on the scene.[8] In both cases the coroner returned the Severn's form of an open verdict: 'found drowned'.

Bathers have notoriously underestimated the strength of the current, and perhaps also the temperature of the water. Among the earliest known cases of drowning to appear in coroners' records are the accidental deaths of bathers. In medieval times they were not of course swimming for pleasure, but in the river to maintain their personal hygiene. For example, on 18 June 1296 William Wegs, a local baker, was drowned, and a day later William Waleus (Welshman) drowned in the same stretch of river in Shrewsbury. Not far away, in August 1303 Isolda, wife of a local saddler, also drowned.[9] All three were bathing in the river upstream of the Welsh Bridge, above the point where the river became contaminated by the town's refuse, including that from local tanneries. At least two of them were local people and it is reasonable to suppose that they had bathed in the river before. John Allen drowned in Newtown in 1857 when he found himself in difficulty one July evening. Two men had narrowly escaped death in the same stretch of river two years previously.[10] The fate of F.T.Y. Molyneux, in 1854 an undergraduate at St John's College Cambridge, shortly to enter holy orders, may have been decided by his unfamiliarity with the river and its currents. The young student had entered the water near Bridgnorth but shortly afterwards, perhaps the water being colder than anticipated, was said to have been seized by a violent and fatal cramp. Unable to swim against the current, 'he turned upon his back, and floated down the stream for some distance, till, the vital power being exhausted, the body twined in a perpendicular position, and

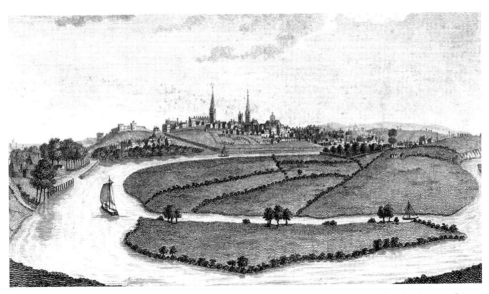

The Severn from Coton Hill in Shrewsbury. In the foreground is the island where a fair was held in 1857 and where several people drowned when the bridge of boats collapsed. (Courtesy of Shrewsbury Museum and Art Gallery)

sank to rise no more'.[11] The body was recovered a couple of hours later, before the river could do its grotesque work. Drink has also been a factor. The landlord of the Wharf Inn at Holt Fleet had refused to serve George Sturdy and his friends on their day trip in September 1906, reckoning that they had already imbibed enough. His friends failed to dissuade George Sturdy from taking a swim.[12]

Accidental drownings have often been lonely affairs, but occasionally spectators who have flocked to the riverbank to enjoy a spectacle have endured the horror of watching people go down to their deaths. In February 1869 a crowd had gathered at the Upper Quay in Worcester to visit Wombwell's Menagerie. When Priscilla Clark, aged only 17, fell into the river her boyfriend, Francis Glover, jumped in after her but, although he managed to reach the girl and they swam together for a short distance, none of the spectators watching the events unfold could throw them a line. His body was soon recovered; they dragged Priscilla's body from the river at Kempsey three months later.[13] The instinct to jump in and rescue a swimmer in distress has often proved fatal. During the construction of the Birmingham Aqueduct over the Severn at Trimpley in 1901 three men who were working on the project were drowned when they went out fishing on their Sunday off. One fell in, the others jumped in to help, but none were aware of or could cope with the strong current.[14]

Perhaps the worst of the Severn's public tragedies happened at Poplars Island near Shrewsbury, where a fete was being held in 1857. The mayor had refused the organisers the use of the Quarry Park. The island, a bylet near Coton Hill on the edge of the town, was a second-best option, but it was necessary to build a bridge of boats to make the island accessible. The riverbank was crowded on the Friday night, during which a firework display was the main attraction. After the show there was a sudden down-pour and spectators rushed on to the bridge to cross quickly and find shelter. People later claimed that some people were deliberately swaying the temporary bridge, but the inquest dismissed that claim. What was not in doubt, however, was that the bridge of boats included one flat-bottomed punt, and it was this that sank and plunged about 100 people into the water.

Among those who had a lucky escape was a local man, Thomas Jones, who gave valuable testimony of the accident, and what it can be like to be plunged into a river at night. 'We were going along the boats and one of the boats was slightly waving; it was the one that sank; the people began to get terrified and ran forward to get to the big barge; just as I was going to put my foot on the big barge the boat sank; I fell in the water over my head with several others; I was there until I lost myself and did not know what I was doing; I laid hold of a piece of rope and a person named Foulkes pulled me out; the mass of people coming forward made it wave; I did not see anyone rocking the boat but a lot of men were making light remarks; I think the cause of the boat sinking was it being too weak.' The punt – a vessel large enough to carry a 13-ton load – did indeed sink, taking down with it the planks laid on top as a makeshift bridge deck. Most of the people were rescued, but ten people were apparently trapped between the deck planks and the punt, and all of them drowned. They included John and Ann Pryce, local siblings aged 11 and 14.[15]

By modern standards, navigating the river was once a dangerous occupation. In some cases the drowned watermen could blame no one but themselves – Samuel Carter had been drinking at the Unicorn Inn at Hampton Loade in 1893 but slipped from the plank when he and his crew members went back on board their narrowboat.[16] Ferries were more dangerous in the lower river and the estuary, as shown by the loss of several passage boats at Aust, but one of the worst ferry disasters happened at night in October 1799. Disaster struck on the daily commute between Coalport and Jackfield of workers at the Coalport chinaworks. The ferry went down close to the bank at nine o'clock at night. Although 15 people reached the shore, in the confusion and the disorientating effect of darkness 28 people drowned: 13 men and boys and 15 women and girls, including three sisters, Jane, Sarah and Anna Bourne.[17] The steersman was blamed for the disaster.

Losses from river vessels were usually blamed on the crew, and often included the crew. Some of them were experienced in river navigation. Richard Matthews, a waterman from Shrewsbury, fell overboard from his barge near Upton-upon-Severn at about two o'clock on a Sunday morning 'from some mismanagement of the tiller'.[18] Four of five people on board a rowing boat were drowned in 1872 near Haw Bridge on their return journey from Tewkesbury, where they had delivered a catch of eels. Coming in the opposite direction was a steam tug hauling four barges and a trow, alongside which was the passenger steamer *Queen Mab*. Instead of navigating toward the bank the steersman, a 40-year-old waterman called Thomas Tarrant, tried to steer a course between the larger vessels. When the boat struck the steamer it turned over and only Joseph Bayliss, a fish-erman, survived, by clinging to the upturned boat until he was rescued by a trowman.[19]

Witnesses to another drowning, that of Arthur Henry Baldwin near Stourport in 1879, claimed that tug-boat crews were not always as careful as they should be. In Baldwin's case, however, an inquest decided that it was unwise to row a small boat into the wake of a tug and its barges. Although the tug was travelling at only 2½ knots, it was enough to overwhelm a small boat.[20] Nor were the barges and narrowboats being tugged always secure. The *Birmingham*, a narrowboat, sank near Haw Bridge in 1879 while carrying a cargo of spelter. Although two of the crew escaped, one of them endured the loss of two sons who were below deck and drowned.[21] Even passenger steamers were not immune to failures in health and safety. Frank Gibbs fell overboard from the steamer *Lady Foley* in 1890, a fatal accident blamed on defective safety barriers.[22]

Murderers and suicides expect the river to offer them complete oblivion, hoping that the body will be washed away never to be found. Perhaps in many cases that remains true, but not always. In 1582 Stephen Prestige pushed his wife over the Stone Bridge at Shrewsbury, but he was caught. A gibbet was set up on the opposite bank, and he was hung from it for three days.[23] In the case of Charrangjit Kaur Gill, murdered in her bed by her own father in 1977, the body was dumped in the river near Bridgnorth in the hope that she could simply be declared a missing person. A gang of men were hoping for the same outcome when they killed 'little Johney Lewis' at Jackfield in 1832. Ben Yates, John Roden, Henry Wae and Noah Potts had tied an iron rail to the body using whip cord, making sure also to tie his cap to it, before dumping the body in the Severn, assuming the ballast would keep him on the bottom forever.[24]

The river destroys evidence, and even if a murder victim is discovered it has not always been possible to solve the crime. The case of a headless corpse discovered at the Haw Bridge in 1938 remains unsolved, and in 1903 a man's body was found in the swollen river at Worcester. His wrists had been bound with a red handkerchief that was then tied to a bush.[25] In 1829 the body of a man was taken out of the river at Coton Hill in Shrewsbury. 'The unfortunate man, who was deranged in intellect … is supposed to have thrown himself into the stream', but the circumstances were more sinister than the newspaper report allows. The man, 'with singular determination, tied his own hands with a handkerchief, to prevent any effort to save himself'.[26] Surely not.

In January 1845 a body was found floating in a whirlpool upstream of Shrewsbury, 'with the head and feet under water, the loins being uppermost, and out of it'. Hauled from the river and taken down to the Fountain Inn in Frankwell, Shrewsbury, the body was quickly identified as that of John Parry, a 38-year-old labourer from Melverley who had vanished from a Severn barge at Montford Bridge two months previously. It was suspected that he had been murdered at the time he disappeared, but the action of the river made it very difficult to prove. On 9 November the boat, laden with Bellan stone and bound for Shelton to be used in road building, was moored near Montford Bridge. The crew drank in the Powis Arms – Parry had three pints of ale, his mates a little more – before returning to the barge before midnight. What happened next is disputed. According to the other crew members, the men retired to bed after smoking their pipes – they all slept in the same cabin, two to a berth – but in the morning Parry was missing. According to a neighbour, around midnight there was a tremendous commotion that sounded like a fist fight, followed by the stamping of several pairs of feet. He did not, however, hear the sound of a body falling into the water. The crew hired another man in Parry's place and completed their journey. Once Parry was reported missing the river was dragged below Montford Bridge, but the Severn still managed somehow to conceal its victim.

A *post mortem* and inquest followed the discovery of the body two months later. All of the crew members were required to give evidence, and all stuck to their original story. The coroner observed that the deceased had a black eye that was sustained before death, although not itself sufficient to be a cause of death. The landlord of the Powis Arms, and a police constable who had seen the party return from the pub, confirmed that Parry did not have a black eye. The injury was consistent with a fist fight, but might also have been caused by the victim falling overboard. Unfortunately the body was too badly decomposed to establish a cause of death, although the coroner noted that the pulmonary arteries were 'not gorged with black blood' as was usual with a drowned man. Evidence of how the man died had perished in the river and so the jury, instructed by the coroner, returned an open verdict of 'found drowned'.[27]

Suicide cases can be ambiguous for different reasons. When the body of Mrs Yapp, missing for three weeks, was discovered by the crew of a tug passing Diglis Lock in 1893 it was assumed to be a simple case of suicide. It was suggested that she had been drinking and that she feared arrest by the police in connection with some stolen money. On the night of her disappearance she was said to have quarrelled with some or all of her seven children. The local community declined to see it that way. At her funeral two days later many of them noisily followed the cortege but were refused admission to the cemetery. Some climbed over the walls and disrupted the ceremony with cries of 'lynch him' and 'duck him' directed at her husband.[28] Emily Harris drowned herself and her two children in August 1859 in the aftermath of a heated domestic argument. Her mother-in-law was arrested on a charge of threatening behaviour, although was not subsequently charged. Her husband was convicted of assault and received a three-month jail sentence.[29]

Richey Edwards of the Manic Street Preachers is the most high-profile of recent Severn suicides. In 1995 his car was found abandoned at Aust Service Station by the Severn Bridge. Did he walk on to the bridge and jump, or did he leave his car there to give the impression that he had committed suicide, only to start a new life anonymously somewhere else? This is fertile territory for conspiracy theorists. But there is a mystery to the story that is common with all suicides, where the information in the public domain gives only a simplified snapshot of a life gone wrong. William Farrington, of St John's Hill in Shrewsbury, was said to have been 'in a low desponding way during the greater part of the severe weather' of 1795 and took his opportunity when the river was in flood. He 'went out (as his wife thought about his business) but in the afternoon his hat and coat were found by the waterside near the Quarry'.[30] His body was recovered two days later quite close to where he was supposed to have entered the water.

The saddest river deaths are of course those of children. Asenath Pardoe drowned herself in 1895 at Worcester along with her 18-month-old daughter Gertrude. The mother had suffered from what we now recognise as post-natal depression and had strapped her infant to her chest when she jumped into the river. The inquest gave verdicts of 'suicide while temporarily insane' for the mother and murder for the child.[31] In at least two other cases the identity of the child remained unknown. In 1847 fishermen fished out a bundle from the water at Lower Parting, Gloucester, during the early hours. 'The outside covering was composed of a dark coloured cloth, sewed tightly with worsted. On cutting this open he found another piece of cloth with something tied up inside, and on unfastening the knot, he discovered a fine full grown female infant. It appeared to have been in the water a long time, and decomposition had commenced.'[32] A similar case occurred only four months later at Stourport, when watermen picked up a green merino bag lying in 18 inches of water. The bag had been sewn up and contained the body of an infant girl of about three months, and a brick. The surgeon who examined the body reported that she had been well-dressed in her night clothes, but had received a blow from the head and had been at least partially suffocated. The child was reckoned to have been in the water for only six or seven hours.[34] Behind these infant tragedies lay the tragedies of despairing mothers or third parties living with the consequences of what had happened. In their desperation they had sought out the river, recognising its power and mystery, hoping that it would never give up its secrets.

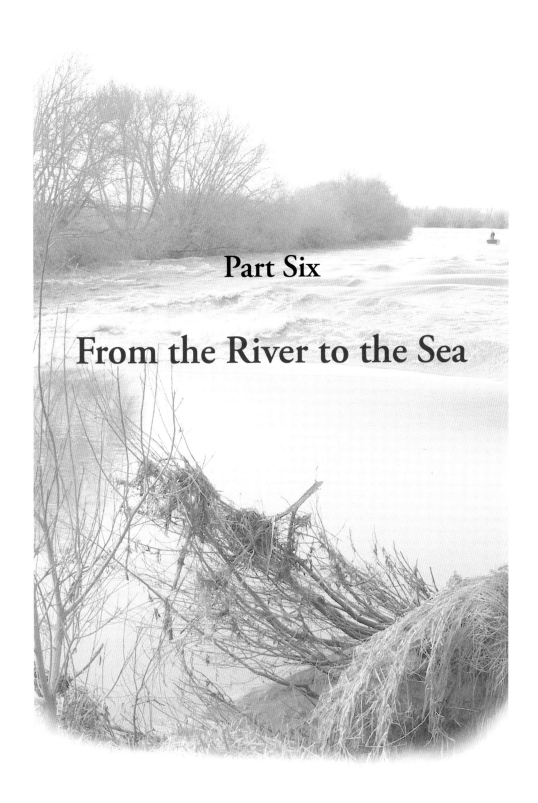

Part Six

From the River to the Sea

∽ 15 ∾
The Severn Bore

That the Severn Bore is one of the natural wonders of Britain was declared by the Welsh historian Nennius, writing as early as the 9th century, in what is the earliest known description of the phenomenon. Not that the Severn is unique; other British rivers also have tidal bores. The Parrett has the next strongest bore in the south-west, and there are also bores on the Humber and the Solway Firth. The latter was described in Sir Walter Scott's novel *Redgauntlet* (1824). And yet none is of the magnitude of the Severn Bore, the primacy of which was emphasised in Michael Drayton's *Poly-Olbion* (1613), an extended rhapsody on the 'renowned Isle of Great Britaine' in which the Severn Bore, or 'hygre', contributes to the glory and beauty of the nation.

> In *Sabrins* Soveraigne armes: with whose tumultuous waves
> Shut up in narrower bounds, the *Higre* wildly raves;
> And frights the stragling rocks, the neighbouring shores to flie
> A farre as from the Maine it comes with hideous cry,
> And on the angry front the curled foam doth bring,
> The billowes gainst the banks when fiercely it doth fling;
> Hurles up the slimie ooze, and makes the scalie brood
> Leap madding to the Land affrighted from the flood
> Oerturnes the toylinge Barge …[1]

The bore was known as the *Hygre* or *Eagre* (pronounced eager) until at least the 18th century.[2] The origin of the word has exercised scholars over the centuries, but as yet there have been no really convincing answers. It is not a local word specific to the Severn. John Ingelow's 1571 poem *High Tide on the Coast of Lincolnshire* spells the bore on the Humber as *eygre*. *Eagre* may have derived ultimately from *eau-guerre* or water-war. Bore is a comparatively recent term, probably derived from the Old Norse *bara*, meaning a wave, but was used by Daniel Defoe in 1725 to describe the tide at Aust.

As Sir Robert Atkyns put it in 1712, the Severn 'swells not by degrees but comes in an heap'.[3] Or to put it in more technical terms, the Severn Bore is a tidal surge wave, caused by the sharp narrowing of the channel at the mouth of the river, coupled with the high tidal reach of the Severn Sea, up to a maximum of 14 metres between high and low tides. (The Bay of Fundy, located between Nova Scotia and New Brunswick in Canada, is the only place in the world with a larger rise between low and high tide.) When this mass of water is funnelled into a narrow channel the tidal surge is formed. A bore needs a channel of particular shape and proportion in plan and in the slope of its bed. It is not simply a matter of the tide coming in; the bore develops a power and momentum of its own. It travels for 25 miles between Awre and Gloucester and moves at up to 14 miles per hour. When it is rolling upstream from Minsterworth the tide is already ebbing at Sharpness. The height of the waves is variable. It has been known to reach over 6 feet (2 metres) but this is exceptional. In most years the largest waves are up to 4 feet (1.3 metres) high – powerful enough to re-deposit river sediments back up the river. The cut made in 1793 to link the river with the Hereford and Gloucester Canal has gradually become blocked by material thrown back by the bore.[4]

There are tidal bores on approximately 130 days of the year, but the most powerful of them coincide with the spring tides either side of the spring and autumn equinoxes. Factors like high rainfall and wind direction can also affect its size. High freshwater levels in the river and opposing winds will reduce its height and delay its arrival, whereas a following wind has the opposite effect.

Nennius described the bore as '*Dau Ri Hafren*, that is, the two kings of the Severn. When the sea floods into the Severn estuary in the Bore, two heaped-up wave crests are built up separately, and fight each other like rams. One goes against the other, and

The Severn Bore in 1930 at what is considered one of the best places to see the bore, Stonebench, to which carriage trips were organised.

they clash in turn, and then one withdraws from the other, and they go forth again at each tide. This they have done, from the beginning of the world to the present day.[5] In the time of Nennius the only place where 'the two kings of the Severn' could have been observed was at Hook Cliff near Frampton. Here the river divides into two channels either side of a sandbank known as the Noose, and the wave in the east channel breaks against and rebounds off Hook Cliff.

Steering boats into the bore is a sport of long standing, but the phenomenon was also a boon to commercial vessels travelling upstream. Barges and trows could make the 30-mile journey from Sharpness to Gloucester in a little over two hours if they could ride the bore. The vessels invariably followed behind the wave, which swelled the river sufficient to give a good depth of water. It was said that the men could pass by a single orchard with one stroke of the oars. Vessels navigating downstream had to take precautions against the advancing bore, which was perfectly manageable for those experienced on the lower river and estuary. The bore can be faced when in a boat, as long as it is taken headlong. If the bore strikes a boat at an angle it will capsize.[6] Exactly that appears to have happened to the Newnham ferry, which sank in 1809 in full view of the horrified and helpless spectators on each bank. Its two-man crew and a passenger were all drowned. The bore was higher than expected, and although the boatmen attempted to turn their vessel end on, the wave engulfed their boat.[7]

Bore-watching has been popular at least since the time of Nennius. By the end of the 18th century, if not earlier, it was attracting large crowds – when Sir Charles Blagdon went to see it at Lower Parting near Gloucester at the turn of the 18th/19th century he found an expectant and knowledgeable crowd gathered there. Favourable conditions for the bore were by then well known. The best ones occurred when the river was relatively low, at a full or new moon, and would be augmented by a south-westerly onshore wind. Sir Charles Blagdon noted that some people watched from the shore, while others were waiting in boats for the thrill of riding a powerful wave. Just below Lower Parting were 'commonly some men in boats to meet the tide, and some dogs are thrown in just as it comes, to observe their howling and distress. On a sudden, the boats and dogs are instantaneously raised up and thrown into violent agitation, and at the same time a vast wall of water, reaching across the whole channel of the Severn ... is seen approaching with extreme rapidity.'[8] Where the river channel narrowed Blagdon reckoned that the wave could rise to 8-9 feet high (2.4-2.75 metres). Blagdon tried to chase the bore on horseback, but reached Over Bridge too late, reckoning that the wave had travelled 20 miles in 65 minutes. In 1819 Lady Hawkins watched the bore from the same position at Lower Parting, and commented how the meeting of tide and stream threw up water that flooded the riverside meadows.

By the late 19th century, trips to see the bore at Stonebench and Elmore were advertised in Gloucester, Cheltenham and Stroud. In April 1901 it was reported that people came from Bristol, Bath, Dursley, Cirencester, Cheltenham and Stroud, and the Great Western Railway had put on special trains.[9] The bore is visible between Awre and Over, but the most popular viewing points are Minsterworth, Framilode, Weir Green, Stonebench, Lower Parting and Over Bridge, mainly because at these points the river is easily accessible. But the bore can be seen to good effect at all places on this stretch of river, all of which is accessible on either bank by public footpaths. During the 1930s the bore was floodlit and attracted huge crowds – it is said that over 100,000 people viewed the spectacle in under two years. Night-time bores still attract visitors and surfers.

The bore can be dangerous. Sightseers have got into difficulties, as in the case of William Glass and his two friends, who had come to Gloucester on Good Friday 1884 hoping to see the equinoctial bore. At Westgate Bridge the three men hired a boat rowed by a local man, Charles Schollard. When the rowing boat was overwhelmed by the bore at Hempsted the men all swam for the shore but William Glass went under. It was assumed that the spring tides would have swept the body far downstream, but in the event his body was recovered two days later only yards from where he was last seen.[10]

The magnitude of the bore has made it attractive to surfers in recent years. Bore-surfing has become a global sport, but it began on the Severn, where surfers have been competing since the 1950s to take the longest ride on the Bore. Colonel Jack Churchill surfed the bore for one and a half miles in 1955; Rodney Sumpter rode it for six miles in 1965. Surfing a bore is not easy, given that the river carries down trees and other debris, and stamina is required to stay on the board for a long period. In 2006 Steve King, from Saul, near Framilode, mastered the Bore to gain the Guinness World Record by staying on his board in the Severn estuary for 7.6 miles. Bores are categorised by their expected strength, and when a rare five-star bore was predicted in March 2010 there were so many surfers at Newnham that they struggled to surf it without getting in each other's way. The fact that a surfer can ride the bore for far longer than it is possible to ride a sea wave, even on the best surfing beaches, explains why the sport has gone global. Even so, the Severn remains one of only a handful of bores that can be surfed. The other main ones are on the Kampar river in Indonesia, the mouth of the Amazon and its tributaries in Brazil, where it is known as a *Pororoca*, and, the largest in height of them all, Qiantang river in Hangzhou province in China.

There is still strong interest in the Severn Bore, as I found when I made the pilgrimage to the riverbank at Lower Parting below Gloucester. Perhaps its special attraction is that it is the biggest bore in Britain. Lower Parting is one of the best places to view the bore because, as the two river channels reunite here on their downstream journey, when the bore rolls in it is directed straight towards the spectators. Ten minutes before it was due, the turnout looked poor, but a steady trickle of visitors followed and a couple of minutes before the appointed time the riverbank was suddenly quite crowded. Behind us in the distance we could see Over Bridge, the only bridge under which the bore passes, where a line of people extended right across the deck of the bridge. Apparently the bore is sometimes early but more often late. This probably accounted for the unhurried demeanour of the spectators, who were mainly Gloucester folk, including regular dog walkers who have seen large and small bores many times. Even two surfers making their way downriver, lying on their boards and paddling with their hands, aided by the river's strong current, seemed in no hurry.

Half an hour after the due time the river was as calm as a summer's day and it was difficult to imagine that anything was about to happen at all. When it did arrive, it

The Severn Bore at Lower Parting, 2012

came silently at first, heralded by three or four surfers, some of whom may still have been riding it as it made its way up the west channel. Someone who has never seen the bore before might expect the wave to break and then peter out, but it keeps moving at a steady, relentless pace. As it approached, the wave broke over the shallow bed, and as it reached the parting of the river there was a rush of water against the bank, ferocious enough to frighten small children. After the bore had passed the river water convulsed for a couple of minutes, and in less than a minute, a river channel that had looked more than half empty had filled up. The direction of flow was now upriver and stronger than the previous downward flow. Part of a tree trunk that had floated gently downstream was now floating back upstream in double quick time, and the same was true of the surfers I had seen gliding down; they had already been defeated by the bore. Over 45 minutes later the direction of flow was still upriver.

The very power of the tide in the estuary that makes the Severn Bore unforgettable has made it attractive in another sense: for electricity generation. Schemes for damming the mouth of the river were mooted in the 19th century; the plan was to replace the Old Passage with a road and rail crossing, which would have facilitated the creation of a freshwater harbour and lake easier to navigate than the river in its natural state. The idea of a barrage surfaced again in the 1920s and 1930s, when there were serious proposals to dam the estuary and generate electricity using turbines. Various schemes have been proposed during the post-war period for barrages built in various places, as far into the Bristol Channel as a line between Cardiff and Weston-super-Mare. Smaller tidal-power schemes have already been successful, the earliest of which, on the Rance estuary in France, began generating in 1966. The Severn estuary would be a much bigger under-taking, and presents the added problem of the high silt load of the Severn, which would quickly reduce the output of any turbines. Following the Severn Tidal Power Feasibility Study concluded in 2010, the government has decided that there is no case for building a barrage at the moment, but that the idea remains a possibility. A tidal-power barrage may prove to be a prohibitively expensive infrastructure project, but if it was ever built, the Severn bore would no longer exist and the lower Severn would cease to be tidal, a reminder of how vulnerable natural wonders can be.

❧ 16 ❧
The Severn Sea

Goat's Hole Cave is one of several caves in the cliffs of the Gower peninsula in south Wales, overlooking the Severn Sea towards the north Devon coast. Here, in 1823, was made one of the luckiest finds in British archaeology, popularly known as the Red Lady of Paviland (in fact neither red, nor a lady, and nor, to be perfectly correct, is the cave called 'Paviland'). That human and animal bones could be found in the Gower caves was well known to locals. It only became known to the wider world when Professor William Buckland, one of the first professional geologists, was called down to investigate a new discovery. What he found was the grave of a man whose clothes had been smeared with ochre, and who was accompanied by a variety of grave goods. We now know that he had lain there undisturbed for 26,000 years, during which time the world outside the cave was transformed beyond recognition.[1]

The cave once overlooked a vast and fertile plain watered by the river Severn and its many tributaries, and stretching westwards well beyond the tip of Cornwall and Pembrokeshire. Much of it was grassland, known as mammoth-steppe, where roamed mammoth, woolly rhinoceros, lion, bear, giant deer, horse, spotted hyena and wolf. A mammoth skull was placed by the grave of the dead man. Hyenas and bears had once found winter dens in what were then hilltop caves, but later on it was humans who colonised them in the summertime. Goat's Hole Cave and others like it were used by hunters as convenient shelters overlooking their summer hunting grounds. Perhaps the cave was a regular haunt of the dead man's family when they visited the area each year, and perhaps they had come specifically looking for valuable ivory. In the millennia following the burial, the world changed immeasurably. Ice sheets advanced southwards into Wales, while another ice sheet from Ireland swept eastwards over the mammoth-steppe. All life retreated southwards – humans to the Loire valley and further south – and by the time the ice melted, the world of the early hunters had been completely forgotten.

When Britain was still joined to the European continent and the Thames was a tributary of the Rhine, the Severn was the only major river that flowed to the sea. The rivers of Somerset, Devon and south Wales – including the Axe, Parrett, Torridge, Taw, Usk, Rhymney, Taf, Neath, Tawe, Towy – are all erstwhile Severn tributaries. Beneath sea level, vestiges of their valley topography have been mapped in many places. Submerged forests and peat beds are found around the coast, and were noted as long ago as 1171 by Giraldus Cambrensis, who saw the stumps of an ancient forest laid bare by a sandstorm at Newgale in Pembrokeshire. The stumps bore hatchet marks, evidence that at the time Giraldus saw it, the timber was still in good enough condition to be used for firewood. When excavations were made for the construction of Barry Docks in 1895 peat beds and oak logs were found 33 feet (10 metres) below sea level.[2] Forget the notion of stone-age fishermen – the 'Red Lady of Paviland' is one of the few relics of this drowned world.

The Severn Sea formed slowly as ice melted and the sea level gradually rose. Changes to the landscape in the aftermath of the Ice Age were, however, more complicated. Rivers that were blocked by glacial boulders, gravel and sand had to cut new channels, depositing more silt into the Severn valley and altering the lie of the land. As the climate warmed, birch, followed by oak, hazel and alder afforestation, made the valley green again before it was progressively drowned. More than 5,000 years ago the builders of the Tinkinswood megalithic chambered tomb in the Vale of Glamorgan, so similar in style to the tombs of the Cotswolds, probably reached beyond Cardiff by land rather than by sea. If the bluestones at Stonehenge really did come from Carn Meini in Pembrokeshire then almost certainly the Severn Sea carried them a shorter distance on their journey to Wiltshire than it would today. There was no Severn Bore at that time because the sea had not yet advanced into the narrow channel upstream of Sharpness. By the onset of the Roman colonisation of Britain, however, sea level had reached what it has been in historic times, the only significant subsequent changes being to the coastline.

As sea level slowly rose the land routes across the broad Severn Vale were gradually cut off and people made their journeys by water instead. The important point is that they kept making those journeys. If today the Severn Sea seems like a formidable barrier separating the coasts of south Wales and south-west England, it has only been seen that way in comparatively recent times. The Severn channel is relatively narrow between north Somerset and south Wales. Minehead is only 12½ miles (20 kilometres) from the Vale of Glamorgan coast, to the west of which the sea widens, but even Swansea is only 27 miles (43 kilometres) from the north Devon coast. The Severn Sea therefore once united rather than divided the people of south Wales and south-west England. An English traveller to south Wales in the late 17th century was surprised to find little Welsh spoken by the local people of Llantwit Major, in the Vale of Glamorgan, and remarked of their English that 'their dialect [is] approaching nearer to a broad Somersetshire than to any other'. A little further west in Coychurch a local source confirmed the same thing: 'the language is partly English, partly Welsh, our tradeing being for the most parte with Summer and Devon Shires which spoiles our Welsh'.[3]

The Severn Sea was for long characterised by cross-channel cultural and trading links. Romans regularly made the crossing from the port at Sea Mills (near Bristol) to Caldicot Pill, which was close to the town of Caerwent and the legionary fortress at Caerleon. Celtic Christian missionaries also crossed the Severn Sea from south Wales, as the dedications of parish churches show. For example, St Cyngar was a Pembrokeshire saint who helped found Christian communities on the Somerset coast, hence the village of Congresbury. Dyfrig was a 6th-century bishop associated with Caerleon, to whom Porlock church in Somerset is dedicated (in the Latin form of his name, Dubricius). At the Somerset port of Watchet the church is dedicated to St Decuman, a 6th-century monk from Pembrokeshire who came to live in the area as a hermit. His cult became well established in his adopted county at Wells Cathedral and Muchelney Abbey. Keyne was one of the daughters of the Welsh patriarch Brychan but, refusing to marry, she crossed the sea to live as a hermit on the Somerset or Devon coast, before moving west to Cornwall. She is especially associated with the well of St Keyne in Cornwall, but her dedication is also found at Llangeinor in Glamorgan. St Samson was a novice in the monastery at Llantwit Major in the 6th century. Subsequently he retired to Caldey Island off Tenby, where he eventually became abbot, before being ordained bishop and travelling across to Cornwall, where he was especially active in missionary work. Petroc also came from south Wales and established a monastery in Cornwall at Padstow. Cornwall was the centre of his cult in the Middle Ages, but churches were dedicated to him in Cornwall, Devon and south Wales.

The Severn Sea links the Celtic lands of Wales and Cornwall (which, in its ancient constitution, also included Dartmoor). In the story from the *Mabinogion* of 'How Culhwch won Olwen' the Severn Sea is the Celtic territory where much of the story takes place. Culhwch is set a list of nigh-impossible tasks by Ysbadadden which he must complete before he can marry his daughter Olwen. The hero enlists the help of Arthur and his court. Arthur has his own ship, *Prydwen*, in which he sails at one point in the story from Gloucester to Milford Haven. One of the chief tasks that must be performed is the hunting of Twrch Trwyth, son of Taredd Wledig, a king who has been transformed into a boar. There was a comb and shears between his ears, and only these implements could be used to dress Ysbadadden's beard. The elusive Twrch Trwyth was tracked down to Aber Hafren (literally 'mouth of the Severn'), where Arthur ordered his men, as well as his Celtic cousins in Devon and Cornwall, to stand up to the boar, who had already killed many of Arthur's men. Ambushed, the boar was driven into the Severn: 'And they grabbed him first by his feet, and soused him in the Hafren until it flooded over him.' They managed to seize the shears, but not the comb. The boar found its feet and escaped, and Arthur pursued it all the way to Cornwall. Two of Arthur's men were drowned by the Severn, which now played a malign role: 'As Cacamwri [Arthur's servant, who also magically appears in the following task] was pulled up, two millstones pulled him back into the depths. As he was running after the boar, Osla Gyllellfawr's knife fell from its sheath and he lost it, and after that his sheath was full of water; as he was pulled up, it pulled him back into the depths.'[4] The comb was at last won by Arthur in Cornwall, and the boar was finally driven into the sea and drowned.

These cultural links across the Severn Sea thrived in the medieval period too. The closeness in style of 13th-century architecture between the church at Haverfordwest, Llandaff Cathedral and Wells Cathedral is well known. The great landowners of the Middle Ages – the barons and the monasteries – had a surprising number of links across the sea. The coastal lowlands of Gwent and Glamorgan were quickly seized by Norman barons, either by sea-borne routes or, in the case of the Fitz Hamo family as successive earls of Gloucester, by land. Bonvilston near Cardiff derives its name from the land-owning de Bonvil family of Minehead; Carmarthen Castle was built in 1094 by William FitzBaldwin, who came from Devon; Henry I persuaded a number of Flemish immi-grants living in Devon to settle in Pembrokeshire, but they retained their English land-holdings. English monasteries like Tewkesbury, Montacute, Gloucester and Glastonbury, were patrons of churches in south Wales, and had daughter religious houses there. Neath Abbey was founded by the Devon knight Richard de Granville and had substantial land-holdings in Devon and Somerset. Writing in the reign of Edward VI in the mid 16th century, Dr Thomas Phaer claimed that most of the coast between Chepstow and Burry Port was owned by the earls of Worcester and Pembroke.[5]

It was John Leland who coined the term 'Severnside' and it was he and his contem-porary Dr Thomas Phaer, when compiling an official report on the harbours and ports of Wales, who described the coastal towns and villages in south-west England and south Wales in relation to one another. So Newport lies against Clevedon, Barry against Minehead and Bridgwater, Mumbles and Oxwich against Combe Martin, Burry Port and Carmarthen against Barnstaple.[6] Apart from these routine crossing routes there was significant trade between the major ports, of which Carmarthen was pre-eminent on the Welsh coast in the Middle Ages, including the ports of the river navigation from Gloucester upwards. But the coastal trade was of course dominated by Bristol.

The importance of Bristol eventually supplanted the ancient link to the Severn in the naming of the sea. It was known as the Severn Sea at least from the time of Ptolemy, and is referred to as such by English and Welsh authors like Giraldus Cambrensis, Leland and Edward Lhuyd. The alternative, Bristol Channel, came about probably from the

St Pierre Pill, near Mathern in Monmouthshire, is seen here in the early 19th century. It was part of the busy cross-channel traffic that characterised life by the Severn Sea.

end of the 17th century and derives presumably from use by sailors to the port of Bristol. A French sea chart of 1693 by Jaillot refers to it as 'Canal de Bristol'.[7] The old name has been left to the versifiers who romanticised the Severn Sea as a conduit of trade and adventure, like T.H. Warren, writing at Minehead in 1892:

> A noble flood, more proudly wide,
> From our dear island's mother breast
> Pours none, nor swirls a fuller tide
> To barter with the boundless West
> For many a costly argosy
> Than this broad stream of Severn Sea.[8]

By the end of the 19th century the former importance of the Severn Sea as a coastal region had evidently been forgotten, overshadowed by the rich international heritage of the port of Bristol. Bristol was an important port even before the Norman Conquest and by the 14th century had established lucrative overseas trade with Gascony, Anjou and Poitou, where wool was traded for wine. The discovery of the New World transformed Bristol as a port. By the end of the 17th century about half of its ships sailed for Virginia, the Caribbean or Newfoundland. Its heyday, the first half of the 18th century, was sustained by the trade of slaves and Caribbean sugar, but it also stimulated an industrial revolution in miniature within Bristol itself. Many new and innovative industries were set up in the city, such as brass, pottery and glass manufacture, often importing raw materials from the Severn river ports. Abraham Darby had a brassworks and an iron foundry in Bristol before he moved to Coalbrookdale in 1708 and applied his innovatory spirit to iron smelting. Bristol and Coalbrookdale may now seem far apart and unconnected, but to Darby's contemporaries that connection was much closer and more logical.

Bristol was also a regional port. When a new quay was built in the mid 12th century it took large vessels trading with France and the Mediterranean, leaving the older quay near Bristol Bridge, known as the Back, and later Welsh Back, to deal with inland and coastal trade with the Severn, south-west England, south Wales and Ireland. It was this coastal trade that brought people from south Wales and the south-west to Bristol as the economic focus of the region.

Many Severnside merchants and landowners, including the monasteries, had commercial premises in Bristol, and many Bristol merchants had property interests in Severnside ports. Thus, Severnsiders took part in Bristol's growing international trade in the Middle Ages and in its voyages of discovery. On a trading expedition to Spain in 1507, John Benett, a Bristol merchant, composed his will, in which he left 20 marks to the church at Mumbles, near Swansea, his place of birth. John Lloyd, a Welshman, captained a ship that embarked from Bristol in 1480 in search of the Isle of Brasil.[9]

The decline of Bristol as a port is attributable to one of the most obvious natural characteristics of the Severn Sea. Anyone who has visited Somerset beaches like Blue Anchor or Weston-super-Mare and has watched the sea stretching far away into the distance at low tide will have noticed that the tide goes out a very long way. The Severn has an enormous tidal reach. The Bristol Avon was only navigable at high tide, and even then, the narrowness of the channel prevented its use by the larger modern ships of the later 19th century. The point was driven home in 1851 when the newly launched Bristol steamship *Demerara* ran aground and broke up in the Avon Gorge, before it had even reached the open sea.

The Severn Sea is fringed with low-lying areas on either side of its channel – the Gwent Levels and the Somerset Levels. Both of these areas are protected by sea defences which have, at times, been breached. A Severn Sea flood is not, technically, a tsunami, but can happen as suddenly and with a similar magnitude of devastation. On the night of 13 December 1981 a 25-foot (7.6 metres) tide was expected but was swelled a further 8 feet (2.4 metres) by a south-westerly storm. When the wind shifted north-westerly at high tide a slab of water was trapped against the Somerset coast, breaking through the sea defences in 15 places between Porlock and Clevedon, inundating Burnham-on-Sea and threatening Hinkley Point's two nuclear power stations. Next to it stood Morris Ingram's eel farm, where water welled up through the floor and overturned the fibre-glass tanks in which the eels were housed, releasing them back into the sea. Livestock were the principal casualties. Sheep were afloat inside houses. Harold Reason of Stretcholt, near the mouth of the Parrett, lost all but two of 1,200 fattened pigs which were just hours from being dispatched to the slaughter house.[10]

The most infamous Severn tidal wave occurred in 1607 and devastated the levels of both Somerset and Gwent.[11] On 20 January 1607 the sea surged over the defences

The Severn Sea, bridged since 1995 by the Second Severn Crossing

in a flood that was described by contemporaries in the same manner as the duke of Buckingham's flood in 1483 – as a divine intervention rather than a natural disaster. 'Sin overflowes our soules: The Seas of all strange impieties have rusht in uppon us: we are covered with the waves of abhomination and uncleanness: we are drowned in the black puddles of hellish iniquity: wee swim up to the throates, nay even above the chins in Covetousness.' And yet it was only a mere taste of God's judgement. We must change our ways unless 'these water-flouds in particular, prove but forerunners unto some fear-full calamities'.

On the Welsh side the sea penetrated as far as four miles inland, over a coastline of some 22 miles from Mathern (by Chepstow) to Rumney (on the edge of Cardiff). On the English side the inundations occurred mainly on the Somerset Levels where the sea defences were breached near Weston-super-Mare. The sea flowed inland for up to five miles at a depth said to have been up to 12 feet (3.7 metres). Escape from the surging waters was almost impossible. The waters, 'having gotten over their wonted limittes, are affirmed to have ranne at their first entrance with a swiftnesse so incredible, as that no Gray hounde coulde have escaped by running before them'. Livestock and agricultural produce stand little chance in sudden floods. In Monmouthshire 'all kinds of Cattle … were drowned; Rakes and mowes of corne torne out of their place and carried away'. In Somerset 'whole heards of Cattle, struggling for life with the flouds, Oxen in great numbers were caryed away with the streame, and looked like so many Whales in ye Sea; their bellowing made a noise in the water as if it had bin a tempest'. Rabbits were driven from their burrows and clung to the backs of sheep to escape the rising waters, until they

The Severn has the world's second highest tidal reach.
Low tide leaves the characteristic square miles of slime and seaweed and rocks.

and their hosts were all drowned. A shepherd climbed a tree for safety and had a bird's eye view of the terrified confusion and annihilation of his flock below.

It is a story of human tragedy and miraculous escapes. It was estimated that nearly 2,000 people perished on the Welsh side. Many sought safety in their houses, on rooftops or up trees, only for their refuges to be swept away. The victims drowned and 'theyr dead bodies floate hourly above water and are continually taken uppe'. There was little time to escape. One man who floated to safety by clinging to one of the roof trusses of his house was washed ashore. But it was a mixed blessing, as 'the tirranous streame presented unto him the Tragedy of his deere Wife and deerest children, She, they ... whorried to their deaths by the torrent before his face, and drowned doubly, in his teares'. But there were also stories of lucky escapes: babies floating to safety in their cradles, a man and a woman who climbed into a butt that floated past as they were clinging to the wreckage of their house, a mother who placed her baby on a roof beam in her house, where the child was found after the water had subsided.

When set against disasters of recent years, such as the tsunami of Thailand in 2005 and Japan in 2011, the melodramatic language does not seem so exaggerated. It has been suggested that the tidal wave of 1607 was also a tsunami triggered in the aftermath of an earthquake (which has serious implications for a coastline with nuclear installations).[12] There was no mass communication in 1607 that could have warned people of imminent danger. We have that now, up to a point. What we cannot predict, however, is the long-term behaviour of the sea and its effect on the low-lying areas of Somerset and Gwent. The Somerset Levels exist in their present form only by pumping and by the installation of gates to shut out the sea water at high tide. Here, where several rivers drain into a flat, unfinished sorting of land from water, the earliest evidence of a tidal gate, or 'clyse', is as early as 1485. Perhaps the slow rise is more to be feared that the sudden inundation. Sea level is certainly rising, and the Severn Sea is only a comparatively recent formation, its business unfinished.

᠀ Afterword ᠀
The Present and Future River

At the end of a book that has portrayed the Severn as part of our cultural history it is reasonable to ask in what sense the river still matters, and what role the Severn is likely to play in our lives in the future. The Severn has been a frontier, a highway, a source of sustenance, a playground and a sewer, but the way we have used the river has changed in many ways. It was rivers that enticed us down from the hilltops where once our civilisation was based, because only a river, flowing through a fertile valley and offering an easy means of communication, could sustain a large number of people together in one place. Riverside towns became centres of commerce and wealth precisely because they were by the river, but commerce has long departed from the river bank. Industry has also left, and what light industry there is in the region looks to the motorway network. The Severn is now behind railways and canals in the story of outmoded transport systems, and its wharfside buildings have either found new uses or disappeared. Many places along the river bear no trace of the great events that once occurred there, like the battlefields at Worcester and Buttington, while some remnants of the past have eluded the heritage industry and are largely forgotten, like the caves at Redstone. Fishing has declined and its culture almost vanished. The river is only navigated for pleasure and no longer needs specialist craft such as trows and coracles to negotiate its shallow waters. The ferry at Hampton Loade is a tourist attraction.

In other ways our relationship with the river has scarcely changed, even if it is largely unrecognised. The Severn provides drinking water for six million people and is likewise integral to the treatment of our sewage. We take this for granted, having forgotten the epic struggle that took place to improve public health in Victorian Britain. The investment in flood defences is a statement about the future, but when floods will occur may become increasingly unpredictable. In previous centuries there was a flooding season from January to March, often exacerbated by thawing ice and snow, but whether that pattern will remain the same in the long term is uncertain. Flash floods, which assailed the Severn area in the summer of 2007, and have occurred in other parts of Britain in recent years, may become the norm. Flood protection relies on the ability to construct temporary barriers, which makes heavy demands on manpower, and perhaps one day the complex logistics needed to erect them will go awry, or the floodwater may even overtop them. The Severn remains hazardous even at times of modest flow. If drowning in the river has been made to seem as though it is consigned to history, it is not so, as was brought home when three men drowned in the river at Shrewsbury in the space of a little over 12 months in 2009 and 2010. It is a reminder that however innocent it may seem by day, the river is a different animal at night.

In physical terms the Severn has been relatively stable over the last two millennia. The old course at Gloucester silted up, as did the eastern channel by the Stone Bridge at Shrewsbury. Otherwise it has shifted remarkably little, except for the cutting of the Maisemore channel at the end of the 15th century. Such a major event would no longer be tolerated, and today would hasten canalisation of the river course, but in the fullness of time we would probably filter out these facts and see it again as a natural river. Indeed, this has already happened. River flow is managed by release of water from the Clywedog reservoir which, coupled with the construction of weirs in the 19th century, means that the flow of the Severn is no longer 'natural', although we instinctively resist the idea of it as a work of hydraulic engineering.

The Severn is unlikely to re-emerge as important in transport and industry, but will find an increasing relevance as a focus for leisure. Some old traditions continue and have been enhanced in recent years. Rowing clubs are as popular as ever. The river has become a fundamental part of the heritage of Ironbridge and has secured an important place in the leisure calendar. A coracle regatta is still held on the river in August, in preparation for which the local Green Wood Centre runs coracle-making courses, giving instruction in how to build a coracle with ash laths and calico, using only simple tools. Swimmers take on the Severn in the Ironbridge triathlon.

The regeneration of Ironbridge and of Gloucester Docks, although neither strictly speaking was aimed at reviving the riverside, began a trend that has been taken up to a certain extent in Worcester and Shrewsbury. Local authorities have been active in promoting the Severn as a natural and cultural asset. With the completion of Diglis Bridge in 2010 it is now possible to make a circular riverside walk that takes in both banks of the Severn at Worcester, passing close to the site of the battle of Worcester in the process. In Shrewsbury, redevelopment of the riverside at Frankwell began with municipal offices, and was followed by the construction of the Theatre Severn, which opened in 2009, a building on a completely different scale to earlier generations of Frankwell buildings. It is also in one of the most flood-prone districts of the town, which shows a determination to make the most of the riverside. Opposite the theatre is the sculpture known as Quantum Leap, erected on the river bank to commemorate the bicentenary of Charles Darwin, although it did not officially open until 2010, a year late. Squeezed in awkwardly on the tree-lined bank, almost in the position of the old Welsh Bridge, it is little frequented because it is beside a busy road detached from the pedestrian areas of the town. Quantum Leap is like a vertebra twisted and formed into an arch, an unnecessary reminder of the arches of the Welsh Bridge, which is only a few yards away. But it recognises the importance of the river to Shrewsbury, which enhances the aesthetic appeal of the town.

Not all of our recent interest in the river is driven by official bodies. The revival of interest in Sabrina taps a latent appetite for a distinctive regional culture of the Severn. The Severn Way emerged with the proliferation of new long-distance walking routes in the 1980s. Counter-intuitively, the best thing about it is that it receives a very modest footfall outside of the towns and cities, and near the source on Plynlimon. The river bank is still a lonely place, whether in the exposed and breezy lower reaches like Arlingham or in places upriver near Llandrinio, where the river is not closely followed by a main road and the riverside water meadows are all but deserted. Resort to the river is not just an escape from the everyday world. The river has its own timescale, not quite geological, but not a human timescale either. In some stretches of the river a fly-fisherman from centuries ago would only register a shift in time by the different fish caught in its waters.

The status of the river Severn in regional and national life will be gauged to some extent by the outcome of two proposed infrastructure projects, about which no final decision has been made at the time of writing. Both are ambitious renewable energy projects that would have a considerable impact on the landscape of the Severn, and both reveal society's ambivalent attitude to nature and heritage.

'Mid Wales Connections' is the brand-name given to a proposal to channel the power from existing and proposed wind farms in mid Wales and connect it to the National Grid. Emphasis on wind farm development in the energy policy of the national government and the Welsh Assembly will mean that the existing infrastructure, which is working at near full capacity, will not be able to cope. The scheme requires the development of a significant new sub-station, which is proposed to be built by the Severn at Abermule, to which a network of pylons will be directed. The job of the transmission station is to transform the voltage from 132kv to 400kv and then transmit the energy via pylons in the Severn valley as far as the Breiddin Hills, from where the intended route diverges from the river to the National Grid in Shropshire.

The scheme has met with opposition within the Severn valley, partly because of the visual impact of pylons in the landscape, but also because wind farms are perceived to generate very little power. It has also exposed the myth that renewable energy is always harmonious with the environment. One of the reasons that the Severn is a viable trans-mission route is that its landscape is not deemed worthy of special protection against such visual intrusions. While there are areas protected for their natural beauty, such as Areas of Outstanding Natural Beauty (AONBs) and National Parks, no part of the Severn Uplands enjoys such a designation. This is significant because when a route from the wind farms of mid Wales was mapped out, National Parks, AONBs, World Heritage Sites and 'Welsh Historic Landscapes' were among the features that the project sought to avoid. Tastes have clearly changed over the centuries. Henry Wyndham, writing in 1774, expressed the views of several authors who passed this way when he described the landscape around Abermule as 'a beautiful valley, which was enriched with the Severn meadows and pastures, and bounded, on each side of the river, with moderate hills generally mantled with woods'.[1] Four years earlier Joseph Cradock had observed of this same stretch of river valley that 'some even venture to affirm that it is not equalled by any in Britain'.[2] The historical significance of the Severn and the valley is self-evidently underrated and in any case there is no mechanism for protecting a natural landscape as a cultural asset. Cultural heritage is measured in terms of exclusively cultural features, like castles, bridges and churches, but what this book has been at pains to show is that the most significant cultural entity is the river itself. A river can at present only be designated for its natural history.

At the mouth of the river the two issues are a future nuclear power station at Oldbury, which is surely a long way off, and a tidal barrage. Corlan Hafren is the leading player in a possible Severn barrage, arguing that a privately-funded £30 billion 10-mile barrage from Lavernock Point to Brean Down could produce up to 5% of the nation's electricity needs. If it went ahead it would be the largest single source of renewable energy in Europe. In addition it would protect homes from the storms that have devastated the coastline in the past and are likely to increase in the future, given that the sea level is now rising. It would also provide a considerable boost to the economy of south Wales, which is why a former cabinet minister and south Wales MP has offered to front the project and pilot the necessary legislation through Parliament. In the past, conservation groups have advocated renewable energy and have agreed in principle that harnessing the tidal power of the Severn estuary would be beneficial, but have so far concluded that the benefits are outweighed by the destruction of wildlife habitats. The Severn bore itself is not protected by any form of statutory designation. Efforts by one section of society to champion the Severn bore as a unique asset that helps to create a distinctive character for the area could easily be overridden by demands for energy. A recent report by the government's Department of Energy and Climate Change considers the bore only insofar as tourist revenue will be impacted if the bore is tamed and rendered unsurfable. Promoters have of course taken account of environmental concerns and have tried to minimise environmental impacts. There have even been claims that the natural state of the Severn estuary is a problem that can be alleviated by a barrage. It has been argued that a barrage would sustain the estuary at a much more stable level than in its present natural state, which is a harsh environment for fragile ecosystems. In slowing down the tide it would introduce more light and oxygen into the estuarine waters, which would attract more fish and a greater variety of birds. In terms of nature conservation, however, an artificially contrived habitat can never have more validity than the natural river, however unhelpful it is to wildlife.

Objectors have pointed out that a network of small generators across the estuary would have a smaller environmental impact than one monolithic concrete dam between Cardiff and Weston-super-Mare, whether or not its turbines are fish-friendly. Nor has every technical problem been overcome. The Severn has a high sediment load and what impact that will have on turbines in the medium or long term is not as yet well-enough understood. But if the present schemes falter then new ones will surely replace them. The ideas behind them will not go away. Whether it is wind power around the Severn Uplands or a tidal barrage at the mouth, the future of the Severn landscape seems unlikely to be determined by environmental or cultural values but will be at the mercy of a national economic and political agenda.

✦ Select Bibliography ✦

Aston, Michael (ed), *Medieval Fish, Fisheries and Fishponds in England*. BAR British series 182(i), Oxford, 1988

Atkin, Michael and Laughlin, Wayne, *Gloucester and the Civil War: A city under siege*. Alan Sutton, Stroud, 1993

Baker, Nigel, *Shrewsbury: An archaeological assessment of an English Border town*, Oxbow Books, Oxford, 2010

Baker, Nigel, and Holt Richard, *Urban Growth and the Medieval Church: Gloucester and Worcester*, Ashgate, Aldershot, 2004

Blackwall, Anthony, *Historic Bridges of Shropshire*, Shropshire Libraries, Shrewsbury, 1985

Blakemore, Phyllis, *Gentlemen of the river: The last coraclemen of the Severn Gorge*, Stenlake Publishing, Catrine, 2009

Cossons, Neil and Trinder, Barrie, *The Iron Bridge: symbol of the industrial revolution*, Phillimore, Chichester, 2002

Giles, Colum, *Stourport-on-Severn*, English Heritage, Swindon, 2007

Green, Colin, *Severn Traders*, Black Dwarf, Lydney, 1999

Hayman, Richard & Horton, Wendy, *Ironbridge: History and Guide*. 2nd edition, Tempus, Stroud, 2003

Hurle, Pamela, *Upton: Portrait of a Severnside Town*, Phillimore, Chichester, 1979

Huxley, Ron, *The Rise and Fall of the Severn Bridge Railway, 1872-1970*, Alan Sutton, Stroud, 1984

Jenkins, J. Geraint, *Nets and Coracles*, David & Charles, Newton Abbot, 1974

Jordan, Christopher, *Severn Enterprise: the story of the old and new passage ferries*, Arthur Stockwell, Ilfracombe, 1977

Morriss, Richard (ed), *The Shropshire Severn*, Shropshire Books, Shrewsbury, 1995

Owen, Sue, Pooley, Colin, Folkard, Andrew, Park, Chris, Clark, Gordon and Watson, Nigel, *Rivers and the British Landscape*, Carnegie Publishing, Lancaster, 2005

Phelps, Humphry, *A glance back at Newnham-on-Severn*, Black Dwarf, Lydney, 2003

Richards, Maurice, *A History of Newtown*, Powysland Club, Welshpool, 1993

Snell, Lawrence (ed), *Essays Towards a History of Bewdley*, Bewdley Research Group, 1973

Trinder, Barrie, *The Industrial Revolution in Shropshire*, 3rd edition, Phillimore, Chichester, 2000

Trinder, Barrie, *Barges and Bargemen: A social history of the Upper Severn navigation*, Phillimore, Chichester, 2005

Trinder, Barrie (ed), *The Most Extraordinary District in the World: Ironbridge and Coalbrookdale*, 3rd edition, Phillimore, Chichester, 2005

Trinder, Barrie, *Beyond the Bridges: The Suburbs of Shrewsbury 1760-1960*, Phillimore, Chichester, 2006

Ward, A.W., *The Bridges of Shrewsbury*, Wilding & Son, Shrewsbury, 1935 (facsimile Shropshire Libraries, 1983)

Waters, Brian, *Severn Tide*, J.M. Dent, London, 1947

Waters, Brian, *Severn Stream*, J.M. Dent, London, 1949Witts, Chris, *Disasters on the Severn*, Tempus, Stroud, 2002

Witts, Chris, *The Severn Bore: an illustrated guide*, Amberley, Stroud, 2011

❧ References ❧

Abbreviations used

IGMT   Ironbridge Gorge Museum Trust
SA   Shropshire Archives
VCH   Victoria County History

Introduction: Queen of Rivers

1 *Henry IV, Part 1*, act 3, scene 1; G.A. Cooke, *Topographical and Statistical Description of the County of Worcester* (1805), p.26
2 M. Lobel & J. Tann, 'Gloucester', in M. Lobel (ed), *Historic Towns* (1976), i, p.4
3 D. Defoe, *A Tour through the Whole Island of Great Britain*, ii (2001), p.179
4 J. Byng, *The Torrington Diaries containing the tours through England and Wales of John Byng*, edited by C.B. Andrews, i (1934), p.137
5 M. Kennedy, *Portrait of Elgar* (1968), pp.202, 268, 3
6 S.Owen et al, *Rivers and the British Landscape* (2005), pp.230-2

Chapter 1 The Natural River

1 J. Fletcher, *A Dreadful Phenomenon Described and Improved, being a particular account of the sudden stoppage of the river Severn … May 27th 1773* (2nd edition, 1774); *Gentleman's Magazine* (1773), pp.281-2
2 Numbers, 16, 30
3 P.D. Triccas, 'Two and a half centuries of ideas relating to the origin of the river Severn and the gorge at Ironbridge', *Proceedings of the Birmingham Natural History Society*, 22.4 (1974), pp.269-86
4 Ibid, p.282; D. Pannett, 'The Physical Background', in R. Morriss (ed), *The Shropshire Severn* (1995), pp.48-50
5 F.B. Young, *The Island* (1944), xi, Songs of the Three Rivers, lines 52-65
6 I. Gurney, 'By Severn', lines 1-2, 5-6
7 D. Defoe, *A Tour through the Whole Island of Great Britain* (2001), ii, p.160
8 J. Rhodes, 'The Severn flood plain and Gloucester in the Medieval and Early Modern Periods', *Transactions of the Bristol & Gloucestershire Archaeological Society*, 124 (2006), p.33
9 C. Park, 'Introduction to British rivers', in S. Owen

et al, *Rivers and the British Landscape* (2005), p.24
10 J. Lewin, 'Historical river channel changes', in K. Gregory et al, *Palaeohydrology in Practice: A river basin analysis* (1987), pp.163-65
11 IGMT Oral History Collection, 167/2003
12 *VCH Gloucestershire*, x, pp.155-60, 139-43
13 J.R.L. Allen, 'The landscape archaeology of Lydney level, Gloucestershire: natural and human transformations over the last two millennia', *Transactions of the Bristol and Gloucestershire Archaeological Society*, 119 (2001), pp.41, 48
14 R. Atkyns, *The Ancient and Present State of Gloucestershire* (1712), p.346; S. Rudder, *A New History of Gloucestershire* (1779), pp.524, 668
15 *VCH Gloucestershire*, x, pp.79-85
16 Rhodes, 'Severn flood plain', p.11
17 N. Baker & R. Holt, *Urban Growth and the Medieval Church: Worcester and Gloucester* (2004), p.77
18 Rhodes, 'Severn flood plain', p.13

Chapter 2 Plynlimon

1 M. Lanchester, *The river Severn from Source to Mouth* (1915)
2 J. Harvey (ed), *William Worcestre: Itineraries* (1969), pp.66-8
3 L. Toulmin Smith (ed), *Leland's Itinerary in England and Wales*, iii (1964), p.124
4 J. Randall, *The Severn Valley* (1862), p.9
5 E. Hamer, 'A parochial account of Llanidloes', *Montgomeryshire Collections*, 5 (1872), p.22
6 E. Hamer, 'A parochial account of Llanidloes', *Montgomeryshire Collections*, 4 (1871), p.418
7 D. Bick, *The Old Metal Mines of mid Wales, part 4: West Montgomeryshire* (1977), pp.28-32
8 A.G. Bradley, *A Book of the Severn* (1920), p.4
9 G. Borrow, *Wild Wales* (1888 ed), p.580
10 B.H. Malkin, *The scenery, antiquities and biography of south Wales* (1807), ii, pp.43ff
11 T. Pennant, *Tours in Wales*, iii (1883), pp.185-6
12 Borrow, *Wild Wales* (1888 ed), pp.576-7
13 quoted in Hamer (note 6), p.424
14 Randall, *Severn Valley*, p.3

15 G. Jones and K. Rowntree, *A Prospect of Wales* (1948), p.6

16 E.R. Henken, *National Redeemer: Owain Glyndwr in Welsh Tradition* (1996), pp.77, 152

17 *The Mabinogion*, translated by Sioned Davies (2007), p.206

18 M. Drayton, *Poly-Olbion*, song vi, lines 103-7, 115-123

19 *Poly-Olbion*, song viii, lines 16-19

20 L Booker, *The Springs of Plynlimmon* (1834), 'Vaga', lines 44-51

21 F.B. Young, *The Island* (1944), xi, Songs of the Three Rivers, lines 1-16

Chapter 3 Sabrina

1 W. Harrison, *Description of Britain* (1587), xiii, lines 65-6

2 Geoffrey of Monmouth, *History of the Kings of Britain*, translated by Lewis Thorpe (1966), ii, 1-5 (pp.75-7)

3 W. Camden, *Britannia* (1695), p.649

4 quoted in L. Thorpe, 'Introduction' to *History of the Kings of Britain*, p.17

5 H. Owen and J.R. Blakeway, *A History of Shrewsbury* (1824), i, p.328

6 E. Spenser, *The Faerie Queene*, ii, canto x.19

7 *The Lamentable Tragedie of Locrine*, act 5, scene 5

8 Ibid

9 quoted in R. Rooksby, *A.C. Swinburne: A poet's life* (1997), p.258

10 A.C. Swinburne, *Locrine*, act 2, scene 1

11 Ibid, act 5, scene 2

12 M. Drayton, *Poly-Olbion*, song vi, lines 173-178

13 J. Milton, *Comus*, lines 824-34

14 Ibid, lines 839-43

15 Ibid, lines 855-7

16 L. Booker, *The Springs of Plynlimmon*, 'Sabrina', lines 267-71

17 Ibid, lines 309-16

18 Ibid, lines 343-50

19 C. Burne, *Shropshire Folk-lore* (1883), p.413

20 J. Dyer, *The Fleece*, book 1

21 B. Waters, *Severn Stream* (1949), p.49

22 T. Pennant, *Tours in Wales*, iii (1883), pp.175-6

23 J. Randall, *The Severn Valley* (1862), p.30

24 *Springs of Plynlimmon*, 'Vaga', lines 81-3

25 Ibid, 'Sabrina', lines 58-60

26 Ibid, lines 570-5

27 Ibid, lines 601-4

28 G. Noszlopy & F. Waterhouse, *Public Sculpture of Herefordshire, Shropshire and Worcestershire* (2010), pp.166-7

29 Ibid, pp.126-7

Chapter 4 A River of Churches

1 B. Waters, *Severn Stream* (1949), pp.187-8

2 R. Bradley, *An Archaeology of Natural Places* (2000), especially pp.25-8

3 A. Gibson, 'The Carreg Beuno prehistoric landscape', *Montgomeryshire Collections*, 83 (1995), pp.41-58; idem, 'Excavations at a Neolithic enclosure at Lower Luggy, near Welshpool, Powys', *Proceedings of the Prehistoric Society*, 72 (2006), pp.163-91

4 A. Gibson, 'Survey and excavation at a newly discovered long barrow at Lower Luggy, Berriew, Powys', *Studia Celtica*, 34 (2000), pp.11-2

5 C. Richards, 'Henges and water: towards an elemental understanding of monumentality and landscape in Late Neolithic Britain', *Journal of Material Culture*, 1 (1996), pp.313-36

6 A. Gibson, 'Excavations at the Sarn-y-bryn-caled cursus complex, Welshpool, Powys, and the timber circles of Great Britain and Ireland', *Proceedings of the Prehistoric Society*, 60 (1994), especially pp.143-91

7 A. Brooks & D. Verey, *The Buildings of England: Gloucestershire* ii (2002), p.586

8 M. Green, *Dictionary of Celtic Myth and Legend* (1992); S. Yeates, *The Tribe of Witches: the religion of the Dobunni and Hwicce* (2008)

9 N. Baker & R. Holt, *Urban Growth and the Medieval Church: Gloucester and Worcester* (2004), pp.197-98

10 Ibid, pp.97-98

11 *Buchedd Beuno*, chapter 8, translated in A.W. Wade-Evans, 'Beuno Sant', *Archaeologia Cambrensis*, 85 (1930), pp.316-17

12 G.A. Cooke, *Topographical and Statistical Description of the County of Worcester* (1805), p.83; F. Laird, *A Topographical and Historical Description of the county of Worcester* (1820), p.271

13 Bede, *Ecclesiastical History of the English People*, ii, 1-2

14 A.R. Williams, *Legends of the Severn Valley* (1925), pp.36-46

15 *VCH Gloucestershire*, x, pp.73-8

16 A.H. Smith (ed), *The place-names of Gloucestershire*, iii (1964), p.265

17 B. Waters, *Severn Tide* (1947), p.154

18 T. Habington, *A Survey of Worcestershire*, edited by J. Amphlett, ii (1899), pp.17-18

19 Laird, *County of Worcester*, p.275

20 Ibid, p.38, where it is claimed that the river had recently diverted its course away from Blackstone Rock and that the hermitage was once next to the river, although this seems unlikely

21 W. Stukeley, *Itinerarium Curiosum* (1724), p.71

22 Cooke, *County of Worcester*, p.124; Laird, *County of Worcester*, p.260

23 R. Atkyns, *The Ancient and Present State of Gloucestershire* (1712), p.375; S. Rudder, *A New History of Gloucestershire* (1779), p.734; Melverley church guide

24 D. Horovitz, 'The Hermitage Caves, Bridgnorth – a myth explained?', *Transactions of the Shropshire Archaeological and Historical Society*, 84 (2009), p.11

25 C. Burne, *Shropshire Folk-lore* (1883), pp.85-86

26 Baker & Holt, *Urban Growth*, pp.20, 100-1; Brooks & Verey, *Gloucestershire*, p.393

27 D. Stephenson, 'Entries relating to Arwystli and Powys in the Welsh Chronicles', *Montgomeryshire Collections*, 99 (2011), p.48

28 J. Davies, *A History of Wales* (1993), p.211; D.M. Robinson, *Buildwas Abbey* (2002), p.30

29 E. Mason, *St Wulfstan of Worcester c1008-1095* (1990), p.109

30 H. Hurst, 'Excavations at Gloucester, 1971-73: second interim report', *Antiquaries Journal*, 54 (1974), p.41; R.M. Clay, *The Medieval Hospitals of England* (1909), p.156

31 G. Bellett, *The Antiquities of Bridgnorth* (1856), pp.88-89

32 Baker & Holt, *Urban Growth*, p.97

33 Bellett, *Bridgnorth*, pp.12-13

34 T. Harral & S. Ireland, *Picturesque Views of the Severn* (1824), ii, p.67

35 J. Allies, *The Ancient British, Roman and Saxon Antiquities and Folk-lore of Worcestershire* (1852), p.37

36 Baker & Holt, *Urban Growth*, p.208

37 Waters, *Severn Tide*, p.166

38 *An Essay on the ancient borough of Bewdley and the Beauties of the adjacent country* (1802), p.17

39 Laird, *County of Worcester*, p.261

40 R. Fenton, *Tours in Wales 1804-1813* (1917), p.35

41 Brooks & Verey, *Gloucestershire*, p.613

Chapter 5 Fords and Ferries

1 R. Fenton, *Tours in Wales, 1804-1813* (1917), p.36

2 F. Laird *A Topographical and Historical Description of the county of Worcester* (1820), p.39

3 T. Bridges & C, Mundy, *Worcester: A pictorial history* (1996), p.xii

4 S. Rudder, *A New History of Gloucestershire* (1779), p.47

5 H. Phelps, *A glance back at Newnham-on-Severn* (2003), p.4

6 B. Waters, *Severn Tide* (1947), p.85

7 J. Davies, *A History of Wales* (1993), pp.146-48

8 J. Davies, 'Rhyd Chwima – the ford at Montgomery – Aque Vadum de Mungumeri', *Montgomeryshire Collections*, 94 (2006), pp.323-24

9 Ibid, p.34

10 Ibid, p.27

11 Lady C. Guest, 'Cyngrog and Rhyd y Groes', *Montgomeryshire Collections*, 22 (1888), p.118

12 P.T. Underdown, 'The navigation of the river Severn 1750-1950', *Transactions of the Worcestershire Archaeological Society*, 3rd series 9 (1984), p.95

13 *VCH Gloucestershire*, viii, p.140

14 M. Gelling & A. Cole, *The Landscape of Place Names* (2000), p.82

15 *VCH Gloucestershire*, x, pp.155-60

16 *VCH Worcestershire*, iv, p.301

17 *VCH Gloucestershire*, viii, p.97

18 J. Bennett, *A Tewkesbury Guide* (1847), p.120

19 *VCH Gloucestershire*, viii, p.140

20 Ibid, p.198

21 B. Trinder, *Barges and Bargemen* (2005), p.44

22 Ibid, pp.55-56

23 J. Randall, *The Severn Valley* (1862), p.189

24 Ibid, p.205

25 M. Lanchester, *The river Severn from source to mouth* (1915), p.43

26 quoted in B. Trinder, *The Most Extraordinary District in the World: Ironbridge and Coalbrookdale* (3rd edition, 2005), p.100

27 Phelps, *Newnham-on-Severn*, p.4

28 *VCH Gloucestershire*, x, pp.29-36

29 J. Lee, 'Cherry Orchard: the growth of a Victorian suburb', in B. Trinder (ed) *Victorian Shrewsbury* (1984), pp.125-26

30 IGMT Oral History Collection, 167/2003

31 T. Harral & S. Ireland, *Picturesque views of the Severn* (1824), ii, p.247

32 Ibid, pp.264-65

33 D. Defoe, *A Tour through the Whole Island of Great Britain* (2001), ii, p.160

34 Rudder, *New History of Gloucestershire*, p.47

35 H.P. Wyndham, *A Tour through Monmouthshire and Wales* (1781), p.208

36 *Monmouthshire Merlin*, 16/3/1844

37 C. Jordan, *Severn Enterprise: the story of the old and new passage ferries* (1977), p.28

38 T. Rolt, *Thomas Telford* (1958), pp.134-35

39 quoted in Jordan, *Severn Enterprise*, p.27

40 J. Simmons & G. Biddle, *The Oxford Companion to British Railway History* (1997), p.331

41 Jordan, *Severn Enterprise*, p.69

Chapter 6 Severn Bridges

1 M.O.H. Carver, 'Medieval Worcester: an Archaeological Framework', *Transactions of the*

Worcestershire Archaeological Society, 3rd series 7 (1980), p.20

2 Julius Caesar, Gallic Wars, iv, 17

3 J. Davies, 'Baldwin's Bridge', Montgomeryshire Collections, 98 (2010), pp.1-3

4 J. Harvey (ed), William Worcestre: Itineraries (1969), pp.66-68

5 quoted in D. Whitehead, 'John Gwynn and the building of Worcester Bridge', Transactions of the Worcestershire Archaeological Society, 3rd series 8 (1982), p.32

6 quoted in J. Plymley, General View of the Agriculture of Shropshire (1803), pp.315-16

7 N. Cossons & B. Trinder, The Iron Bridge (2002), pp.47-49

8 J. Rhodes, 'The Severn flood plain and Gloucester in the Medieval and Early Modern Periods', Transactions of the Bristol & Gloucestershire Archaeological Society, 124 (2006), pp.12-13

9 W. Camden, Britannia (1695), p.543

10 T. Harral & S. Ireland, Picturesque views of the Severn (1824), i, p.206

11 J. Ingram, The Anglo-Saxon Chronicle (1912), p.74

12 D. Harrison, The Bridges of Medieval England (2004), p.26

13 Ibid, pp.165-66; P. McGurk (ed), The Chronicle of John of Worcester, iii (1998), p.55

14 Rhodes, 'Severn flood plain', pp.12-13

15 N. Baker, Shrewsbury: An archaeological assessment of an English Border town, (2010), p.109

16 Matthew 25, 31-46

17 E.H. Pearce (ed), The Register of Thomas de Cobham, Bishop of Worcester 1317-27 (1930), p.164; Harrison, Bridges, p.198

18 W. Langland, Piers the Ploughman, translated by J.F. Goodridge (1966), book vii, p.92

19 H. Hurst, 'Excavations at Gloucester, 1971-73', Antiquaries Journal, 54 (1974), pp.48-49; Rhodes, 'Severn flood plain', p.13

20 M. Bazeley, 'The Forest of Dean', Transactions of the Bristol and Gloucestershire Archaeological Society, 33 (1910), p.275; Hurst, 'Excavations at Gloucester', p.41; Rhodes, 'Severn flood plain', pp.15-16; N. Baker & R. Holt, Urban Growth and the Medieval Church: Worcester and Gloucester (2004), pp.118-19

21 Harrison, Bridges, pp.44-45

22 A. Cooper, Bridges, Law and Power in Medieval England (2006), p.157

23 S. Rudder, A New History of Gloucestershire (1779), p.543

24 C. O'Connor, Roman Bridges (1993), p.140

25 N. Brooks, 'Medieval bridges: a window onto changing concepts of state power', Haskins Society Journal, 7 (1995), p.20

26 O'Connor, Roman Bridges, pp.140, 2

27 H.C. Maxwell Lyte, 'Manuscripts of the Corporation of Bridgnorth', Transactions of the Shropshire Archaeological Society, 10 (1887), p.139

28 Bewdley Historical Research Group, Bewdley in its Golden Age: life in Bewdley 1660-1760 (1991), pp.4, 86

29 T. Phillips, The History and Antiquities of Shrewsbury (1779), p.145

30 D. Farmer, Oxford Dictionary of Saints (1997), p.512

31 Cooper, Bridges, Law and Power, pp.156-65

32 C.H. Drinkwater, 'Montford Bridge: Tolls, customs & Co AD1285 – AD1412', Transactions of the Shropshire Archaeological Society, 3rd series, 7 (1907), pp.65-69, 74

33 A. Dyer, The City of Worcester in the Sixteenth Century (1973), p.65

34 Harrison, Bridges, p.109

35 L. Toulmin Smith (ed), Leland's Itinerary in England and Wales, ii (1964), pp.57-58

36 Rhodes, 'Severn flood plain', p.20

37 Harrison, Bridges, p.93

38 H. Owen, Some Account of the Ancient and Present State of Shrewsbury (1808), pp.81, 83

39 N. Baker, Shrewsbury Abbey: a medieval monastery (1990), p.12

40 M.H. Ellis, 'The bridges of Gloucester and the hospital between the bridges', Transactions of the Bristol and Gloucestershire Archaeological Society, 51 (1929), p.174; Baker & Holt, Urban Growth, p.79

41 D. Cromarty, Everyday Life in Medieval Shrewsbury (1991), p.53; B. Champion, Everyday Life in Tudor Shrewsbury (1994), p.86

42 Phillips, History of Shrewsbury, p.213

43 A.W. Ward, The Bridges of Shrewsbury (1935), p.133

44 A.W. Ward, 'The Stone or East Bridge, Shrewsbury, 1765', Transactions of the Shropshire Archaeological Society, 53 (1950), p.251

45 J.W. Bund, Diary of Henry Townshend of Elmley Lovett 1640-1663 (1920), pp.40-41

46 J. Noake, Worcester in Olden Times (1849), p.112

47 A. Blackwall, Historic Bridges of Shropshire (1985), p.12

48 VCH Worcestershire, iv, p.213

49 G.A. Cooke, Topographical and Statistical Description of the County of Worcester (1805), p.54

50 A. Brooks & N. Pevsner, The Buildings of England: Worcestershire (2007), p.741

51 quoted in Whitehead, 'Worcester Bridge', p.31

52 T. Rolt, Thomas Telford (1958), p.32

53 Harral & Ireland, Picturesque Views of the Severn, i, p.18

54 T. Pennant, *Tours in Wales*, iii (1883), p.177

55 R. Fenton, *Tours in Wales* (1917), p.35

56 quoted in Rhodes, 'Severn flood plain', p.35

57 Cossons & Trinder, *Iron Bridge*, pp.77-78

58 Ibid, p.11

59 This account is based on Cossons & Trinder, *Iron Bridge*, pp.12-30

60 N. Scarfe, *Innocent Espionage* (1995), pp.95-96

61 quoted in B. Trinder (ed), *The Most Extraordinary District in the World* (2005), p.49

62 Cossons & Trinder, *Iron Bridge*, p.78

63 *Shrewsbury Chronicle*, 11/1/1828

64 R. Haslam, *The Buildings of Wales: Powys* (1979), p.85

65 R. Huxley, *The Rise and Fall of the Severn Bridge Railway, 1872-1970* (1984)

66 R. Christiansen, *Regional History of the Railways of Great Britain, 13: Thames & Severn* (1981), pp.124-28

67 Waters, *Severn Tide*, p.124

68 B. Carne, 'Thomas Fulljames 1808-74: Surveyor, Architect and Civil Engineer', *Transactions of the Bristol and Gloucestershire Archaeological Society*, 113 (1995), pp.16-17

69 A. Brooks & D. Verey, *The Buildings of England: Gloucestershire* ii (2002), pp.158-59

70 J. Newman & N. Pevsner, *The Buildings of England: Shropshire* (2006), p.549

71 E. Lawson, *Records and Traditions of Upton-on-Severn* (1869), p.155

Chapter 7 Castles and Kings

1 Tacitus, *Annals*, xii, 31

2 R. White & P. Barker, *Wroxeter: Life and Death of a Roman City* (1998), pp.38-40

3 Tacitus, *Annals*, xii, 33-37

4 G. Webster, *Rome Against Caratacus: The Roman campaigns in Britain AD 48-58* (1993), p.29; White & Barker, *Wroxeter*, pp.39-41 suggest Llanymynech on the Vyrnwy

5 White & Barker, *Wroxeter*, pp.42-43

6 Webster, *Rome Against Caratacus*, p.55

7 P. Crew, 'Forden Gaer, Montgomery', *Bulletin of the Board of Celtic Studies*, 28/4 (1980), p.741; N.W. Jones, 'Caersws Roman fort and vicus', *Montgomeryshire Collections*, 81 (1993), p.85

8 Webster, *Rome Against Caratacus*, p.107; N.W. Jones, 'Excavations within the Roman vicus at Caersws', *Montgomeryshire Collections*, 84 (1996), p.15

9 D. Horovitz, 'A tale of two bridges: *Cwatbrycge* and Bridgnorth revisited', *Transactions of the Shropshire Archaeological and Historical Society*, 83 (2008), p.9

10 W.B. Dawkins,' One some human bones found at Buttington, Montgomeryshire', *Montgomeryshire Collections*, 6 (1873), pp.144-45

11 A. Smyth, *King Alfred the Great* (1995), pp.127-28

12 N. Baker & R. Holt, *Urban Growth and the Medieval Church: Gloucester and Worcester* (2004), p.133

13 J. Davies, *A History of Wales* (1993), p.101

14 *VCH Worcestershire*, iv, pp.378, 380

15 P. and A. Duckers, *Castles of Shropshire* (2006), p.69

16 P. Barker, 'Hen Domen revisited', in J. Kenyon and R. Avent, *Castles in Wales and the Marches* (1987), pp.51-54

17 Duckers, *Castles of Shropshire*, p.144

18 T. Rowley, *The Welsh Border: Archaeology, History & Landscape* (2001), p.106

19 Duckers, *Castles of Shropshire*, p.99

20 Ibid, p.18

21 J. Beverley Smith, *Llywelyn ap Gruffudd: Prince of Wales* (1998), p.360

22 Ibid, pp.415-16

23 H.P. Wyndham, *A Tour through Monmouthshire and Wales* (1781), p.191

24 L. Butler, 'Dolforwyn Castle, Montgomeryshire, Powys: the second report', *Archaeologia Cambrensis*, 144 (1995), pp.128-29

25 Beverley Smith, *Llywelyn ap Gruffudd*, pp.578-79

26 *VCH Worcestershire*, iv, p.303

27 J. Bennett, *A Tewskesbury Guide* (1847), p.50, A.H. Burne, *The battlefields of England* (2002), p.283

Chapter 8 Civil Wars

1 C. Carlton, *Going to the wars: the experience of the British Civil Wars, 1638-1651* (1992), p.103

2 J.W.W. Bund, *The Civil War in Worcestershire 1642-1646, and the Scotch Invasion of 1651* (1905), p.169

3 T. Bracher & R. Emmett, *Shropshire in the Civil War* (2000), p.77

4 J. Corbet, *An Historical Relation of the Military Government of Gloucester* (1645), reprinted in J. Washbourn, *Bibliotheca Gloucestrensis* (1823), pp.12-13

5 Bund, *Civil War in Worcestershire*, p.41

6 Ibid, p.46, E. Hyde (Earl of Clarendon), *The History of the Rebellion and Civil Wars in England* (1703), ii, p.20

7 Bund, *Civil War in Worcestershire*, p.49

8 Bracher & Emmett, *Shropshire in the Civil War*, p.86

9 Corbet, *Military Government of Gloucester*, p.28

10 Ibid, pp.32-33

11 Bund, *Civil War in Worcestershire*, pp.94-96

12 Corbet, *Military Government of Gloucester*, p.150

13 M. Atkin & W. Laughlin, *Gloucester and the Civil War: A city under siege* (1992), p.167

14 J. Dorney, *A Briefe and exact relation of the … siege laid before the city of Gloucester* (1643), reprinted in Washbourn, *Bibliotheca Gloucestrensis*, p.211

15 Ibid, p.218; Corbet, *Military Government of Gloucester*, p.49

16 Dorney, *siege laid before the city of Gloucester*, p.222

17 Bund 1905, *Civil War in Worcestershire*, p.102

18 The bridge is described as a ruse in H. Foster, *A True and Exact Relation of the Marchings of the Two Regiments of the Trained Bands of the City of London … for the Reliefe of the City of Gloucester* (1643), reprinted in Washbourn, *Bibliotheca Gloucestrensis*, p.261

19 Corbet, *Military Government of Gloucester*, pp.63-64, 72

20 Ibid, p.71; Bund, *Civil War in Worcestershire*, pp.118-19

21 D. Hill & M. Worthington, *Offa's Dyke: history & guide* (2003), pp.148-52

22 Corbet, *Military Government of Gloucester*, pp.116, 123-24

23 B. Whitelocke, *Memorials of the English Affairs* (1732), p.107

24 Corbet, *Military Government of Gloucester*, p.147; Atkin & Laughlin, *Gloucester and the Civil War*, p.17

25 W. Maurice 'An Account of the Civil War in north Wales', *Archaeologia Cambrensis*, 1 (1846), p.37; Bracher & Emmett, *Shropshire in the Civil War*, p.83

26 Bracher & Emmett, *Shropshire in the Civil War*, p.85

27 Ibid, 36-37

28 Bund, *Civil War in Worcestershire*, p.163

29 Carlton, *Going to the wars*, p.174

30 G. Bellett, *The Antiquities of Bridgnorth* (1856), pp.166-68

31 J.W.W. Bund (ed), *Diary of Henry Townshend of Elmley Lovett 1640-1663* (1920), p.167

32 Ibid, p.157

33 Bund, *Civil War in Worcestershire*, p.226

34 Ibid, p.231

35 Whitelocke, *Memorials of the English Affairs*, p.505

36 Bund, *Civil War in Worcestershire*, p.234

37 Whitelocke, *Memorials of the English Affairs*, p.507

38 Ibid, p.508

39 Atkin & Laughlin, *Gloucester and the Civil War*, p.50; Clarendon, *Civil Wars in England*, ii, p.475

40 Bellett, *Bridgnorth*, pp.131-32

41 P. Styles, 'The city of Worcester during the Civil Wars 1640-1660', in R.C. Richardson (ed), *The English Civil Wars: Local Aspects* (1997), p.199; Bund, *Civil War in Worcestershire*, p.129

42 Bund, *Civil War in Worcestershire*, p.156

43 Capt R. Blackhouse, *A True Relation of a Wicked Plot … against the City of Gloucester* (1644), reprinted in Washbourn, *Bibliotheca Gloucestrensis*

44 T. Harral & S. Ireland, *Picturesque Views of the Severn* (1824), ii, p.264; C. Jordan, *Severn Enterprise: the story of the old and new passage ferries* (1977), p.16

45 Styles, 'Worcester during the Civil Wars', p.203; Whitelocke, *Memorials of the English Affairs*, p.81

46 Dorney, *siege laid before the city of Gloucester*, p.229

47 quoted in Bracher & Emmett, *Shropshire in the Civil War*, p.40

48 Ibid, p.21

49 Bund, *Civil War in Worcestershire*, p.119

50 Styles, 'Worcester during the Civil Wars', p.201

51 Bund, *Civil War in Worcestershire*, p.141

52 Bellett, *Bridgnorth*, p.170

53 M. Wanklyn, 'Urban revival in early Modern England: Bridgnorth and the river trade 1660-1800', *Midland History*, 18 (1993), p.38

Chapter 9 Industry

1 C. Hulbert, *The History and Description of the County of Salop* (1836), quoted in B. Trinder (ed) *The Most Extraordinary District in the World: Ironbridge and Coalbrookdale* (3rd edition 2005), pp.108-9

2 C. Morris (ed), *The Journeys of Celia Fiennes* (1949), p.232

3 P.G. Barton, 'A history and conspectus of Montgomeryshire water corn mills', *Montgomeryshire Collections*, 87 (1999), pp.6-7, 72

4 Ibid, p.64; P.G. Barton, 'The Beander Mill, Newtown, Montgomeryshire, 1330-1851', *Montgomeryshire Collections*, 93 (2005), p.39

5 Barton 'Montgomeryshire water corn mills', pp.13, 72

6 Ibid, p.70

7 quoted in M. Richards, *A History of Newtown* (1993), p.58

8 J.G. Jenkins, *The Welsh Woollen Industry* (1969), p.150; Barton, 'Montgomeryshire water corn mills', p.63

9 Barton, 'Montgomeryshire water corn mills', p.72

10 Jenkins, *Welsh Woollen Industry*, p.131

11 Ibid, p.132; Barton, 'Montgomeryshire water corn mills', p.70

12 B. Trinder, *Beyond the Bridges: the suburbs of Shrewsbury 1760-1960* (2006), pp.82-83

13 B. Trinder, *The Industrial Archaeology of Shropshire* (1996), p.44

14 J.E. Vize, 'The parish of Forden', *Montgomeryshire Collections*, 15 (1882), p.158

15 Barton, 'Montgomeryshire water corn mills', p.77

16 Trinder, *Most Extraordinary District in the World*, pp.78, 138-9

17 Trinder, *Industrial Archaeology*, p.11

18 *VCH Gloucestershire*, viii, p.97

19 T. Harral & S, Ireland, *Picturesque views of the Severn* (1824), i, p.197

20 B. Trinder, The *Industrial Revolution in Shropshire* (3rd edition, 2000), pp.11-3

21 R. Hayman, 'Lloyds Engine House, Ironbridge', *Transactions of the Shropshire Archaeological Society*, 72 (1997), pp.38-51

22 quoted in Trinder, *Most Extraordinary District in the World*, pp.19-20

23 Ibid, p.20

24 Trinder, *Industrial Revolution*, p.20

25 J.F.A. Mason, *The Borough of Bridgnorth, 1157-1957* (1957) pp.13, 41

26 Trinder, *Most Extraordinary District in the World*, p.84

27 Trinder, *Industrial Revolution*, p.133; R. Hayman & W. Horton, *Ironbridge History & Guide* (2003), p.144

28 Trinder, *Industrial Revolution*, p.227

Chapter 10 The Working River

1 G. Perry, *The Gentleman's Magazine* (1758), 178-9, quoted in B. Trinder, *Barges and Bargemen* (2005), pp.143-4

2 *VCH Gloucestershire*, x, pp.139-43

3 M.G. Fulford et al, 'The medieval quay at Woolaston Grange, Gloucestershire', *Transactions of the Bristol and Gloucestershire Archaeological Society*, 110 (1992), p.119

4 J.R.L. Allen, 'The landscape archaeology of Lydney level, Gloucestershire: natural and human transformations over the last two millennia', *Transactions of the Bristol and Gloucestershire Archaeological Society*, 119 (2001), p.33

5 N. Baker, *Shrewsbury: An archaeological assessment of an English Border town* (2010), p.216

6 J. Rhodes, 'The Severn flood plain and Gloucester in the Medieval and Early Modern Periods', *Transactions of the Bristol & Gloucestershire Archaeological Society*, 124 (2006), p.22

7 R.N. Fisher & C.M. Pagett, 'A brief history of transportation and communication in Bewdley', in L. Snell (ed), *Essays Towards a History of Bewdley* (1973), pp.69-70

8 Fisher & Pagett, 'transportation and communication in Bewdley ', p.73

9 A. Dyer, *The city of Worcester in the sixteenth century* (1973), p.61

10 Trinder, *Barges and Bargemen*, p.38

11 quoted in M. Wanklyn, 'The Severn Navigation in the seventeenth century', *Midland History*, 13 (1988), p.52

12 Ibid, p.37

13 Trinder, *Barges and Bargemen*, p.80

14 Wanklyn, 'Severn Navigation', p.37

15 Fisher & Pagett, 'transportation and communication in Bewdley', p.71

16 Trinder, *Barges and Bargemen*, p.84

17 quoted in Ibid, p.143

18 R.R. Angerstein, *R.R. Angerstein's Illustrated Travel Diary 1753-1755* (2001), pp.175, 329

19 Dyer, *Worcester*, p.64

20 *Berrow's Worcester Journal*, 5/4/1832; SA 1649, commonplace book of Thomas Beard, 24/8/1829, 25/3/1836

21 N.M. Herbert, 'The Newnham and London Traders', *Transactions of the Bristol and Gloucestershire Archaeological Society*, 98 (1979), p.94

22 Trinder, *Barges and Bargemen*, p.29

23 *Shrewsbury Chronicle*, 25/3/1859

24 SA 1649, commonplace book of Thomas Beard, 15/10/1832, 6/12/1831, 2/11/1832, 23/7/1831

25 M. Wanklyn, 'Urban revival in early Modern England: Bridgnorth and the river trade 1660-1800', *Midland History*, 18 (1993), p.49

26 Ibid, p.52

27 R. Hayman, *Ironmaking* (2005), p.61; John Rylands University Library, Manchester, Botfield Collection 1/4/6, letters dated 18/1/1827, 21/2/1827

28 *Berrow's Worcester Journal*, 24/1/1822

29 Trinder, *Barges and Bargemen*, p.70

30 *Shrewsbury Chronicle*, 10/9/1858

31 SA 1649, 1/5/1833; 24/3/1830

32 Ibid, 29-31/1/1831, 7/11/1831

33 C. Morris (ed), *The Journeys of Celia Fiennes* (1949), p.232

34 Fisher & Pagett, 'transportation and communication in Bewdley', p.74

35 W. Owen, 'Narrative, travels etc of Captain William Owen', *Montgomeryshire Collections*, 16 (1883), p.240

36 *Gentleman's Magazine* (1783), i, p.374

37 R. Pococke, *The Travels through England*, i (1888), 13/7/1734

38 Trinder, *Barges and Bargemen*, pp.93-4

39 Fisher & Pagett, 'transportation and communication in Bewdley', p.76

40 Trinder, *Barges and Bargemen*, pp.94, 111

41 Herbert, 'Newnham and London Traders', p.93

42 J.G. Jenkins, *Nets and Coracles* (1974), pp.186-90

43 IGMT Oral History Collection 167/2003

44 Ibid; B. Trinder (ed), *The Most Extraordinary District in the World: Ironbridge and Coalbrookdale* (2005), p.58

45 A.S. Davies, 'The river trade and craft of Montgomeryshire and its borders', *Montgomeryshire Collections*, 44 (1936), p.48

46 IGMT Oral History Collection 167/2003; P. Blakemore, *Gentlemen of the river* (2009), pp.27, 33-5, 41

47 C.H. Drinkwater, 'Montford Bridge: Tolls, customs & Co AD1285 – AD1412', *Transactions of the Shropshire Archaeological Society*, 7 (1907), pp.67-9

48 *VCH Gloucestershire*, x, p.140

49 C. Hart, *The Industrial History of Dean* (1971), pp.415-7

50 B. Trinder, *Industrial Archaeology of Shropshire* (1996), p.170

Chapter 11 Fish

1 *Shrewsbury Chronicle*, 11/4/1828

2 J. Smyth, *A description of Berkeley in the county of Gloucester and its inhabitants* (1885 edition); *VCH Gloucestershire*, x, pp.139-43

3 J. Plymley, *General View of the Agriculture of Shropshire* (1803), p.84

4 T. Harral & S. Ireland, *Picturesque Views of the Severn* (1824), i, p.171; C. Hulbert, *The Manual of Shropshire Biography* (1839), p.73

5 *The Mabinogion*, translated by Sioned Davies (2007), p.204

6 M. Low, *Celtic Christianity and Nature* (1996), p.77

7 W. Pitt, *A General View of the Agriculture of the County of Worcester* (1810), p.15

8 *VCH Gloucestershire*, x, pp.109-114

9 C.J. Bond, 'Monastic fisheries', in M. Aston (ed), *Medieval Fish, Fisheries and Fishponds in England* (1988), pp.84-6

10 D.J. Pannett, 'Fish weirs of the river Severn with particular reference to Shropshire', in Aston, *Fish, Fisheries and Fishponds*, p.385

11 Bond, 'Monastic fisheries', p.86

12 T. Habington, *A Survey of Worcestershire by Thomas Habington*, edited by J. Amphlett (1899), p.39, for Hallow, i.e. Norwycke and including a river island known as an eyte

13 Bond, 'Monastic fisheries', pp.87-9

14 Pannett, 'Fish weirs', p.371

15 Ibid, p.376

16 J. Rhodes, 'The Severn flood plain and Gloucester in the Medieval and Early Modern Periods', *Transactions of the Bristol & Gloucestershire Archaeological Society*, 124 (2006), p.21

17 G. Jenkins, *Nets and Coracles* (1974), pp.45, 62

18 Ibid, pp.54-55

19 B. Waters, *Severn Tide* (1947), p.126

20 Ibid, pp.39-41; Jenkins, *Nets and Coracles*, pp.257-8

21 *VCH Worcestershire*, iv, p.213

22 Waters, *Severn Tide*, pp.189-94

23 A.S. Davies, 'The river trade and craft of Montgomeryshire and its borders', *Montgomeryshire Collections*, 44 (1936), pp.46-9

24 F. Laird, *A Topographical and Historical Description of the county of Worcester* (1820), p.40

25 Waters, *Severn Tide*, p.7

26 Ibid, pp.42-43

27 R.U. Sayce, 'Food through the ages', *Montgomeryshire Collections*, 49 (1946), p.57

28 Waters, *Severn Tide*, pp.135-7

29 A. Dyer, *The city of Worcester in the sixteenth century* (1973), p.139

30 Plymley, *Agriculture of Shropshire*, p.84

31 J. Chambers, *A General History of Worcester* (1819), p.398; J. Noake, *Worcester in Olden Times* (1849), p.43

32 Jenkins, *Nets and Coracles*, pp.16-9

33 P. Blakemore, *Gentlemen of the river* (2009), p.35

34 Chaucer, *Complaint of Mars*, lines 237-240

35 R. Cornes, 'A short topographical account of Bridgnorth, 1736', in *Transactions of the Shropshire Archaeological and Natural History Society*, 9 (1886), p.197

36 Jenkins, *Nets and Coracles*, p.269

37 Waters, *Severn Tide*, p.47

38 Ibid, p.57

39 J. Randall, *The Severn valley* (1862), p.63

40 H. Pidgeon, *Memorials of Shrewsbury* (1836), p.184

41 C.C. Dyer, 'The consumption of freshwater fish in medieval England', in Aston, *Fish, Fisheries and Fishponds*, p.35

42 H. Green, *Pack my bag: a self-portrait* (1979), p.52

43 R. Green, *A Brief History of Worcester* (1806), p.115

44 *Shrewsbury Chronicle*, 7/12/1860

45 Waters, *Severn Tide*, pp.113-4

46 Harral & Ireland, *Picturesque Views*, ii, p.210

47 *Shrewsbury Chronicle*, 7/12/1860

48 A.G. Bradley, *A Book of the Severn* (1920), pp.44, 42

49 Chambers, *History of Worcester*, pp.337-8

50 Plymley, *Agriculture of Shropshire*, p.84; Laird, *Description of Worcester*, p.39

51 Waters, *Severn Tide*, pp.20-1

52 quoted in Ibid, p.136

53 Laird, *Description of Worcester*, p.40

54 Chambers, *History of Worcester*, p.338

55 Pitt, *Agriculture of Worcester*, p.16

56 Dyer, *Worcester*, p.138

57 S. Paston-Williams, *The Art of Dining: A history of cooking and eating* (1993), p.26

58 C.A. Wilson, *Food and Drink in Britain from the Stone Age to recent times* (1984), p.53

59 T. Austin (ed), *Two fifteenth-century cookbooks* (1888), pp.32, 52, 98-9

60 C. Morris (ed), *The Journeys of Celia Fiennes* (1949), p.235

61 T. May, *The Accomplisht Cook, or the Art and Mystery of Cookery* (1660), pp.334-5

62 H. Glasse, *The Art of Cookery made plain and easy* (1758), pp.179, 231

63 S. Buczacki, *Fauna Britannica* (2002), p.119

64 Waters, *Severn Tide*, p.118

65 Jenkins, *Nets and Coracles*, p.282

Chapter 12 Water of Life

1 Tacitus, *Annals*, xii.32

2 *Shrewsbury Chronicle*, 13/2/1795

3 E. Lawson, *Records and Traditions of Upton-on-Severn* (1869), p.177

4 N. Baker & R. Holt, *Urban Growth and the Medieval Church: Gloucester and Worcester* (2004), p.334

5 B. Trinder, *Barges and Bargemen* (2005), p.61

6 R. White & P. Barker, *Wroxeter: Life and Death of a Roman City* (1998), pp.98-100

7 M. Lobel & J. Tann, 'Gloucester', in M. Lobel (ed), *Historic Towns*, i, (1976), p.11

8 J. Dorney, *A Briefe and exact relation of the ... siege laid before the city of Gloucester* (1643), p.212

9 *VCH Gloucestershire*, iv, pp.262-9

10 A. Dyer, *The city of Worcester in the sixteenth century* (1973), pp.206-7

11 G.A. Cooke, *Topographical and Statistical Description of the County of Worcester* (1805), pp.53, 128; T. Harral & S. Ireland, *Picturesque views of the Severn* (1824), ii, p.43; P. Hughes & A. Leech, *The Story of Worcester* (2011), pp.241ff

12 J. Chambers, *A General History of Worcester* (1819), p.336

13 C. Gwilt, *A History of Bridgnorth* (2009), p.90

14 R. Cromarty, 'The water supply in Shrewsbury 1550-1835', *Transactions of the Shropshire Archaeological Society*, 75 (2000), pp.17-8; T. Minshull, *The Shrewsbury Visitors' Pocket Companion, or Salopian Guide and Directory* (1804), pp.39, 71, 74; W. Ranger, *Report to the General Board of Health on a preliminary enquiry into the sewerage, drainage and supply of water, and the sanitary condition of the inhabitants of the borough of Shrewsbury* (1854), p.39

15 C. Morris (ed), *The Journeys of Celia Fiennes* (1949), p.227

16 Cromarty, 'water supply', pp.20-2

17 Harral & Ireland, *Picturesque Views*, i, p.177; T. Minshull, *The Shrewsbury Guide* (1809), p.28

18 Cromarty, 'water supply', pp.23-5

19 Gwilt, *Bridgnorth*, p.91; B. Trinder, *Industrial Archaeology of Shropshire* (1996), p.74

20 Gwilt, *Bridgnorth*, p.82

21 *Shrewsbury Chronicle*, 11/2/1831

22 H. Pidgeon, *Memorials of Shrewsbury* (1836), pp.185-86; Trinder, *Industrial Archaeology*, p.200

23 Ranger, *Report to the General Board of Health*, passim

24 Ibid, pp.44, 62

25 SA 1649, commonplace book of Thomas Beard, 25/8/1828

26 *VCH Shropshire*, x, p.285

27 Ranger *Report to the General Board of Health*, p.57

28 B. Trinder, *Beyond the Bridges: The Suburbs of Shrewsbury 1760-1960* (2006), pp.83, 86

29 *Eddowes Salopian Journal*, 15/8/1876

30 Trinder, *Industrial Archaeology*, p.73

31 quoted in P. Stamper, *Historic Parks and Gardens of Shropshire* (1996), pp.70-1; Dyer, *Worcester*, pp.206-7; J. Rhodes, 'The Severn flood plain and Gloucester in the Medieval and Early Modern Periods', *Transactions of the Bristol & Gloucestershire Archaeological Society*, 124 (2006), p.18

32 J. Noake, *Worcester in Olden Times* (1849), pp.94-5

33 R. Green, *A Brief History of Worcester* (1806), p.39

34 Rhodes, 'Severn flood plain, p.22

35 B. Champion, *Everyday Life in Tudor Shrewsbury* (1994), p.53

36 Ranger, *Report to the General Board of Health*, pp.14, 45, 109

37 *VCH Shropshire*, x, p.285

38 Champion, *Tudor Shrewsbury*, p.80

39 J. Randall, *The Severn Valley* (1862), p.162

40 K. Hobson, 'Every Other House ... Bewdley Inns', in L. Snell (ed), *Essays Towards a History of Bewdley* (1973), pp.119-22

41 Trinder, *Barges and Bargemen*, p.63

42 SA 1649

43 J. Butt, 'Red lights in Roushill', in B. Trinder (ed), *Victorian Shrewsbury* (1984), pp.69-70

44 Trinder, *Barges and Bargemen*, p.69

45 J. Byng, *The Torrington Diaries containing the tours through England and Wales of John Byng*, edited by C.B. Andrews, i (1934), p.31

46 Noake, *Worcester*, p.35

47 H. Fielding, *The History of Tom Jones* (1746), book x, chapter 4

48 Ibid, book ix, chapter 3

49 I. Walton, *The Compleat Angler* (1983 ed), p.70

50 IGMT Oral History Collection, 161/2003

51 Gwilt, *Bridgnorth*, p.82

52 R. Pococke, *The Travels through England*, i (1888), v, letter dated 13/7/1734

53 H. Owen, *Some Account of the Ancient and Present State of Shrewsbury* (1808), pp.54-5

54 J. Nightingale, *A Topographical and Historical Description of the County of Salop* (1810), p.75

55 Byng, *Torrington Diaries*, i (1934), p182; iii (1936), pp.233-4

56 Pidgeon, *Memorials of Shrewsbury*, p.179

57 F. Laird, *A Topographical and Historical Description of the county of Worcester* (1820), p.138

58 Green, *Worcester*, p.61

59 Randall, *Severn Valley*, pp.197-9

60 *Berrow's Worcester Journal*, 11/7/1891

61 Randall, *Severn Valley*, p.202

62 A. Hare, *Shropshire* (1898), p.288

63 *Shrewsbury Chronicle*, 23/6/1854, 14/7/1854, 18/8/1854, 1/9/1854; *Eddowes Salopian Journal*, 27/6/1855

64 *Shrewsbury Chronicle*, 16/9/1854

65 Pidgeon, *Memorials of Shrewsbury*, p.109

66 Minshull, *Shrewsbury Visitors' Pocket Companion*, pp.21-25

67 *Shrewsbury Chronicle*, 23/6/1854

Chapter 13 Flood and Freeze

1 J. Chambers, *A General History of Worcester* (1819), pp.60-1

2 B. Champion, *Everyday Life in Tudor Shrewsbury* (1994), p.112

3 *Shrewsbury Chronicle*, 11/2/1831

4 Environment Agency, *Creating a better place: Bewdley Flood Defences* (c2005)

5 *VCH Gloucestershire*, viii, pp.137-46

6 A.W. Ward, *The Bridges of Shrewsbury* (1935), p.21

7 W.R., *A Concise History of Worcester* (1808), p.91

8 Psalm 147, 16-17

9 T. Phillips, *The History and Antiquities of Shrewsbury* (1779), pp.18-9

10 C. Hulbert, *The Manual of Shropshire Biography* (1839), pp.68-70

11 R. Holinshed, *Chronicles* (1586), iii, p.265

12 E. Lawson, *Records and Traditions of Upton-on-Severn* (1869), p.178

13 *Shrewsbury Chronicle*, 13/2/1795, 20/2/1795; L. Snell, *Essays Towards a History of Bewdley* (1973), p.83

14 W.R., *Worcester*, p.88

15 *Shrewsbury Chronicle*, 20/2/1795

16 Severn Trent Water, *The Impact of the July Floods on the Water Infrastructure and Customer Service: Final Report* (2007), p.10

17 Environment Agency, *Review of 2007 Summer Floods* (2007), p.22

18 Chambers, *History of Worcester*, p.397

19 quoted in Lawson, *Upton-on-Severn*, p.177

20 Phillips, *History of Shrewsbury*, p.149

21 *Shrewsbury Chronicle*, 17/2/1809

22 *VCH Gloucestershire*, viii, pp.137-46

23 M. Barrett, 'Bewdley Bridge', in L. Snell (ed), *Essays Towards a History of Bewdley* (1973), p.87

24 Champion, *Tudor Shrewsbury*, p.86; *Shrewsbury Chronicle*, 15/12/1848

25 *Shrewsbury Chronicle*, 13/2/1795

26 *Shrewsbury Chronicle*, 13/2/1852; Champion, *Tudor Shrewsbury*, p.112

27 Severn Trent Water, *Impact of the July Floods*, pp.13-4

28 Environment Agency, *Summer Floods*, p.46

29 *Daily Telegraph* 24/7/2007

30 *Shrewsbury Chronicle*, 13/2/1795

31 Ward, *Bridges of Shrewsbury*, p.21

32 P. Blakemore, *Gentlemen of the river* (2009), p.27

33 SA 1121/12/25, number 59

34 *Shrewsbury Chronicle*, 13/2/1852

35 *Shrewsbury Chronicle*, 11/2/1831

36 *Shrewsbury Chronicle*, 13/2/1795

37 W. Camden, *Britannia* (1695), p.231

38 R. Atkyns, *The Ancient and Present State of Gloucestershire* (1712), pp.292, 346

39 J. Bishton, *A General View of the Agriculture of the County of Salop* (1794), p.16

40 Lawson, *Upton-on-Severn*, p.178

41 quoted in R. Ward, *Floods: A geographical perspective* (1978), p.115

Chapter 14 'Found Drowned'

1 E. Lawson, *Records and Traditions of Upton-on-Severn* (1869), p.179

2 *Gloucester Citizen*, 24/3/1903, 7/5/1903

3 *Berrow's Worcester Journal*, 25/12/1886, 12/11/1887

4 IGMT Oral History Collection, 167/2003

5 *Shrewsbury Chronicle*, 18/4/1828

6 *Berrow's Worcester Journal*, 22/1/1859

7 *Berrow's Worcester Journal*, 13/8/1825

8 *Berrow's Worcester Journal*, 11/9/1869

9 D. Cromarty, *Everyday Life in Medieval Shrewsbury* (1991), p.66

10 *Shrewsbury Chronicle*, 16/9/1857

11 *Shrewsbury Chronicle*, 14/7/1854

12 *Gloucester Citizen*, 19/9/1906

13 *Berrow's Worcester Journal*, 29/5/1869

14 *Gloucester Citizen*, 8/7/1901

15 *Eddowes Salopian Journal*, 8/7/1857

16 *Gloucester Citizen*, 18/1/1894

17 *Shrewsbury Chronicle*, 1/11/1799
18 *Eddowes Salopian Journal*, 21/1/1818
19 *Berrow's Worcester Journal*, 26/10/1872
20 *Gloucester Citizen*, 28/6/1879
21 *Gloucester Citizen*, 2/1/1886
22 *Gloucester Citizen*, 18/8/1890
23 T. Phillips, *The History and Antiquities of Shrewsbury* (1779), p.208
24 SA 1649, Commonplace book of Thomas Beard, 29/4/1839
25 *Gloucester Citizen*, 7/1/1903
26 *Shrewsbury Chronicle*, 4/9/1829
27 *Eddowes Salopian Journal*, 29/1/1845; *Shrewsbury Chronicle*, 22/11/1854, 31/1/1855
28 *Gloucester Citizen*, 11/3/1893, 1/4/1893, 3/4/1893
29 *Berrow's Worcester Journal*, 15/10/1859, 22/10/1859
30 *Shrewsbury Chronicle*, 13/2/1795
31 *Berrow's Worcester Journal*, 4/5/1895
32 *Berrow's Worcester Journal*, 27/5/1847
33 *Berrow's Worcester Journal*, 2/9/1847

Chapter 15 The Severn Bore

1 M. Drayton, *Poly-Olbion* (1613), song vii, 9-17
2 Ibid; R. Atkyns, *The Ancient and Present State of Gloucestershire* (1712), p.18
3 Ibid
4 J. Rhodes, 'The Severn flood plain and Gloucester in the Medieval and Early Modern Periods', *Transactions of the Bristol & Gloucestershire Archaeological Society*, 124 (2006), p.9
5 Nennius, *British History and the Welsh Annals*, edited and translated by John Morris (1980), p.68
6 B. Waters, *Severn Tide* (1947), pp.67-68
7 *Shrewsbury Chronicle*, 10/2/1809
8 'Observations on the head of tide in the river Severn', *Transactions of the Bristol & Gloucestershire Archaeological Society*, 97 (1979), p.124
9 *Gloucester Citizen*, 22/4/1901, p.3
10 *Gloucester Citizen*, 24/3/1894, 26/3/1894; *Berrow's Worcester Journal*, 31/3/1884

Chapter 16 The Severn Sea

1 S. Aldhouse-Green, *Paviland Cave and the Red Lady: a definitive report* (2000)
2 F. North, *The Evolution of the Bristol Channel* (1955), pp.60-61
3 R. Griffiths, *Conquerors and Conquered in Medieval Wales* (1994), p.8
4 *The Mabinogion*, translated by Sioned Davies (2007), pp.211-2
5 W.R.B. Robinson, 'Dr Thomas Phaer's Report on the harbours and customs administration of Wales under Edward VI', *Bulletin of the Board of Celtic Studies*, 24 (1972), p.496
6 Ibid, pp.494-96
7 North, *Bristol Channel*, p.10
8 T.H. Warren, *By Severn Sea* (1898), lines 1-6.
9 Griffiths, *Conquerors and Conquered*, p.13
10 A. Nicolson & P. Sutherland, *Wetland: Life in the Somerset Levels* (1986), pp.24-25
11 The following account is drawn from two pamphlets, *Lamentable Newes out of Monmouthshire* (1607); *A true report of certain wonderfull overflowings of Waters, now lately in Somersetshire* (1607)
12 S. Haslett, *Earthquakes, Tsunami and Nuclear power: relevance of the 1607 flood in the Bristol Channel* (2011)

Afterword: the present and future river

1 H.P. Wyndham, *A Tour through Monmouthshire and Wales* (1781), p.191
2 J. Cradock, *Letters from Snowdon descriptive of a tour through the northern counties of Wales* (1770), 104

✥ Index ✥

Italicized page numbers indicate illustrations